# Financing
the
## 1996
# Election

# Financing
the
1996
# Election

John C. Green, Editor

*M.E.Sharpe*
Armonk, New York
London, England

**Library of Congress Cataloging-in-Publication Data**

Financing the 1996 election / edited by John C. Green.
p.  cm.
Includes bibliographical references and index.
ISBN 0-7656-0384-5 (cloth : alk. paper)
ISBN 0-7656-0385-3 (pbk. : alk. paper)
1. Campaign funds—United States.  2. Presidents—United States—
Election—1996.  3. United States—Congress—Elections, 1996.
4. United States—Politics and government—1993– .
I. Green, John Clifford, 1953– .
JF1991.F566  1999
324.7′8′097309049—dc21          99-31066
CIP

Printed in the United States of America

The paper used in this publication meets the minimum requirements of
American National Standard for Information Sciences—
Permanence of Paper for Printed Library Materials,
ANSI Z 39.48-1984.


∞


BM (c)  10   9   8   7   6   5   4   3   2   1
BM (p)  10   9   8   7   6   5   4   3   2   1

# Contents

# About the Editor and Contributors

**Herbert E. Alexander** is director emeritus of the Citizens' Research Foundation; he currently serves as senior adviser. For more than forty years, he has been an observer, scholar, and active participant in shaping campaign reforms at the federal, state, and local levels. Alexander has published extensively on political finance and campaign finance reform. He initiated the series this book represents, beginning with *Financing the 1960 Election* and published every four years since. In 1996 he received the Samuel J. Eldersveld Career Achievement Award from the Political Organizations and Parties Section of the American Political Science Association, for a lifetime of outstanding scholarly and professional contributions to the field.

**Robert Biersack** is supervisory statistician at the Federal Election Commission. He has written numerous articles on campaign finance, political parties, and interest groups.

**Anthony Corrado** is associate professor of government at Colby College. He has published extensively on campaign finance and related topics. He is the author of *Let America Decide* (1996) and *Creative Campaigning* (1992), and is a coauthor of *Campaign Finance Reform: A Sourcebook* (1997) and *Financing the 1992 Election* (1995).

**Diana Dwyre** is assistant professor of political science at the California State University, Chico. She has written a number of articles on campaign finance and federal elections, on topics ranging from soft money and congressional elections to party campaign innovations, party issue advocacy advertising, and party campaign finance strategies. Professor Dwyre served as the 1998 American Political Science Association Steiger Congressional Fellow, where she worked with key House members on campaign finance reform legislation that passed the House of Representatives.

**Peter L. Francia** is a Ph.D. candidate in the Department of Government and Politics at the University of Maryland.

**Rachel E. Goldberg** is a graduate student in the Department of Government at Georgetown University.

**John C. Green** is the director of the Ray C. Bliss Institute of Applied Politics and professor of political science at the University of Akron. He has published on campaign finance, political parties, and religion and politics. He is coeditor of *The State of the Parties: The Changing Role of Contemporary American Parties* (1994, 1996, and 1999).

**Melanie Haskell** is a graduate student at the Ray C. Bliss Institute of Applied Politics at the University of Akron. She is currently employed by SDR Technologies, Inc. as project manager for the FEC's electronic filing system.

**Paul S. Herrnson** is professor of government and politics at the University of Maryland, College Park. He has written numerous articles on Congress, campaign finance, political parties, and elections. He is the author of *Congressional Elections: Campaigning at Home and in Washington,* 2nd ed. (1998) and *Party Campaigning in the 1980s* (1988). He is coeditor of several volumes, including *After the Revolution: PACs, Lobbies, and the Republican Congress* (1998), *The Interest Group Connection: Electioneering, Lobbying, and Policy Making in Washington* (1998), and *Risky Business? PAC Decisionmaking in Congressional Elections* (1994).

**Wesley Joe** is a graduate student in the Department of Government at Georgetown University.

**Robert E. Mutch** is the author of *Campaigns, Congress, and Courts: The Making of Federal Campaign Finance Law* (1988), a political history of federal campaign funding regulations from 1907. In 1991 he wrote a comparative history of U.S. and Canadian campaign finance law for Canada's Royal Commission on Electoral Reform. In addition to several articles on campaign finance, political parties, and U.S. political history, he has written op-ed pieces and provided expert testimony.

**Clyde Wilcox** is professor of government at Georgetown University. He has published extensively on campaign finance, religion and politics, gender politics, and many other topics. He is the coauthor of *Serious Money: Fundraising and Contributing in Presidential Campaigns* (1995), and coeditor of *Risky Business? PAC Decisionmaking in Congressional Elections* (1994), *Interest Group Connection: Electioneering, Lobbying, and Policy Making in Washington* (1997), and *Interest Groups in National Elections* (1998).

# Tables and Figures

**Tables**

## Figures

# Acknowledgments

This study updates and extends analyses and categories of data developed over the years by Professors James Pollock, Louise Overacker, and Alexander Heard; the Senate Subcommittee on Privileges and Elections (under the chairmanship of Senator Albert Gore of Tennessee) in 1956; and the nine previous volumes authored or coauthored by Herbert E. Alexander in his quadrennial series on elections and their financing. All of the work in this volume owes an intellectual debt to these predecessors in the study of campaign finance.

The editor would like to express his gratitude to the colleagues who shared their expertise in the chapters for this book. Herbert Alexander, Anthony Corrado, Clyde Wilcox, and Paul Herrnson provided guidance throughout the project, while Robert Mutch and Diana Dwyre were helpful with their advice and commentary. Robert Biersack was an unfailing source of information on federal campaign finance and insights as to its meaning.

The cooperation and encouragement received from Herbert Alexander, Gloria Cornette, and officers and members of the board of trustees of the Citizens' Research Foundation are also deeply appreciated. A special thanks goes to The Joyce Foundation and Lawrence N. Hansen for the financial support for this project, as well as support for the research efforts of several of the authors. However, none of these organizations or individuals are responsible for any errors of omission or commission, nor do the interpretations presented here necessarily represent their views. All such matters are the sole responsibility of the individual authors.

This project would not have been possible without the support of the Ray C. Bliss Institute of Applied Politics at the University of Akron, and, in particular, the diligent work of Kimberly Haverkamp on the manuscript. Patricia Kolb and her associates at M.E. Sharpe provided invaluable assistance as well. Even editors are indebted to the patience and affection of their families, which in this case knows no bounds.

John C. Green

# Financing
the
# 1996
# Election

JOHN C. GREEN

# The End of an Era:
# Introduction and Overview

Whatever its political significance, the 1996 election revealed dramatic changes in the way for which federal campaigns are paid. These changes mark the end of one era of the campaign finance regulation and herald the start of a new one. Although still substantially in place, the campaign finance system enacted after the Watergate scandal in the 1970s has been seriously undermined by newly prominent practices, often sanctioned by regulatory and judicial rulings. These changes threaten to erode the contribution limitations, disclosure requirements, and public financing provisions that define the *hard money* (federally regulated) relationships between federal candidates and contributors (Wilcox and Joe 1998). As a result, features once common in federal campaigns reappeared in 1996 to the dismay of many observers: very large donations by individuals and institutions, unlimited and undisclosed spending by organized interests, and the systematic flouting of campaign finance laws by presidential campaigns and the major political parties (Wilcox 1999). There is every reason to expect these trends to continue in the 2000 election.

Chief among the newly prominent practices are *soft money* donations and *issue advocacy* spending. Soft money is raised outside of the federal campaign finance regulations, principally through the state affiliates of the Democratic and Republican parties (Corrado et al. 1997, ch. 6). Issue advocacy is spending to influence the outcome of federal elections, but that does not expressly advocate the election of a specific candidate (Corrado et al. 1997, ch. 7). Issue advocacy gives political parties a new way to expend funds, especially soft money. It also allows interest groups to raise and spend money entirely outside of the federal campaign finance system. These new practices have revitalized the debate over campaign finance reform, although as of this writing, no reform legislation has been enacted.

This book catalogues the new finance practices in 1996 and their consequences for the future, and the end of an era of campaign finance regulation is a persistent theme in the chapters that follow. This theme arises in the context of a detailed description of campaign finance in 1996, work that continues a series of research reports on the subject dating back to the 1950s (Alexander and Corrado 1995; Alexander and Bauer 1991; Alexander and Haggerty 1987, 1983; Alexander 1979, 1971, 1966, and 1962; Alexander et al. 1976; Heard 1960). Unlike its predecessor studies, however, this book is a collective effort, drawing on the expertise of a dozen scholars, some well established and others new to the field. This collaboration is warranted by the sea change in federal campaign finance evident in 1996. Federal campaign finance has become increasingly complex, and the authors offer a number of different perspectives, assessments, and measures of financial activity in 1996.

The organization of the book reflects new issues as well as traditional patterns of analysis. The book begins with an overview of spending in the 1996 election (chapter 2), followed by three chapters on the finances of presidential and congressional candidate committees (chapters 3, 4, and 5). The next three chapters cover important kinds of campaign contributors: individual donors, political parties, and interest groups (chapters 6, 7, and 8). The book concludes with a consideration of campaign finance reform (chapter 9).

## The Costs of Democracy in 1996

Chapter 2, the first substantive chapter in the book, offers a detailed overview of spending in the 1996 election by Herbert Alexander, the dean of campaign finance scholars. Alexander uses categories employed by the Citizens' Research Foundation for more than forty years, thus allowing for comparison over time. By these measures, democracy was quite expensive in 1996, with the total bill estimated at about $4.2 billion, an increase of nearly one-third over a comparable estimate in 1992 (see Table 2.1). These figures represent real growth in the cost of democracy in recent times. If presidential spending is taken as a guide, then real spending has increased some 440 percent since 1952 (see Table 2.5). To put the 1996 figures in perspective, political actors expended approximately $21 per person in the voting-age population; because of the low voter turnout, the cost per vote cast was $43 (using presidential turnout as the standard).

A large portion of the 1996 expenditure was directly associated with federal candidates, with roughly one-sixth spent on the presidential campaigns ($700 million) and one-fifth on congressional races ($838 million). Other political organizations spent slightly less, with political parties accounting for one-fifth ($834 million for national, state, local, and soft money funds) and interest groups one-eighth ($505 million) of the total. The remaining funds, almost one-third of the total, were accounted for by state, local, and ballot-issue campaigns ($1.3 million). Alexander also reviews the rate of participation in the finance system generally (about one-eighth of the citizenry reported making a contribution of some sort in 1996; see Table 2.9) and utilization of the income tax check-off to support public financing (about one-eighth of all federal income tax returns in 1996; see Table 2.10).

Interestingly, soft money (6 percent overall) and issue advocacy (some 13 percent of total presidential spending) made up a relatively small percentage of total expenditures. But these practices have a great capacity to expand in the future. Indeed, Alexander concludes that the Federal Election Campaign Act (FECA) was shown to be outdated by the 1996 election. One aspect, expenditure limitations associated with the public financing of presidential campaigns, was especially ineffective. Such limitations failed to control spending in any phase of the presidential selection process in 1996.

**Candidate Spending in 1996**

The next three chapters describe the 1996 finances of federal candidate committees. Wesley Joe and Clyde Wilcox describe spending in the presidential prenomination campaigns (chapter 3), followed by Anthony Corrado's account of the general election (chapter 4), and Paul Herrnson's review of congressional campaigns (chapter 5).

Joe and Wilcox put the primary campaign in historical context, noting that, in political terms, 1996 most closely resembled 1984, when a popular incumbent president (Ronald Reagan) was unopposed for renomination, and the party out of power (the Democrats) experienced a tight contest. In both years, the leading out-party candidate (Walter Mondale in 1994, Bob Dole in 1996) won the nomination in a bruising battle that exhausted his legal spending limit. Indeed, once the GOP nomination was secured, Dole was unable to counter Clinton's "primary" spending against him. This problem was remedied by millions of dollars of issue advocacy by the Republican National Committee, in partial imitation of the issue advocacy spending by the Democratic National Committee on behalf of President Clinton. Indeed, the Clinton effort broke new ground with a multimillion-dollar issue advocacy campaign in 1995 and 1996, mostly paid for with soft money. Given these and other forms of "creative campaigning," Joe and Wilcox conclude that 1996 may well be the "last regulated" campaign under FECA (chapter 3).

Anthony Corrado surveys the 1996 presidential general election finances (chapter 4). He, too, notes the similarity between 1996 and 1984: a popular incumbent buoyed by a strong economy was reelected over a prominent challenger regarded as out of touch with the mood of the country. But as in the prenomination campaign, the general election finances marked a departure from the past. This departure produced an unusual result: For the first time under FECA, campaign finance was an issue in the presidential campaign. Leaving aside soft money and issue advocacy (covered in chapters 7 and 8), Corrado notes three important innovations within the context of FECA. The first involved "general election legal and accounting compliance" (GELAC) funds, private contributions allowed for the purpose of paying for compliance with the campaign finance regulations. The clever use of GELAC funds allowed the presidential campaigns to stretch their spending. Second, the major parties did not spend the legal limit in "coordinated expenditures" on behalf of their presidential nominees, opting instead to engage in unlimited issue advocacy spending. A third innovation was the public financing of the Reform Party and Ross Perot's presidential campaign. This chapter also covers innovations in presidential campaign advertising in 1996. Corrado concludes that the 1996 campaign revealed the flaws in the current campaign finance system and that FECA has been rendered nearly meaningless by constant abuses.

Next, Paul Herrnson describes the finances of the 1996 campaigns for the Senate and House of Representatives (chapter 5). Unlike the presidential campaign, the congressional elections were extremely competitive, being the first held after the Republicans' historic takeover of the Congress in 1994. With control of the legislative branch at stake, congressional campaign finance reflected both continuity and change. On the first count, congressional finances once again set new records, and funding remained tilted toward incumbents. On the second count, Republicans took advantage of their position to outspend their Democratic opponents for the first time under FECA. In addition, there was an unprecedented increase in independent and issue advocacy spending on behalf of congressional candidates. This last change paralleled the use of soft money and issue advocacy in the presidential campaign. Responding to court decisions, the major party committees deployed millions of dollars in marginal Senate and House races, and interest groups engaged in high levels of issue advocacy spending for candidates they favored. Herrnson notes that these new vehicles for campaign spending may well undermine FECA further.

**Sources of Campaign Funds in 1996**

The next three chapters report on the major sources of campaign funds in 1996. Peter Francia, Rachel Goldberg, John Green, Paul Herrnson, and Clyde Wilcox discuss individual campaign contributors (chapter 6), followed by Robert Biersack and Melanie Haskell's account of party finance (chapter 7), and then Diana Dwyre's report on interest-group spending (chapter 8).

Francia, Goldberg, Green, Herrnson, and Wilcox describe the characteristics of individual donors in 1996. Individual contributors were the single largest source of campaign funds, providing the bulk of the money for candidate, party, and political action committees. The authors first compare the major donors to the presidential and congressional campaigns with the population at large. They found major donors to differ substantially from ordinary citizens. Major donors were mostly wealthy, well-educated white men, who tended to be Republican and conservative, and were very active in other aspects of politics. Despite these characteristics, major donors were not monolithic. Important differences existed between Democratic and Republican donors as well as significant factional divisions within each party's financial base. Such divisions were especially prominent among Republican presidential primary donors in 1996. These findings are a reminder of what is at stake in campaign finance regulation: Money can give some people a louder voice in the political process (chapter 6).

Robert Biersack and Melanie Haskell describe the financial activities of the major political parties in the 1996 election (chapter 7). Party committees were granted a prominent role by the FECA, and over the past two decades they have become an increasingly significant source of campaign funds. Biersack and Haskell identify two sides of this activity: first, hard money raised and spent under FECA, and then soft money raised under state law, but coordinated and spent with national direction. Hard money still dominated party finance in 1996, with the parties raising $638 million. But 1996 was a "break-out" year for soft money, which grew to $252 million, equaling almost two-fifths of party hard money. Soft money was attractive to the parties because it could be raised in amounts vastly larger than the FECA limits (the top ten soft money donors gave in excess of $500,000 each) and from sources that were otherwise prohibited from contributing to federal campaigns (such as the treasuries of business corporations and labor unions). The development of issue advocacy spending made soft money even more attractive because soft money could be used directly in campaigns. Biersack and Haskell detail the complex web of party finance in 1996, supporting the conclusion of other chapters that soft money and issue advocacy have eroded the FECA. They find the attitudes of the major parties toward the Federal Election Commission (FEC) akin to "spitting on the umpire."

Diana Dwyre completes the picture with a review of the financial activities of interest groups in 1996 (chapter 8). Interest groups were also given a role in campaign finance by the FECA, principally via political action committees (PACs). Recently, interest-group financial activity has expanded beyond the FECA. Hard money activities still dominated interest-group involvement in 1996, with PACs spending $430 million. Issue advocacy spending was at least $70 million, however, and interest groups were the prime source of party soft money. These kinds of funds may have equaled three-quarters of PAC hard money. The imprecision of these numbers reflects a very serious problem, namely, the lack of full and accurate disclosure of these new practices. Dwyre describes the variety of activities paid for under these arrangements and the complex set of transactions they entail. She argues explicitly that the volume of interest-group activity outside of the FECA has inaugurated a "postreform era" in federal campaign finance.

## The Prospects for Reform

In the final chapter of the book, Robert Mutch considers the debate over campaign finance reform since the 1992 election (chapter 9). This debate was influenced by both the 1994 elections, when the Republicans gained control of Congress, and the 1996 campaign, when the new finance practices became an issue. The 1996 elections reinvigorated the debate because Republicans and reformers each had incentives to respond to the campaign finance scandals. Mutch explains in detail the issues, actors, and reform proposals prominent before and during the "window of opportunity" for reform afforded by the 1996 campaign. His account helps explain the failure of the reform efforts, which fell victim to partisan wrangling and disagreements among reformers.

Mutch argues that reformers and their opponents could agree on two things: There was no strong demand for federal campaign finance reform from the public, and in the absence of such a demand, the Congress was unlikely to enact reform legislation. He suggests that the "scandal-reform" cycle critical to past legislation, including the post-Watergate reforms, may be a thing of the past. Ironically, the culprit could be the disclosure provisions of the FECA: A steady stream of information on campaign finance may have left the public so jaded that it cannot summon the outrage necessary for reform.

In sum, the United States is likely to enter the 2000 election with a system of campaign finance regulation that is increasingly irrelevant. The new practices so prominent in 1996, especially soft money donations and issue advocacy spending, are likely to become more common. Although the future of campaign finance regulation is far from clear, a new era is upon us.

## 2

Herbert E. Alexander

# Spending in the 1996 Elections

The 1996 elections cost more than any previous elections, yet produced the lowest voter turnout since 1924. During the 1995–96 election cycle, political candidates, committees, and other organizations and individuals spent a total of $4.2 billion on political campaigns. This spending covered not only campaigns for nomination and election to federal offices—the presidency and seats in Congress—but also nomination and election campaigns for state and local offices; campaigns for and against ballot propositions; efforts by political parties and numerous independent organizations to register and turn out voters and engage in issue advertising; and the costs of administering national, state, and local political party organizations and numerous political committees sponsored by interest and ideological groups.

The $4.2 billion represents an increase of 32 percent over the Citizens' Research Foundation (CRF) estimate for the 1991–92 election cycle (Alexander and Corrado 1995). Notably, this increase far exceeded the 11.8 percent rise in the Consumer Price Index (CPI) from 1992 to 1996. This increase was more than enough to stoke the fires of criticism of political campaign costs, compounded by the revelations of high "soft money" spending and other questionable fund-raising and spending practices.

Critics maintain that high campaign costs force candidates to devote an inordinate amount of time to raising money. They also hold that special interest groups seeking to exercise influence by satisfying candidates' needs for campaign funds threaten the integrity of the election and governmental processes. Compared with some other categories of spending, however, the amounts expended for political campaigns are low. The amount spent in 1995–96 is less than the sum that the nation's two leading commercial advertisers—Procter and Gamble and General Motors—spent in 1996 to proclaim the quality of their products (*Advertising Age* 1997, 54). It represents a mere fraction of 1 percent of the $2.4 trillion spent in 1996 by federal, state, and local governments (U.S. Department of Commerce 1998, 57). And it is just a tiny portion of what is spent on cosmetics or gambling.

As with many kinds of spending, there is no universally accepted criterion by which to determine when political spending becomes excessive. Many factors have contributed to what sometimes appear to be high political campaign costs. No candidate wants to lose for having spent too little. During the past two decades, political campaigning at most levels has become a highly professionalized undertaking, involving pollsters, media specialists, computer specialists, fund-raising consultants, and a host of other experts whose services are expensive and, in the estimation of many candidates and committees, essential. The costs of items and services many campaigns must purchase, including travel, telephones, and broadcast time, have risen dramatically. In addition, federal, state, and local laws enacted to compel disclosure of campaign finances and, in some cases, to impose limits on political contributions and expenditures and to provide public funding, have required candidates to hire election attorneys and accountants to ensure compliance. Candidates and political committees must compete for attention not only with each other but also with commercial advertisers that have access to large budgets and are able to advertise regularly—in the electronic and print media—and not just during the campaign season. Finally, the Supreme Court has encouraged greater spending by determining that limits on campaign expenditures are unconstitutional except when voluntarily agreed to by candidates as a condition of accepting public funding. It has ruled further that even when campaigns are publicly funded, no limits may be placed on independent expenditures by individuals and committees that seek to advocate candidates' election or defeat. And the explosion of spending in 1996 on issue advertising—adding at least $150 million to the totals—has been upheld by lower courts (Beck et al. 1997).[1]

## Categories of Political Spending in 1996

The campaign bill of $4.2 billion in the 1995–96 election cycle may be classified in eight major categories (see Table 2.1):

Table 2.1

**Campaign Spending in 1996** (in millions $)

| | |
|---|---:|
| Presidential[a] | $ 700 |
| Congressional[b] | 838 |
| National party[c] | 354 |
| Party—state and local[d] | 209 |
| Soft money (all levels)[e] | 271 |
| Nonparty[f] | 505 |
| State (nonfederal)[g] | 650 |
| Local (nonfederal)[h] | 425 |
| Ballot issues[i] | 225 |
| | $4,177 |

*Source:* Citizens' Research Foundation.

[a]Includes all presidential-election-related spending in prenomination, convention, and general election periods, plus independent expenditures, communication costs, and issue advocacy on their behalf.

[b]Includes all spending by congressional candidates, plus independent expenditures, communication costs, and issue advocacy on their behalf.

[c]Includes all spending by national political party committees except money contributed to presidential and congressional candidates, coordinated expenditures on behalf of presidential candidates, and that portion of money spent on media advertising in presidential campaigns. Includes only hard and soft money.

[d]Includes all hard money spending reported by federally registered state and local party committees, minus money contributed to, or spent on behalf of, presidential candidates; money contributed directly to congressional candidates; and estimated expenditures on grassroots activities to support presidential tickets. Includes only hard money.

[e]Includes all party soft money—national, state, and local.

[f]Includes all spending reported by federally registered, nonparty political committees and their sponsors, except money contributed to federal candidates and political party committees and money spent independently on behalf of presidential and congressional candidates. Includes an estimated $200 million in political action committee administration and fund-raising costs paid by PAC sponsors but not reported to the FEC.

[g]Includes all spending by, or on behalf of, candidates for state offices, and the maintenance of state party committees.

[h]Includes all spending by, or on behalf of, candidates for local offices, and the maintenance of local party committees.

[i]Includes all spending in campaigns to support or oppose state and local ballot issues, and ballot qualification costs.

1. *Spending on presidential campaigns* ($700 million), including spending on prenomination campaigns that began in 1995; spending by nominating convention committees; spending by major-party, minor-party, and independent presidential general election campaigns; and spending by national party committees on behalf of their presidential nominees (Federal Election Commission 1997a).[2] There were twenty-

one presidential candidates filed with the Federal Election Commission (FEC) who were on the general election ballot in at least one state; Republican Dole, Democrat Clinton, Reform Party Perot, and Libertarian candidate Harry Browne qualified on the November ballot in all fifty states. Some eighteen candidates spent at least $5,000 each for minor-party nomination or general election campaigns.

2. *Spending on congressional campaigns* ($838 million), including money contributed directly to candidates by party and nonparty political committees in prenomination, general election, and special election campaigns (Federal Election Commission 1997c). Also included are independent expenditures, communication costs, and related issue advocacy, the latter amounting to $73 million.

3. *Spending by national political party committees* ($354 million), including administration, fund-raising, and other costs, but excluding coordinated expenditures on behalf of presidential candidates and direct contributions to congressional candidates that are already counted in the first two categories (Federal Election Commission 1997b). Also excluded is soft money (see below).

4. *Spending by federally registered state and local party committees* ($209 million), including administrative expenses shared with state-oriented party committees, but excluding money contributed to, or spent on behalf of, presidential candidates and money contributed directly to congressional candidates (Federal Election Commission 1997b). Some of these funds were combined with soft money, as required by FEC formulas, to produce and air issue ads.

5. *Spending of soft money* ($271 million), funds most often routed through special nonfederal committees associated with the national party committees, which then channeled the money to state and local committees regulated by state laws (Federal Election Commission 1997b). This money was mixed in part with hard money to produce and air issue ads, but also was used for local canvassing, registration, and get-out-the-vote campaigns.

6. *Spending by nonparty political committees and their sponsors* ($505 million), including an estimated $200 million in political action committee (PAC) administration and fund-raising costs paid by PAC sponsors but not reported to the FEC, excluding funds contributed directly to federal candidates or spent independently to influence presidential or congressional elections (Federal Election Commission 1997d).

Table 2.2

**U.S. Political Costs, 1952–1996**

| Year | Amount |
|------|--------|
| 1952 | $  140,000,000 |
| 1956 | 155,000,000 |
| 1960 | 175,000,000 |
| 1964 | 200,000,000 |
| 1968 | 300,000,000 |
| 1972 | 425,000,000 |
| 1976 | 540,000,000 |
| 1980 | 1,200,000,000 |
| 1984 | 1,800,000,000 |
| 1988 | 2,700,000,000 |
| 1992 | 3,220,000,000 |
| 1996 | 4,200,000,000 |

*Source:* Citizens' Research Foundation.

7. *Spending on (nonfederal) state election campaigns* ($650 million), including the costs in eleven states to nominate and elect governors and other statewide officials; the money spent on legislative elections; and the maintenance of political party organizations (e.g., Beyle 1998; Moncrief 1998).

8. *Spending on (nonfederal) local campaigns* ($425 million) to nominate and elect county, regional, and municipal officials, and the maintenance of political party organizations.

9. *Spending on (nonfederal) state and local ballot proposition campaigns* ($225 million), pro and con.

Adding together the first six categories, approximately $2.8 billion was spent at the federal level. This represents a full $500 million more than in 1992, and is higher than other estimates (e.g., Abramson 1997b).[3]

From 1952, the first year for which total political costs in the United States were calculated, to 1996, spending in presidential election cycles has steadily increased, as shown in Table 2.2 (Alexander and Haggerty 1987).

## Patterns in Political Spending

Consideration of selected spending patterns in 1996 will illuminate why the political bill was as high as it was, and how the cost factors seem to be forever rising. Simply put, there was greater diversity in spending by many new actors in an expanding electoral arena. There were great increases in both individual and institutional giving. There were also great increases in both hard and soft money, leading to higher party expenditures. And outside spending by interest groups exploded in terms of hard money in independent expenditures and soft money in issue advertising. It is worth noting that spending limits in the publicly funded presidential campaigns failed to control amounts spent in each of the three phases of the presidential selection process— the prenomination campaigns, the national nominating conventions, and the general election campaigns.

### Presidential Elections

A combined total of $700 million was spent on the three phases of the presidential selection process, an increase of 21 percent from the equivalent 1991–92 cost of $550 million (see Table 2.3).

Public funds provided the basic monies in each phase of the presidential selection process. The laws provided for public matching funds for qualified candidates in the prenomination period (including minor-party candidates who qualified), public grants to pay the costs of the two major parties' national nominating conventions, and public grants for the major-party general election candidates. Spending limits were applied to each phase of the process. The laws also established criteria whereby minor parties and new parties could qualify for the public funds to pay nominating convention and general election campaign costs; the general election campaign of the Reform Party's ticket, Ross Perot and Pat Choate, was mainly publicly financed and qualified for eligibility based on Perot's 1992 showing.

Some $234 million, or approximately 35 percent of total spending on the presidential selection process, consisted of public funding provided by the U.S. Treasury on certifications by the FEC; this amount compared with $175.4 million paid out in the 1991–92 election cycle and represented a 45 percent increase, a giant leap from previous totals (see Table 2.4). This put a strain on the presidential public funding system and left a very small balance, about $3 million, toward needs in the presidential elections of 2000.

While the 1996 spending was high, when seen in perspective in Table 2.5, the long-term trends are not so alarming. When adjusted for

Table 2.3

**Costs of Electing a President, 1996** (in million $)

| Prenomination | |
|---|---|
| Spending by major-party candidates | $228.6 |
| RNC spending on Dole nomination campaign | 14.0 |
| DNC spending in Clinton nomination campaign | 17.0 |
| Spending by minor-party candidates | 11.7 |
| Independent expenditures | 0.7 |
| Communication costs | 1.1 |
| Compliance costs | 10.0 |
| Subtotal | $282.5 |
| | |
| Conventions (including host cities and committees) | |
| Republicans | $ 31.0 |
| Democrats | 34.0 |
| Subtotal | $ 65.0 |
| | |
| General election | |
| Spending by major-party candidates[a] | $125.2 |
| Parties coordinated expenditures[b] | 18.4 |
| Compliance | 13.6 |
| Nonparty organizations[c] | 25.0 |
| Spending by minor parties | 27.6 |
| Independent expenditures | 0.7 |
| Labor, corporate, association spending | 20.0 |
| Parties soft money, issue advertising[d] | 68.0 |
| Communication costs | 1.6 |
| Subtotal | $300.1 |
| | |
| Miscellaneous expenses[e] | $ 52.4 |
| | |
| Grand total | $700.0 |

*Source:* Citizens' Research Foundation.

[a]Includes $61.8 million in public funds spent by each major-party ticket.

[b]Includes $11.7 million in hard money coordinated expenditures by RNC and $6.7 million by DNC.

[c]Includes a reasonable portion of funds spent by nonpartisan organizations to conduct voter registration and get-out-the-vote drives that benefited presidential candidates.

[d]Includes soft money expenditures related to the presidential campaigns by the Democratic National Committee and the Republican National Committee.

[e]Miscellaneous out-of-pocket expenditures at all levels.

Table 2.4

**Payouts from the Presidential Election Campaign Fund, 1976–1996**

| Year | Amount (in million $) |
|------|------------------------|
| 1976 | $ 71.4 |
| 1980 | 101.6 |
| 1984 | 132.6 |
| 1988 | 176.9 |
| 1992 | 175.4 |
| 1996 | 234.0 |

*Source:* Federal Election Commission.

inflation since 1960, the costs of presidential campaigns have increased only by a factor of four and one-half, whereas aggregate unadjusted costs have risen almost twenty-four-fold from 1960 to 1996.

*Prenomination Campaigns*

In the presidential prenomination period, some $244.5 million was spent by Democratic, Republican, Reform Party, Libertarian Party, and other candidates; eleven candidates received federal matching funds, accounting for $56.8 million, or 23 percent of the total prenomination costs. Three candidates spent large amounts of their own money:

- Ross Perot spent $8.5 million in founding the Reform Party and contesting its nomination against Richard Lamm, which, if added to his $64 million self-contribution in 1992, makes him the largest contributor in American history;
- Steven Forbes spent $41.6 million, mostly his own money, in seeking the Republican nomination;
- Morris Taylor, an industrialist who also sought the Republican nomination, spent $6.5 million, mostly his own money.

Two other candidates, mostly dependent on contributions from others, did not seek matching funds:

- Richard Lamm, $289,500, spent in contesting the Reform Party nomination won by Ross Perot;
- Harry Browne, the Libertarian Party candidate, $1.3 million.

Both President Clinton and the eventual Republican nominee, Rob-

Table 2.5

**Presidential Spending, 1960–1996** (in million $)

|  | Actual spending | Adjusted spending |
|---|---|---|
| 1960 | $ 30.0 | $ 30.0 |
| 1964 | 60.0 | 57.3 |
| 1968 | 100.0 | 85.1 |
| 1972 | 138.0 | 97.7 |
| 1976 | 160.0 | 83.2 |
| 1980 | 275.0 | 98.9 |
| 1984 | 325.0 | 93.7 |
| 1988 | 500.0 | 126.5 |
| 1992 | 550.0 | 117.8 |
| 1996 | 700.0 | 132.1 |

*Source:* Citizens' Research Foundation.

*Note:* Spending figures include prenomination, convention, and general election costs. Adjusted spending figures are based on 1960 dollars.

ert Dole, accepted public funds and spent up to the $37.1 million limit in seeking nomination. The two campaigns could not have been more different. Clinton had no competition for the Democratic nomination, yet he spent the full amount, some of it in primary and caucus states, but much of it in ways that would be helpful in the November election, thus giving the Clinton-Gore ticket a special advantage. Another advantage for Clinton-Gore consisted of more than $40 million in soft money advertising extolling the ticket's virtues but not expressly advocating their election; the advertising took place both before and after their nomination.

On the other hand, Dole's spending was in a highly competitive field of candidates. Early in the campaign season, front-runner Dole was forced to spend money to fend off vigorous and sometimes well-financed challengers from such rivals as Senator Phil Gramm and commentator Patrick Buchanan. When the independently wealthy Steve Forbes later joined the fray, he upped the ante, forcing Dole to spend even more to remain competitive.

Such spending left the Republican nominee dangerously close not only to the overall prenomination spending limit ($37.1 million) but also to individual state limits in states especially important in the general election campaign. After clinching the nomination in March, he was assisted by "generic" issue advertising on television paid for by

Republican state and local party committees spending soft money. Dole's ability to present his message directly to voters was curtailed by his legal inability to spend raised money in his own way. The spending limit reduced Dole's flexibility and made the campaign process more rigid.

*National Conventions*

The second phase of the presidential selection process consisted of the national nominating conventions. The major-party conventions were financed in part by public funds; in 1996 the two conventions, the Republicans in San Diego and the Democrats in Chicago, were each provided $12.3 million in public funds. Although the public funds were the legal limit of convention spending, the actual costs of the conventions were $31 million for the Republicans and $34 million for the Democrats. Other resources from the convention cities' municipal host committees, tourist bureaus, and corporate and labor sponsors paid for the additional amounts beyond the spending limits. Here the expenditure limits did not control spending.

*General Election*

In the 1996 general election period, three distinct but parallel campaigns were conducted by the major-party candidates or on their behalf. Only one of them operated under legally imposed spending limits. The three campaigns broke down as follows:

1. In the *first campaign,* spending was limited by law to the $61.8 million provided in public funding. This money was supplemented by allowable national party coordinated expenditures of $12 million, making the official spending limit $73.8 million for each of the major-party tickets.

2. In the *second campaign,* however, spending is provided for, but not limited under the law. A small portion represents funds raised under the law to pay compliance costs to ensure that candidates do not violate the law (GELAC funds). A much larger portion was used to pay direct and indirect campaign costs beyond the limits. Much was in the form of soft money contributions raised by the major parties outside federal limits from wealthy individuals, corporations, and labor unions. It also represents money spent on the nominees' behalf by

labor unions, trade associations, and membership groups on partisan communications with their constituencies and on nominally nonpartisan activities directed to the general public but clearly intended to benefit the nominees.

3. In the *third campaign,* independent spending was conducted by individuals and groups legally permitted to spend unlimited amounts to advocate the election or defeat of selected candidates, as long as they do so without consultation or collaboration with candidates and their campaigns.

Adding together the amounts spent on these three aspects of the presidential campaigns in 1996, a total of $156.9 million was spent by or on behalf of the Clinton-Gore ticket, and $131 million by or on behalf of the Dole-Kemp ticket (see Table 2.6). Here, too, the legal spending limits did not control expenditures.

Thus, all three phases of the presidential selection process provided evidence that the spending limits were not effective.

Important components of these amounts were both hard and soft monies raised and spent by or on behalf of the major-party candidates for president and vice president. About one-half of the soft money was spent by the major parties, but there also was a marked increase in spending on behalf of, or against, candidates by labor unions, businesses, and ideological groups, such as the Coalition, some disclosed and some not disclosed. Both major parties were charged with funneling money to outside groups for such spending.

One curiosity in spending occurred as the result of a Supreme Court decision in the case of *Colorado Republican Federal Campaign Committee* v. *Federal Election Commission* (518 U.S. 604 [1996]). This decision opened a new avenue for political party spending, independent expenditures. The National Republican Senatorial Committee spent about $10 million in this category and the Democratic Senatorial Campaign Committee about $1.5 million.

## Minor Parties and Independent Presidential Candidates

Ross Perot was the most important and influential minor-party candidate in 1996, but there were other minor-party and independent candidates as well. Some $28.1 million was spent by Perot and others. Perot accounts for most of the spending, about $25 million of it in the general election campaign. But Perot also spent $8.5 million of his own

Table 2.6

**Sources of Funds, Major-Party Presidential Candidates, 1996 General Election** (in million $)

|  | Sources of funds | Dole | Clinton |
|---|---|---|---|
| Limited campaign | | | |
| Candidate controlled | Federal grant | $ 61.8 | $ 61.8 |
| | National party | 12.0 | 12.0 |
| Unlimited campaigns | | | |
| Candidate may coordinate | Party soft money[a] | 48.2 | 54.1 |
| | Labor[b] | 2.0 | 20.0 |
| | Corporate/association compliance | 6.0 | 8.0 |
| Independent of candidate | Independent expenditures[c] | 1.0 | 1.0 |
| Total | | $131.0 | $156.9 |

*Source:* Citizens' Research Foundation, based on Federal Election Commission and other data.

[a]Includes soft money raised by the national party committees and channeled to state and local party committees from July 1, 1992, through December 31, 1992.

[b]Includes hard and soft money, and internal communication costs (both those in excess of $2,000, which are reported as required by law, and those less than $2,000, which are not reported), registration and voter turnout expenditures, overhead, and related costs. Labor amount includes $2.4 million spent in partisan communication costs.

[c]Does not include amount spent to oppose the candidates: $34,648 against Bush and $506,758 against Clinton.

money in forming the Reform Party and in seeking its nomination, which was challenged by Richard Lamm, who spent $289,500 in losing the nomination to Perot. Thus Perot and the Reform Party spent a total of $33.5 million in 1996-related activities.

## Congressional Elections

The costs of electing a Congress were about $765.3 million. This amount includes (1) direct spending by general election candidates including their primary expenses; (2) candidate spending in special elections; and (3) spending by candidates who lost in the primaries. The FEC has reported the breakdown of candidates' spending as follows: $477.8 million spent on campaigns for the House of Representatives, and $287.5 million on campaigns for the Senate.

Table 2.7

**Congressional Campaign Expenditures, 1972–1996** (in millions $)

| Election cycle | Total | Senate | House |
|---|---|---|---|
| 1971–72 | $ 77.3 | $   30.7 | $ 46.5 |
| 1973–74 | 88.2 | 34.7 | 53.5 |
| 1975–76 | 115.5 | 44.0 | 71.5 |
| 1977–78 | 194.8 | 85.2 | 109.7 |
| 1979–80 | 239.0 | 102.9 | 136.0 |
| 1981–82 | 342.4 | 138.4 | 204.0 |
| 1983–84 | 374.1 | 170.5 | 203.6 |
| 1985–86 | 450.9 | 211.6 | 239.3 |
| 1987–88 | 457.7 | 201.2 | 256.5 |
| 1989–90 | 446.3 | 180.4 | 265.8 |
| 1991–92 | 678.3 | 271.6 | 406.7 |
| 1993–94 | 724.2 | 319.0 | 406.2 |
| 1995–96 | 765.3 | 287.5 | 477.8 |

*Source:* Citizens' Research Foundation compilation based on FEC and other data.

These amounts were for the period from January 1, 1995, through December 31, 1996, and total spending for this election cycle was $40 million higher than for the 1993–94 election cycle (see Table 2.7). This result occurred despite lower spending in Senate campaigns compared with 1994 for two reasons. First, there were no Senate campaigns in the two largest and most costly states, California and New York; and second, fewer wealthy candidates spent large amounts of their own money than in 1994, when Michael Huffington spent $28 million of his own money in a losing campaign in California. For this latter reason, the index of self-spending candidates was down from 1994.

Spending on congressional campaigns reached its peak late in the election season, even though polling results throughout 1996 consistently showed President Clinton ahead of Senator Dole in the presidential campaigns. By October, significant party funds were diverted from the presidential campaigns and focused on the congressional. Party control of both the Senate and House was in doubt, and excess spending, particularly for House campaigns, was thought likely by both parties to influence control of the Congress.

As in the presidential campaigns, these amounts tell only part of the story. In addition to candidate spending, there was party spending, both hard and soft money, and PAC operations (not counting funds given to presidential or congressional candidates), independent expenditures (at least $14.8 million in Senate campaigns, and $5.4 million in House campaigns), and issue advocacy (estimated at $150 million), one-half of it intended to affect the outcome of Senate and House contests. The PAC component accounted for $215.3 million that was contributed to congressional candidates and only $2.5 million to presidential candidates. PACs also spent $10.6 million in independent expenditures for and against federal candidates.

## Political Parties

The total amounts of spending by parties in 1995–96 rose dramatically compared with the previous presidential election cycle of 1991–92, in both hard and soft money categories. In hard money, national, state, and local Republican committees spent $408.5 million, representing a 62 percent increase over the 1991–92 election cycle. In comparison, Democratic committees spent $214.3 million, representing a 36 percent increase. In addition, soft money spending by Democrats totaled $121.8 million, rising a remarkable 271 percent, while Republican spending rose to $149.7 million, representing a notable 224 percent increase (Federal Election Commission 1997b). Of these amounts, both parties spent in hard money less than the legal limit, $12 million, on their presidential general election campaigns, while in soft money the Democrats outspent the Republicans, $54.1 million to $48.2 million; both of these amounts are shown in Table 2.6. When all forms of spending are considered, including corporate, labor, compliance, and independent expenditures, the Clinton-Gore ticket outspent the Dole-Kemp ticket $156.9 million to $131 million.

In congressional campaigns, the parties contributed $5.9 million and paid out in coordinated expenditures some $35.1 million. Of these amounts, the Republican amounts of assistance to their candidates were greater. Despite the large amounts raised and spent, both parties ended the 1996 election year with extensive debts: Republican debts totaled $15 million, and Democratic debts were $17.4 million. While each party had about $5.5 million cash on hand at the end of the year, the rest of the debts seemed manageable with renewed fund-raising efforts by President Clinton and Vice President Gore, on the one hand, and Speaker Gingrich and others, on the other hand. Individuals accounted for 87 percent of Republican receipts, compared with 77 percent for Democrats. PAC support provided $19.2 million for Democratic Party committees at the federal level, and $13.8 million for Republican committees.

## Political Action Committees

The total amounts of spending by PACs in 1995–96, $429.9 million, represented an 11 percent increase over 1994 (Federal Election Commission 1997d). Here the significant factor is how much money went to incumbents, $146.4 million, or 67 percent, compared with amounts to challengers, $31.6 million, or 15 percent, and to open-seat candidates, $39.8 million, or 18 percent. The incumbent advantage is notable, and since Republicans controlled both the Senate and the House, Republican candidates received $115.8 million compared with $98.8 million contributed by PACs to Democrats.

## Patterns of Political Giving

Although the costs of television, the total costs of campaigning, and the general availability of funding have risen dramatically over recent decades, the percentage of those who donate to candidates and parties has not changed much since 1952. An overview of responses to public opinion surveys on political contributions from 1952 to 1996 is given in Table 2.8. Although these figures are subject to a polling error of up to 4 percent, their replication over the years gives confidence that the upper and lower parameters of giving are accurate.

Electoral reform has restrained the large giver, prompting alternative techniques of fund-raising—sophisticated direct-mail appeals, soft money, and other means. Even with the widespread use of these techniques by candidates and political organizations in 1996, the proportion of the population giving to political causes does not appear to have increased. Yet campaign spending has increased because those individuals who give are giving more, and institutional giving by corporations, labor unions, trade associations, and others has increased greatly.

While increased spending in the 1980s and 1990s is not reflected in the results of surveys on giving, the national adult civilian population, on which these surveys are based, has grown, so 4 or 5 percent in later years represents a larger aggregate because the universe is larger than in the earlier years.

Table 2.8

## Percentage of National Adult Population Making Political Contributions, 1952–1992

| Year | Polling organization | Contributed to | | Total[a] |
|------|---------------------|----------------|-----------|----------|
| | | Republican | Democrat | |
| 1952 | SRC | 3 | 1 | 4 |
| 1956 | Gallup | 3 | 6 | 9 |
| 1956 | SRC | 5 | 5 | 10 |
| 1960 | Gallup | 4 | 4 | 9 |
| 1960 | Gallup | | | 12 |
| 1960 | SRC | 7 | 4 | 12 |
| 1964 | Gallup | 6 | 4 | 12 |
| 1964 | SRC | 5 | 4 | 10 |
| 1968 | SRC | 3 | 3 | 8[b] |
| 1972 | SRC | 4 | 5 | 10[c] |
| 1974 | SRC | 3 | 3 | 8[d] |
| 1976 | Gallup | 3 | 3 | 8[e] |
| 1976 | SRC | 4 | 4 | 9[f] |
| 1980 | CPS | 3 | 1 | 4 |
| 1984 | CPS | 2 | 2 | 4 |
| 1988 | CPS | 4 | 2 | 6 |
| 1992 | CPS | 2 | 2 | 4 |
| 1996 | CPS | 3 | 2 | 6 |

*Sources:* Survey Research Center (SRC), and later the Center for Political Studies (CPS), both at the University of Michigan; data direct from the center or from Angus Campbell, Philip E. Converse, and Donald E. Stokes, *The American Voter* (New York: John Wiley and Sons, 1960), p. 91; 1980 data from Ruth S. Jones and Warren E. Miller, "Financing Campaigns: Macro Level Innovation and Micro Level Response, " *Western Political Quarterly* 38, no. 2 (1987); 1984 data from Ruth S. Jones, "Campaign Contributions and Campaign Solicitations: 1984" (Paper presented at the meeting of the Southern Political Science Association, Nashville, Tenn., November 6–9, 1985); Gallup data direct or from Roper Opinion Research Center, Williams College, and from the American Institute of Political Opinion (Gallup poll).

[a]The total percentage may add to a total different from the total of Democratic and Republican contributors because of individuals contributing to both major parties, or to candidates of both major parties, nonparty groups, or combinations of these.

[b]Includes 0.7 percent who contributed to the American Independent Party (AIP).

[c]Includes contributors to the American Independent Party.

[d]Includes 0.7 percent who contributed to both parties and 0.8 percent who contributed to minor parties.

[e]Includes 1 percent to another party and 1 percent to "do not know" or "no answer."

[f]Republican and Democratic figures are rounded. The total includes 0.6 percent who gave to both parties, 0.4 percent to other, and 0.3 percent "do not know."

A broader series of surveys of differentiated contributors has been carried out by the Center for Political Studies at the University of Michigan since 1980. This series, results of which are summarized in Table 2.9, has been conducted every two years, in congressional as well as presidential years.

It is worth noting that the congressional years include many more gubernatorial elections—some thirty-six states—compared with only eleven states in presidential years, so the percentages of organizational contributors (which includes party givers shown in Table 2.8) was relatively steady in congressional as well as in presidential election years. The data also suggest that the opportunity to give to a growing number of PACs has not stimulated an increase in the percentage of the population willing to contribute to an organized group. While PAC contributors were at as high a level as party contributors in 1980 and 1982, the proportion of such donors, which is included in the category "other group" in recent years and presumably includes PAC donors, has remained steady at 4 to 6 percent.

From 1952 to 1996, between 4 and 12 percent of the total adult population said they contributed to politics at some level. Clearly, some persons contribute in more than one category. The conclusion of one study of patterns of giving is insightful:

> While it is true that more and more people are now asked, by phone and mail, to make political contributions, the response rate is generally very low. Modern technology notwithstanding, face-to-face appeals continue to be the most effective way of soliciting political contributions. There does not seem to be a large, undifferentiated electorate just waiting for an invitation to contribute to campaigns. (Jones 1990)

The data seem to bear out this conclusion. It should be noted, however, that one factor in the years 1972 to 1984 was missing since 1986: a federal income tax credit for portions of political contributions. The Tax Reform Act of 1986 repealed the credit (Public Law 99–514). Whatever incentive the tax benefit may once have given contributors has not been available in later years.

## The Federal Tax Checkoff

The Revenue Act of 1971 established a voluntary tax checkoff provision on federal income tax forms that allows individual taxpayers to

Table 2.9.

**Mode of Political Contributions, 1980–1996** (in percentages)

| | 1980 (N = 1,395) | 1982 (N = 1,418) | 1984 (N = 1,944) | 1986 (N = 2,176) | 1988 (N = 1,775) | 1990 (N = 2,000) | 1992 (N = 2,252) | 1994 (N = 1,795) | 1996 (N = 1,714) |
|---|---|---|---|---|---|---|---|---|---|
| Federal tax checkoff[a] | 26.0 | 30.0 | 31.0 | 32.0 | 26.0 | 25.0 | 26.0 | N.A.* | N.A.* |
| State tax checkoff[b] | 6.0 | 7.0 | N.A. | N.A. | N.A. | N.A. | N.A. | N.A. | N.A. |
| Candidate organization[c] | 6.0 | 7.0 | 5.0 | 5.0 | 6.0 | 5.0 | 6.0 | 4.6 | 4.9 |
| Republican | 3.8 | 2.8 | 2.1 | 2.1 | 2.7 | 2.2 | 2.2 | 2.1 | 2.6 |
| Democrat | 2.0 | 4.0 | 2.4 | 2.4 | 2.6 | 2.5 | 3.0 | 1.7 | 1.8 |
| Both | N.A. | N.A. | 0.3 | 0.2 | 0.4 | 0.2 | 0.4 | 0.5 | 0.2 |
| Other[d] | 0.5 | 0.4 | 0.2 | 0.2 | 0.2 | 0.2 | 0.4 | 0.1 | 0.2 |
| Party organization[e] | 4.0 | 4.0 | 5.0 | 5.0 | 6.0 | 4.0 | 4.0 | 4.4 | 5.6 |
| Republican | 3.0 | 2.7 | 2.6 | 2.7 | 4.0 | 1.9 | 1.9 | 2.5 | 2.8 |
| Democrat | 1.0 | 1.3 | 2.0 | 1.9 | 1.9 | 1.8 | 1.8 | 1.3 | 2.2 |
| Both | N.A. | N.A. | 0.2 | 0.3 | 0.1 | 0.1 | 0.1 | 0.3 | 0.2 |
| Other[f] | 0.0 | 0.0 | 0.2 | 0.1 | 0.0 | 0.1 | 0.1 | 0.3 | 0.4 |
| PAC[g] | 7.0 | 8.0 | N.A. | N.A. | N.A. | N.A. | N.A. | N.A. | N.A. |
| Ballot issue[h] | N.A. | N.A. | 2.0 | N.A. | N.A. | N.A. | N.A. | N.A. | N.A. |
| Other group[i] | N.A. | N.A. | 2.0 | 3.0 | 4.0 | 5.0 | 5.0 | 5.0 | 5.0 |

Summary

| | | | | | | | | |
|---|---|---|---|---|---|---|---|---|
| Noncontributor[j] | 68.0 | 63.0 | 65.0 | 64.0 | 68.0 | 69.0 | 69.0 | 89.0** | 88.0** |
| Checkoff only[k] | 20.0 | 21.0 | 26.0 | 27.0 | 20.0 | 20.0 | 20.0 | N.A.* | N.A.* |
| Organizational giver[l] | 11.0 | 15.0 | 10.0 | 9.0 | 12.0 | 10.0 | 11.0 | 11.0 | 12.0 |

*Source:* Based on data of the Center for Political Studies, University of Michigan, and compiled by Professor Warren E. Miller.

*Note:* Entries do not always total 100 percent because of rounding.

[a]"Did you use the $1 checkoff option on your federal income tax return to make a political contribution?" The entries are those who said yes.

[b]"Did you make a political contribution by checking off that item on your state income tax return?" The entries are those who said yes.

[c]"Did you give money to an individual candidate?" The entries are those who said yes.

[d]"Which party did that candidate belong to?" Missing values are not included.

[e]"Did you give money to a political party?" The entries are those who said yes.

[f]"To which party did you give money?" Missing values are not included.

[g]"Did you give money to political action groups?" The entries are those who said yes.

[h]"Did you give any money to help support or oppose any ballot proposition this election year?" The entries are those who said yes.

[i]"Did you give any money to any other group that supported/opposed candidates?" The entries are those who said yes.

[j]The entries are an index that counts those who did not make political contributions at all.

[k]The entries count those who make only checkoff contributions.

[l]The entries count those who make other kinds of contributions and may have used the checkoff.

*This question no longer asked by NES.

**These entries are an index of those who made no organizational contributions.

designate limited tax dollars to the Presidential Election Campaign Fund (PECF), a separate account maintained by the Treasury Department to finance the public funding program for presidential elections. From 1972 to 1992, the law allowed individuals with a federal tax liability to check off a specific amount—$1 for individuals and $2 for married persons filing jointly—without increasing their tax obligation or reducing the amount of any anticipated refund. In 1993, the amount of the checkoff was increased to $3 for individuals and $6 for married persons filing jointly (Federal Election Commission 1994).[4]

The reported checkoff participation rates have steadily declined since 1981. As noted in Table 2.10, the early years of the checkoff were characterized by rising participation and substantial growth in the annual revenues deposited into the PECF. These trends peaked in 1981, when 28.7 percent of all tax returns designated money to the public financing program. Since then, participation has fallen to a low of 12.4 percent in 1997. Annual receipts also declined sharply, dropping from a high of more than $41 million in 1981 to less than $30 million in 1992 and 1993, until the checkoff amount was increased in 1993. In the last three years, the amounts raised have hovered in the range of $66 to $68 million per year.

As shown in Table 2.10, the low balances of funds in the PECF in 1992 and 1996 are explained by the utilization in these presidential election years of current funding available through tax checkoffs in the early months of those years, in order to meet shortfalls in needed monies. Similar shortfalls can be expected in the year 2000 elections. With such a low balance coming out of the 1996 election year—only $3.6 million—the four-year totals will not oversupply the fund for the next presidential election. This situation will put an extra strain on the system for the 1999–2000 election cycle because the presidency will be an open seat, probably with heated competition for nominations in both major parties, and hence very costly.

The discrepancy between the figures on checkoff activity, which are compiled by the Internal Revenue Service (IRS) and Treasury Department and reported by the FEC, and the findings of survey research, may be explained in part by the conclusions of a Twentieth Century Fund study of the tax checkoff system. This 1993 analysis revealed that the decline in participation may not be as steady or steep as is often assumed. It noted that although the rate of checkoff participation has steadily declined since 1981, the actual number of participants has

Table 2.10

**The Federal Income Tax Checkoff**

| Calendar year | Percentage of returns with checkoff[a] | Dollar amount designated | Fund balances |
|---|---|---|---|
| 1997 | 12.4[c] | $66,347,632 | $ 69,907,162 |
| 1996 | 12.5[c] | 66,903,797 | 3,657,886 |
| 1995 | 12.9 | 67,860,127 | 146,862,732 |
| 1994[d] | 13.0 | 71,316,995 | 101,664,547 |
| 1993 | 14.5 | 27,636,982 | 30,779,386[e] |
| 1992 | 17.7 | 29,592,735 | 4,061,061 |
| 1991 | 19.5 | 32,322,336 | 127,144,469 |
| 1990 | 19.8 | 32,462,979 | 115,426,713 |
| 1989 | 20.1 | 32,285,646 | 82,927,013 |
| 1988 | 21.0 | 33,013,987 | 52,462,359 |
| 1987 | 21.7 | 33,651,947 | 177,905,677 |
| 1986 | 23.0 | 35,753,837 | 161,680,423 |
| 1985 | 23.0 | 34,712,761 | 125,870,541 |
| 1984 | 23.7 | 35,036,761 | 92,713,782 |
| 1983 | 24.2 | 35,631,068 | 177,320,982 |
| 1982 | 27.0 | 39,023,882 | 153,454,501 |
| 1981 | 28.7 | 41,049,052 | 114,373,289 |
| 1980 | 27.4 | 38,838,417 | 73,752,205 |
| 1979 | 25.4 | 35,941,347 | 135,246,807 |
| 1978 | 28.6 | 39,246,689 | 100,331,986 |
| 1977 | 27.5 | 36,606,008 | 60,927,571 |
| 1976 | 25.5 | 33,731,945 | 23,805,659 |
| 1975 | 24.2 | 31,656,525 | 59,551,245 |
| 1974[b] | 0.0 | 27,591,546 | 27,591,546 |
| 1973[b] | 0.0 | 2,427,000 | 2,427,000 |

*Source:* Federal Election Commission.

[a]The percentages refer to the tax returns of the previous year. For example, the 17.7 percent of 1991 tax returns that indicated a checkoff of $1 or $2 directed $29,592,735 into the Presidential Election Campaign Fund in calendar year 1992.

[b]The 1973 tax forms were the first to have the checkoff on the first page; in 1972 taxpayers had to file a separate form to exercise the checkoff option. To compensate for the presumed difficulty caused by the separate form, taxpayers were allowed to designate $1 for 1972 as well as 1973 on the 1973 forms. Given these circumstances, total and percentage figures for these returns would be misleading.

[c]The participation rates for 1996 and 1997 were taken from the Taxpayer Usage Study (TPUS), a sample based analysis generated by the Internal Revenue Service.

[d]1994 (1993 tax year returns) was the first year in which the checkoff value was $3.

not (Corrado 1993, 19–25). Between 1983 and 1991, when the rate of participation fell from 24.2 percent to 19.5 percent, the actual number of returns that earmarked a contribution remained relatively stable, ranging from 23.2 million to 22.3 million. In three of those years—

1986, 1988, and 1990—the number of participants was higher than in the previous years. This suggests that the sharpness of the decline is not due simply to the number of participants; it also is a function of the increase in the number of individual tax returns filed each year. For example, in 1985, 22.8 million tax returns designated a contribution, yielding a participation rate of 23 percent. In 1988, the same number of tax returns designated a contribution, but the participation rate fell to 21 percent (Corrado 1993, 19).

It is also important to note that despite the overall decline in participation over the past decade, the checkoff has served to expand the number of individuals who participate financially in the political system. About 80 percent of those who use the checkoff are not organizational or candidate contributors, which suggests that these individuals would not have participated financially had there been no checkoff. Moreover, the 30 million or more individuals represented by the checkoff percentages constitute a large body of support, especially when compared with the numbers of those who contribute money, who give service to parties and candidates, or who vote in congressional election years.

The checkoff system admittedly has experienced a substantial decline in annual receipts. Most observers assume that this decline is a result of the decline in participation. The problem with this assumption is that the annual revenue loss does not correspond to the drop in participation. For instance, between 1983 and 1991, the number of returns that included a checkoff contribution fell from 23.2 million to 22.3 million, and annual receipts fell from $35.6 million to $32.3 million. A decline of 900,000 returns thus resulted in an annual revenue loss of about $3.3 million. But since the maximum amount that could be checked off was $2 in those years (and this only if the return was a joint filing), the total loss should have been no more than $1.8 million, or $1.5 million less than the actual difference. Similarly, in 1986, the number of returns with a contribution rose by 1.1 million, but receipts increased by less than $1.1 million, or by less than the minimum checkoff of $1 per return. The likely explanation for these discrepancies is that some of those who earmarked a contribution had no tax liability and were ineligible to participate in the program. Even though these individuals chose to support the public financing program and marked the yes box on their tax forms, no money was deposited into the fund as a result of their actions because the regulations that govern the checkoff specify that only those with a tax liability may designate a contribution to the fund. The declining PECF revenues, therefore, are not simply a result of declining participation; they also are related to the tax status of checkoff participants.

For years, FEC officials have assumed that the low level of checkoff participation was largely a result of inadequate citizen understanding of the public financing system, a view supported by several research surveys (Sorauf 1988; Market Decisions Corporation 1990).

To address this problem and enhance participation, the FEC initiated a number of projects in advance of the 1992 election to improve public awareness of the checkoff. The agency sponsored focus-group surveys of public attitudes toward the checkoff; produced television and radio public service announcements in English and Spanish; and undertook an extensive public outreach effort that included the distribution of informational brochures, numerous media appearances by commission members, and special information packages for tax preparers and accounting software companies.

The FEC estimated that its announcements and education materials reached a potential audience of more than 90 million citizens in 1991 and about 200 million in 1992 (*Federal Election Commission Broadcast Media Public Education Program on the Tax Checkoff* 1991). While extensive, this effort was relatively modest in its resources and intensity. In most instances, the public service advertisements were broadcast infrequently, if at all. The program did not produce a level of exposure great enough to provide taxpayers with a clear understanding of the relatively complex provisions of the checkoff system. Nor was it strong enough to outweigh the public perception that the system is not working, or the growing feelings of frustration and alienation among the electorate. As a result, the FEC's efforts appear to have had little effect: Checkoff participation did not change appreciably in either 1991 or 1992. The FEC initiative was not repeated in 1995 or 1996.

Yet even if a major improvement in the level of public awareness is achieved, there is no guarantee that participation or checkoff receipts will increase. Studies sponsored by the FEC show that most noncontributors are unlikely to become contributors even with further education (Market Decisions Corporation 1990). There also appears to be limited potential for additional contributions from those who are presumably passive nonparticipants, that is, those who leave the checkoff boxes on their tax forms blank from year to year. Surveys of selected tax returns conducted by the Internal Revenue Service from 1989 to 1994 show that on average only about 16 to 18 percent of tax filers fail to check "no" or "yes" on the checkoff question on their forms (Internal Revenue Service 1994). While some of these individuals may simply be overlooking this question, others surely leave the boxes blank because they have no tax liability and are ineligible to participate. But even if all these individuals were potentially eligible and participated at rates comparable to the rest of the taxpaying population, their contributions would increase participation by only 3 or 4 percent. Thus, there does not appear to be a large bloc of checkoff nonparticipants within the electorate who can easily be identified and encouraged to contribute by means of the income tax checkoff.

In short, neither contributor percentages nor tax checkoff rates seem to hold a promise of large numbers of new persons pursuing these forms of political participation. Accordingly, as campaign costs continue to rise, the search for political dollars will become more intensive—and more costly.

## Conclusion

The 1995–96 election cycle raised serious doubts about the ability of the 1970s campaign finance laws and their enforcement agency, the FEC, to cope with the burgeoning campaigns of the mid-1990s. The Federal Election Campaign Act (FECA) proved itself outdated in 1996. As noted, there was a great diversity of spending by many actors in an expanding political arena. The infusion of money from foreign sources raised concern about the effectiveness of the regulatory system. This trend was compounded by whole new or enhanced categories of money, generated by whole new categories of players, in the form of soft money, party independent expenditures, bundlers, issue advertising by groups spending money to communicate with voters about candidates but not coordinating their activities with any party or candidate, and the utilization of some nonprofit groups to enable donors to avoid public disclosure. The blurring of the boundaries of campaign finance by interest-group spending poses questions of whether candidates and parties are losing control of their election campaigns.

An unremarkable presidential selection process was highlighted in the last month before the election by extraordinary public attention paid to aspects of its financing, leading to increasing calls for campaign reform on the federal level. Of special interest were revelations that the Democratic National Committee returned some $3.5 million in contributions, mainly from foreign sources. In some cases, contributors had been invited to the White House, to meetings and seminars with the president and vice president, and to golf, conventions, Air Force One rides, and other events. The Republicans also received smaller amounts of money from dubious sources, and their leaders met with large contributors at various functions. The Democrats unceasing determination to raise money enabled them to reduce the Republicans traditional advantage in fund-raising.

The "arms race" atmosphere led to numerous demands to reform the regulatory system. Republicans called for an independent counsel to investigate; to achieve this, by law, a Justice Department investigation must lay the groundwork for such an appointment. Intensive investigations were carried on by the Justice Department, leading to a number of indictments. But Attorney General Janet Reno resisted making an independent counsel appointment in three major cases. Meanwhile, the U.S. Senate Committee on Governmental Affairs and the U.S. House Committee on Government Reform and Oversight undertook hearings and investigations, providing the most extensive information about campaign financing since Watergate events in the 1970s. The American people have learned more about improper or questionable, if not corrupt, practices, but that wide media coverage so far has not translated into legislative action. In addition, spending in congressional campaigns continued to escalate in 1996, while outside spending by nonparty groups in some states and districts has exceeded money spent by candidates and parties.

Spending limits in the publicly funded presidential campaigns failed to control amounts spent in each of the three phases of the presidential selection process—the prenomination campaigns, the national nominating conventions, and the general election campaigns. One wonders why spending limits remain an article of faith with campaign finance reformers when the empirical evidence above shows repeatedly and conclusively that they only give the illusion that they are effective, but actually fail to control spending, and instead lead to inevitable spending in soft money and issue advocacy.

Election lawyers are continually testing the parameters of the law, challenging and probing, leading, among other results, to an emphasis on issue advertising that legally is not express advocacy and hence is not regulated or even fully disclosed. By reducing the arsenal of constitutional approaches to reform, the courts play a critical role in restricting the road to change. This frustrates reformers, while it constrains some of the means to bring about meaningful change. The intensifying drive for change is marked by uncertainty as to what public policy remedies are both feasible legislatively and acceptable constitutionally.

## Notes

1. Roughly one-half of the issue advocacy component was spending by party committees and one-half by interest groups.

2. Amount is based on Table 2.3 in this chapter, supplemented by direct assistance of Robert Biersack, supervisory statistician, Federal Election Commission.

3. Based on compilation of the Center for Responsive Politics.

4. This change was made under the Omnibus Budget Reconciliation Act signed into law by President Clinton on August 10, 1993.

WESLEY JOE AND CLYDE WILCOX

# Financing the 1996 Presidential Nominations: The Last Regulated Campaign?

The American process of selecting party nominees for presidential elections is long and complicated, with much as stake. At the beginning of the process, there are often many candidates in both major parties, advocating a range of policy agendas. At the end, only two candidates are left, who define the policy content of their respective parties and, if successful in the general election, the political agenda for the nation as a whole. But even the losing candidates can have an impact on national politics. Sometimes their ideas take root in the campaigns of their party's nominee: In 1988, for example, many observers noted that George Bush borrowed themes from Jack Kemp and Pat Robertson in his general election campaign. Often ideas of losing candidates, such as the flat-tax proposals of Republican candidates Phil Gramm and Steve Forbes in 1996, take on a new life as rallying cries for party factions or are incorporated into more general party appeals. Moreover, losing candidates can often negotiate for changes in party rules, as Jesse Jackson did in 1984 and Pat Robertson in 1988. And they sometimes end up in the cabinet of the party nominee, as did Jack Kemp after the 1988 campaign, or their importance may be symbolically acknowledged through major speeches at the party convention, as occurred in 1992 at the GOP convention.

Candidates who seek their party's nomination for the presidency must mount their own campaigns. They must decide their positions on key issues and which issues will form the core of their campaign. They must develop a strategy to win and a set of tactics to implement this

Table 3.1

**Presidential Prenomination Spending, 1996**

| | |
|---|---|
| Democratic Party | |
| Clinton | $ 38,105,490 |
| Republican Party | |
| Alexander | $ 16,353,539 |
| Buchanan | 24,489,005 |
| Dole | 42,173,706 |
| Dornan | 341,718 |
| Forbes | 41,657,444 |
| Gramm | 28,038,313 |
| Keyes | 4,252,471 |
| Lugar | 7,631,213 |
| Specter | 3,391,843 |
| Taylor | 6,504,966 |
| Wilson | 7,219,912 |
| Reform Party | |
| Perot | $  8,031,229 |
| Lamm | 289,500 |
| Total | $234,378,164[a] |

*Source*: Federal Election Commission.
[a]Includes some minor candidates not identified in this table.

strategy. Above all, they must raise enough money to get their message to the primary election and caucus voters. As the nomination period has become increasingly compressed in recent years, the importance of early money has grown. Money does not buy victory, but without it a candidate cannot get on the plane and fly to the next stop, cannot answer his or her opponents charges with a television advertisement, cannot commission a poll, or even pay for pizza to feed campaign workers. Money is a necessary but not sufficient condition for victory in presidential nomination politics. In 1996, more than a dozen major- and minor-party candidates spent $234 million—of which nearly one-quarter came from federal matching funds—on prenomination campaigns (Table 3.1).

In many ways, the financing of the 1996 presidential nominations resembled closely those of 1984. Like Ronald Reagan, President Bill Clinton was a popular incumbent with a strong economy who faced no intraparty opposition, and was a formidable fund-raiser. Thus, Clinton was able to spend all of his "primary election" money on the general election—either attacking his likely GOP opponent Senator Bob Dole or building his own support. Like Reagan, Clinton raised early soft money to enable his party to expand its machinery and to aid his candidacy indirectly. Like Walter Mondale, Dole was a respected party leader facing a near-impossible task—to hold off a strong set of challengers within his party, while looking ahead to a difficult general election.

Yet the financing of the 1996 campaigns differed importantly from the 1984 and any other earlier election. Clinton helped his party raise prodigious amounts of soft money long before the start of the campaign, and apparently worked closely with Democratic Party officials to fashion advertising designed to bolster Clinton's image. Reform Party candidate Ross Perot ran a second time, accepting matching funds and spending more than $8 million of his own money to finance his campaign. Most importantly, two millionaire businessmen sought the GOP nomination: Maurice Taylor, who spent $6.5 million of his own money, and Steve Forbes, who loaned his campaign $37.5 million. Forbes spent record sums early in the campaign and forced Dole to spend up to the legal limit to win the nomination.

In the end, the campaign finance laws were once again stretched, this time perhaps to the breaking point. Many aspects of the Clinton fund-raising effort were investigated by journalists, a Senate committee, and the Justice Department, calling attention to new and widespread practices (Wilcox 1999). A growing number of observers, including academics, politicians, and practitioners, called for campaign finance reform. As campaign professionals looked ahead to the 2000 campaigns, with an early California primary and an even more frontloaded calendar, they predicted that the scramble to raise campaign funds would be even more frantic. And with the advent of new spending techniques, such as issue advocacy, the 1996 nomination contest may have been the last fought under the post-Watergate campaign finance system embodied by the Federal Election Campaign Act (FECA).

Before we can discuss the specifics of the 1996 campaign, however, we must first describe the regulatory framework that guided this activity. Candidates choose their fund-raising strategies by assessing their resources and then considering the constraints of rules and of existing fund-raising practices.

## The Regulations

The 1974 amendments to FECA serve as the primary set of regulations on presidential nomination finance. This legislation was passed in response to the abuses of President Nixon's Committee to Re-Elect the President (CREEP). The 1972 presidential election was the most expensive to that point in history: The Nixon campaign spent a record $56 million, and the McGovern camp spent $40 million. In the investigations that followed, it was revealed that the Nixon campaign had essentially extorted illegal contributions from major companies and laundered the money. Moreover, there were many very large contributions from individuals who were later rewarded with ambassadorships.

In response to these revelations, Congress passed a set of comprehensive amendments to the FECA that radically transformed the financing of presidential nomination campaigns. Contributions to presidential nomination candidates were limited in size, federal money was provided to help candidates campaign, and a strict system of disclosure was established so that citizens could learn who was financing each candidate's efforts. Amendments to the law in 1979 and subsequent court decisions have further modified the law.

The regulatory regime can be summarized as follows:

1. *Limits:* The law limits contributions from individuals to $1,000 per candidate during the primary elections. Interest groups (through PACs) are limited to $5,000 per candidate, and the candidates themselves can give their own campaigns $50,000 if they accept matching funds (described below).

If candidates do not accept matching funds, they can give or loan unlimited amounts to their own campaigns. Individuals and interest groups can give unlimited amounts to the political parties for party-building activity—these large party gifts are called *soft money*. Soft money cannot be spent on the campaigns of specific federal candidates, and cannot be coordinated with those campaigns. Individuals and interest groups (through PACs) can spend unlimited amounts to advocate the election or defeat of a candidate. Individuals and groups can also spend unlimited amounts to advertise their positions on issues and can feature the images of candidates in these advertisements as long as they do not expressly call for the election or defeat of the candidate. Those advertisements that expressly advocate the election or defeat of a candidate (called *independent expenditures*) must be financed through FECA guidelines, which include contribution limits and the disclosure of spending to the FEC. Those that merely advocate an issue (called *issue advocacy*) need not be disclosed and can be financed from interest group treasuries and from contributions from individuals of unlimited amounts.

2. *Matching funds:* Each year American taxpayers can contribute $3 through a checkoff to a public fund, which is used to help finance the primary election campaigns, the party conventions, and the general election campaigns. During the primary elections, candidates can qualify for public matching funds by raising $100,000 in amounts of $250 or less, with $5,000 coming from each of twenty states. Once a candidate has met this criterion, the first $250 of any contribution from one individual is matched by money from the federal fund. There is an overall cap on total matching funds that any one campaign can receive: In 1996 that amount was slightly more than $13 million. Candidates can lose their ability to qualify for matching funds by doing poorly in primary elections and caucuses.

3. *Spending limits:* All candidates who accept matching funds must abide by state and overall spending limits. The state limits are based on the state's voting-age population, not on the strategic importance of the state. This means that the limits for critical early states, such as New Hampshire, are approximately the same as for Alaska and the District of Columbia. State limits are routinely ignored and evaded with a variety of tactics by all candidates (Wilcox 1991), and by 1996 reported figures on statewide spending were meaningless. The overall limit, however, has more force. In 1996, candidates could spend $30.9 million on campaign costs and another $6.2 million to raise the money.

In 1996, this "hard dollar" regulatory framework was stretched to the breaking point. The Clinton and Dole campaigns benefited from issue advocacy campaigns run by the national party committees and financed with soft money. This spending enabled both campaigns to circumvent federal laws restricting contributions and spending without giving up substantial federal matching funds.

## Regulations, Resources, and Candidate Fund-Raising Strategies

The regulations provide constraints on fund-raising that influence the way candidates raise money. Under FECA regulations, most candidates have relied primarily on three sources to finance their campaigns: individual contributions, the matching funds associated with individual contributors, and loans that can be secured against the promise of matching funds. Although PACs are a major source of funding for congressional candidates, in presidential elections they are mostly invisible (Wilcox 1991). In 1996, no presidential candidate raised as much as 4 percent of their total receipts from PACs (Wayne 1998).

Table 3.2 shows the sources of funds for major presidential nomination candidates from 1980 through 1996. Individuals were the main source for all candidates, and the ratio between individual gifts and matching funds reflects primarily the size of the average contribution: Candidates with relatively more matching funds receive smaller contributions. Thus, in 1996 Patrick Buchanan received 67 percent as much in matching funds as he received in individual contributions, because he relied primarily on small contributions, but Governor Pete Wilson received matching funds that amounted to only 29 percent of his total individual contributions because his fledgling campaign relied more heavily on large donations. A number of candidates borrow money against their matching funds: In 1996 Lamar Alexander was able to borrow money against his matching funds in 1995 to keep his campaign afloat. Candidates can loan their own campaigns unlimited amounts if they do not accept matching funds, and Table 3.2 shows that Steve Forbes ended his campaign owing himself more than $37 million. Candidates loan the money to their campaigns rather than give it outright because if they win they can usually attract sufficient contributions to recoup some of the investment. In 1992 Patrick Buchanan reclassified a contribution to his campaign as a loan and was able to repay that amount to himself when the campaign finished in the black.

Prior to the FECA, candidates often launched their campaigns by asking a few wealthy people for very large contributions. This pattern applied even for candidates with strong ideological appeals: Herbert Alexander reports that Eugene McCarthy in 1968 received $2.5 million from fifty individuals (Alexander 1971). In 1996 it would have taken 2,000 contributors each giving the maximum amount (along with the subsequent matching funds) to have raised that amount. Clearly, the FECA requires candidates to contact many more potential contributors. This means that it is important for candidates to begin their candidacies quite early. In 1968 Robert Kennedy was able to raise $11 million in eleven weeks, mostly from large contributors, but such fund-raising

Table 3.2

**Presidential Prenomination Campaigns: Sources of Receipts: 1980–1996**
(in thousand $)

|  | Individuals | Matching funds | Loans | PACs and parties |
|---|---|---|---|---|
| **1996** |  |  |  |  |
| Clinton | 28,866 | 13,412 | 0 | 3 |
|  |  |  |  |  |
| Alexander | 12,823 | 4,573 | 2,650 | 290 |
| Buchanan | 15,698 | 10,540 | 53 | 18 |
| Dole | 30,564 | 13,546 | 4,300 | 1,237 |
| Dornan | 300 | 0 | 6 | 1 |
| Forbes | 4,297 | 0 | 37,885 | 15 |
| Gramm | 16,128 | 7,356 | 2,434 | 420 |
| Keyes | 3,517 | 1,263 | 1 | 4 |
| Lugar | 4,844 | 2,657 | 1,435 | 129 |
| Specter | 2,326 | 1,010 | 551 | 163 |
| Wilson | 5,776 | 1,724 | 160 | 253 |
| **1992** |  |  |  |  |
| Brown | 4,560 | 857 | 600 | 0 |
| Clinton | 14,179 | 4,240 | 1,900 | 3 |
| Harkin | 2,780 | 1,734 | 0 | 330 |
| Kerrey | 3,457 | 1,784 | 10 | 280 |
| Tsongas | 4,775 | 1,443 | 550 | 2 |
|  |  |  |  |  |
| Buchanan | 4,817 | 2,877 | 0 | 27 |
| Bush | 23,969 | 6,785 | 0 | 36 |
| **1988** |  |  |  |  |
| Babbitt | 2,265 | 1,079 | 905 | 1 |
| Dukakis | 19,401 | 9,040 | 0 | 9 |
| Gephardt | 6,313 | 2,896 | 2,528 | 661 |
| Gore | 8,015 | 3,853 | 1,560 | 517 |
| Jackson | 12,282 | 7,608 | 5,169 | 47 |
| Simon | 6,147 | 3,603 | 3,037 | 300 |
|  |  |  |  |  |
| Bush | 22,567 | 8,393 | 50 | 673 |
| Dole | 17,430 | 7,618 | 0 | 849 |
| du Pont | 5,502 | 2,551 | 828 | 0 |
| Kemp | 10,568 | 5,877 | 3,300 | 65 |
| Robertson | 20,637 | 9,691 | 9,553 | 0 |
| **1984** |  |  |  |  |
| Glenn | 6,683 | 3,325 | 2,655 | 398 |
| Hart | 8,919 | 5,328 | 7,720 | 9 |
| Jackson | 5,139 | 3,061 | 637 | 31 |
| Mondale | 17,415 | 9,495 | 7,672 | 1 |
|  |  |  |  |  |
| Reagan | 16,485 | 10,100 | 200 | 131 |

*(continued)*

Table 3.2 *(continued)*

| 1980 | | | | |
|---|---|---|---|---|
| Carter | 13,000 | 5,052 | 0 | 500 |
| Kennedy | 7,761 | 3,863 | 2,653 | 240 |
| Anderson | 3,910 | 2,680 | 175 | 24 |
| Bush | 10,929 | 5,716 | 4,467 | 131 |
| Connally | 11,784 | 0 | 578 | 210 |
| Crane | 3,480 | 1,755 | 40 | 2 |
| Dole | 902 | 446 | 50 | 46 |
| Reagan | 13,886 | 7,193 | 5,513 | 288 |

*Source*: FEC Reports on Financial Activity: Final Presidential Reports 1980, 1984, 1988, and final press releases for 1992, 1996.

*Note:* Final receipts exclude any repaid loans.

---

speed is unthinkable today, since it would take 8,000 contributors giving the maximum amount to raise that much money, and first the candidate would need to qualify for matching funds.

Because the maximum contribution limit was not indexed to inflation, the value of a $1,000 contribution, and the difficulty of raising it, has declined over time. Consequently, many candidates seek to raise substantial portions of their individual contributions in large donations of $750 or more. To do this, candidates enlist a few top-level campaign solicitors, who build networks of solicitors. Each solicitor is asked to raise a certain amount—for example, $1 million. Solicitors ask others to give and then raise an additional $100,000 apiece. The resulting pyramid of contributions usually raises substantial sums, often through invitations to fund-raising dinners and other events (Brown, Powell, and Wilcox 1995). The success of a fund-raising campaign often depends on how many layers exist in the fund-raising pyramids.

The availability of matching funds makes profitable impersonal forms of solicitation. Candidates rent lists of donors to organizations, party committees, and even to other candidates; they then solicit those lists through direct-mail letters and telephone calls. For example, the Buchanan campaign solicited members of conservative organizations such as pro-gun groups. In the 1992 campaign, Buchanan also rented Jack Kemp's contributor list and raised more money from those donors than Kemp ever had. Although direct-mail fund-raising is an expensive way to raise money, it is made more profitable by matching funds. A $50 contribution to Buchanan was worth $100 to the campaign because it was fully matched from the federal fund. Moreover, it is not uncommon for individuals who make one small donation to a campaign through the mail to respond to multiple solicitations (Brown, Powell, and Wilcox 1995).

Most campaigns use a mix of these networks of personal solicitations and impersonal appeals, but the resources available to each candidate help determine the precise blend of fund-raising tactics. Brown, Powell, and Wilcox (1995) reported that more than 70 percent of Bob Dole's contributors in the 1988 campaign were contacted through personal solicitation networks, and that the overwhelming majority of Buchanan's 1992 contributors were solicited through the mail.

Candidates with influence over the congressional agenda (party leaders, committee chairs, policy entrepreneurs) can often assemble national networks of personal solicitation, working through businesses and groups that seek access to Congress. Washington lobby firms can help assemble the networks, which may include substantial numbers of contributors who do not really care if the candidate wins the presidency, since giving is also a way of securing access for lobbying. Candidates who are sitting or former governors often can tap into business networks in their home state. Indeed, governors usually rely on in-state money for a substantial amount of their early cash. Candidates can also use their religion and ethnicity to develop networks of personal solicitation. In 1988, Michael Dukakis raised substantial sums through networks of Greek restaurateurs (Berke 1987; Brown, Powell, and Wilcox 1995) and Jews, while Jesse Jackson raised money in black churches (Hertzke 1993; Brown, Powell, and Wilcox 1995).

In contrast, candidates with more extreme ideological views can often develop large direct-mail lists that can raise substantial sums. In 1988, televangelist and Christian Right leader Marion "Pat" Robertson raised record amounts of money through direct-mail solicitations: His first report to the Federal Election Commission (FEC) contained the names of 70,000 contributors and was delivered in a sixteen-foot truck (Wilcox 1992).

The 1996 campaigns involved candidates with a range of resources. Bill Clinton ran unopposed for the Democratic nomination (except for the perennial fringe candidate Lyndon LaRouche) and therefore could count on the party apparatus and the trappings of the presidency as key fund-raising resources. In addition, although Clinton had governed as a centrist Democrat and coopted GOP issues such as the death penalty and welfare reform, he could count on the ideological wing of the party to support him when control of Congress shifted to the GOP in 1994.

Bob Dole had a long and well-established network of solicitors from his 1980 and 1988 presidential bids, and from his multiple Senate reelection campaigns as well. A survey of Dole's 1988 contributors found an unusual number of lobbyists, many of whom cared little about whether he would ultimately win the White House, since he remained a valuable friend in the Senate even if he lost (Brown, Powell, and Wilcox 1995). Lamar Alexander and Pete Wilson could count on in-state networks to generate their early money. Patrick Buchanan, Bob Dornan, and Alan Keyes could use their ideological credentials to solicit conservative money through direct-mail appeals.

Table 3.3 shows the distribution of contributions by size for major nomination candidates from 1980 through 1996. The trend toward increasing reliance on large contributions, especially among GOP candidates, continued. In 1996, Alexander, Dole, Gramm, Specter, and Wilson all raised at least one-half of their money in large contributions, mostly of $1,000. In contrast, candidates representing the ideological extreme of the GOP relied more on small contributions: Patrick Buchanan raised a record 91 percent of his money in small contributions, and Dornan and Keyes both raised more than 80 percent of their far less impressive totals in this fashion. Bill Clinton used a mix of mail appeals and large fund-raising events and therefore received a mix of small and large contributions.

Table 3.4 shows the percentage of individual contributions received in-state by each candidate. Alexander, Gramm, Lugar, Specter, and Wilson all raised significant sums from their home states. This reflects two realities. First, most campaigns begin by soliciting past contributors to the candidate's gubernatorial, Senate, or House campaigns, and most of these donors reside in the candidate's home state. Second, unsuccessful campaigns seldom expand beyond that initial core of support, which means that they ultimately receive little money outside their state. In contrast, more successful campaigns rely on in-state donors for "seed money," then build networks that extend beyond the state. In 1991 Clinton raised more than one-third of his early money from Arkansas, hardly a money center in American politics, but in 1992 Arkansas provided just slightly more than 5 percent of his total individual contributions. Similar trends are evident for Lamar Alexander in the 1996 cam-

Table 3.3

**Presidential Prenomination Campaigns: Individual Contributions by Size, 1980–1992** (in percentages)

|  | $1–$499 | $500–$749 | $750–$1,000 |
|---|---|---|---|
| **1996** | | | |
| Clinton | 38 | 5 | 57 |
| | | | |
| Alexander | 17 | 17 | 66 |
| Buchanan | 91 | 3 | 6 |
| Dole | 39 | 7 | 55 |
| Dornan | 87 | 5 | 7 |
| Forbes | 41 | 10 | 49 |
| Gramm | 37 | 10 | 53 |
| Keyes | 86 | 6 | 9 |
| Lugar | 51 | 13 | 36 |
| Specter | 38 | 11 | 50 |
| Wilson | 14 | 15 | 71 |
| **1992** | | | |
| Brown | 100 | 0 | 0 |
| Clinton | 38 | 20 | 42 |
| Harkin | 73 | 8 | 19 |
| Kerrey | 41 | 16 | 43 |
| Tsongas | 60 | 13 | 26 |
| | | | |
| Buchanan | 83 | 6 | 12 |
| Bush | 9 | 9 | 82 |
| **1988** | | | |
| Babbitt | 35 | 12 | 54 |
| Dukakis | 37 | 20 | 42 |
| Gephardt | 43 | 19 | 38 |
| Gore | 44 | 17 | 39 |
| Jackson | 88 | 4 | 7 |
| Simon | 61 | 12 | 27 |
| | | | |
| Bush | 22 | 12 | 66 |
| Dole | 36 | 12 | 51 |
| du Pont | 45 | 14 | 40 |
| Kemp | 68 | 9 | 22 |
| Robertson | 89 | 3 | 8 |
| **1984** | | | |
| Glenn | 37 | 18 | 45 |
| Hart | 68 | 10 | 23 |
| Jackson | 86 | 6 | 8 |
| Mondale | 52 | 17 | 31 |
| | | | |
| Reagan | 63 | 9 | 29 |

*(continued)*

Table 3.3 *(continued)*

1980

| | | | |
|---|---|---|---|
| Carter | 32 | 18 | 50 |
| Kennedy | 59 | 11 | 31 |
| | | | |
| Anderson | 87 | 6 | 8 |
| Bush | 57 | 18 | 25 |
| Connally | 43 | 13 | 44 |
| Crane | 91 | 4 | 5 |
| Dole | 43 | 18 | 39 |
| Reagan | 59 | 11 | 30 |

*Source:* FEC Reports of Financial Activity: Presidential Final Reports 1980, 1984, 1988, and final press release for 1992.

paign, who raised 47 percent of his individual contributions in 1995 in his home state, but only 27 percent in 1996.

In contrast, Bob Dole raised relatively little money in Kansas. Dole had amassed a long list of national supporters, both from his days as Senate majority leader and from his two presidential campaigns. His tax-exempt foundation had also helped him develop a reliable list of national contributors. The ideological candidates—Buchanan and Keyes—both raised most of their money out of their home state. Dornan's short-lived campaign drew heavily from his home district in California: Apparently his attempts at national direct mail failed. Steve Forbes also drew from diverse geographic constituencies, although if his personal loans to his campaign were figured in, nearly all of his money would have come from New Jersey.

**The Money Chase in 1996**

As in previous campaigns, in 1996 the candidates struggled to win the early fund-raising race, often called the "invisible primary" (Buell 1996). Journalists of all types devoted considerable air time, column space, and web pages to stories about that financial contest—who was raising the most money, who had the most money on hand, who was running up the largest debts. These stories were written on the assumption that money is an important indicator of a candidate's support and that money was a vital tool in helping candidates reach the voters. Indeed, articles as early as October 1995 began to discount candidates who had done less well than expected in the fund-raising race—nearly five months before the first caucus or primary was held (Fritsch 1995a). In 1996 the candidates raised

Table 3.4

**Presidential Prenomination Campaigns: Percentage of Individual Contributions Raised in the Home State, 1996**

| | |
|---|---|
| Clinton | 4.71 |
| Alexander | 43.08 |
| Buchanan | 4.15 |
| Dole | 4.73 |
| Dornan | 22.20 |
| Forbes | 11.72 |
| Gramm | 39.35 |
| Keyes | 1.47 |
| Lugar | 64.51 |
| Specter | 53.91 |
| Wilson | 61.64 |

*Source:* Federal Election Commission.

money earlier than ever: Three candidates had raised more than $20 million by the end of 1995, and two others had raised more than $10 million. Once again, the two candidates who had raised the largest amounts by December in the year prior to the primary elections—Bill Clinton and Bob Dole—won the party nomination.

## The Democrats

Although Clinton's popularity began rebounding almost as soon as the GOP took control of Congress in 1994, the Clinton White House was greatly worried by the 1996 reelection campaign, and this led them to raise prodigious amounts of soft money very early in the electoral process. Two specters haunted President Clinton and his close advisers: Gingrich and Carter. The 1994 midterm elections produced an electoral earthquake, giving the GOP control of both the Senate and House of Representatives for the first time since the Eisenhower era. Many White House officials believed that the voters had not so much embraced the Republicans' Contract with America as they had rebuked Clinton. Early in 1995, journalists, commentators, and others publicly questioned the president's relevance, and Clinton and his advisers feared that the president's weak political position would invite a challenge to his renomination campaign and even cost him his office.

The top White House point man for the reelection effort, Deputy Chief of Staff Harold Ickes, knew this road well. A veteran of Senator Edward M. Kennedy's challenge to President Jimmy Carter's renomination in 1980, Ickes remembered how an acrimonious primary campaign mortally wounded Carter, who ultimately lost reelection in a surprisingly lopsided defeat. The Clinton administration's fears were well founded. Senator Bob Kerrey, a Clinton rival for the presidential nomination in 1992, contemplated such a challenge.

Determined to avoid Carter's fate, Clinton and his staff began the active renomination campaign earlier than had any previous incumbent president. The Clinton campaign helped the Democratic Party raise prodigious amounts of soft money in 1995, and afterward the methods of this fund-raising came under close scrutiny. It was widely alleged that Clinton had hosted intimate coffees in the White House where he asked for contributions, that he had allowed future "friends of Bill" to have pajama parties in the Lincoln bedroom if they made large contributions, and that convicted felons and other dubious characters had attended fund-raising events. The media coverage of these stories was extensive, and this eventually led to a congressional investigation and widespread criticism from even usually sympathetic sources. Reports that Vice President Albert Gore had solicited contributions from his White House office telephone, and that he had attended a fund-raiser at a Buddhist temple where contributors were reimbursed by the temple, led to calls for an independent counsel, although after a lengthy investigation Attorney General Janet Reno declined. More importantly, an entire network of foreign money, some of which appears to have come from the Chinese government, forced the DNC to return millions of dollars in contributions, and led some Republicans to charge that the administration had sold national security for foreign money. Overall, the Clinton administration and the DNC appear to have relaxed their usual scrutiny of fund-raising after the 1994 elections and to have taken previous practices to new lows of decorum (Wilcox 1999).

The Clinton campaign aired some advertising in 1995, praising Clinton's position on gun control (Corrado 1997a). But the campaign hit on a more innovative strategy—to use party soft money to run "issue advertisements" that did not specifically call for the reelection of Clinton but that would serve to bolster his image. At the urging of consultant Dick Morris, Clinton raised enough soft money to fund an $18 million advertising campaign during the summer and fall of

1995. One such ad charged that the "Dole-Gingrich" budget tried to cut Medicare, but Clinton cut taxes for working families. Eventually, this kind of spending topped $44 million (Marcus and Babcock 1997). An FEC preliminary audit of the Clinton campaign held that this party spending was really campaign spending and asked for a repayment of $7 million. Nevertheless, the Commission itself voted 6–0 that the spending was issue advocacy and that no repayment was needed (Abramson 1998). The decision sets the stage for a potential radical change in the financing of presidential campaigns, which we discuss in the conclusion to this chapter.

Clinton also had no difficulty raising hard money for the campaign. Indeed, the campaign had raised fully $25 million by the end of 1995, a record amount. The campaign even considered forgoing matching funds and thus avoiding any spending limits, although it eventually decided that such a move would undermine the president's image as a supporter of campaign finance reform. Instead, the campaign accepted the more than $9 million for which its 1995 fund-raising qualified, meaning that Clinton had essentially completed his hard money fund-raising before the 1996 campaign got under way. Overall, Clinton spent perhaps $5 million less than Dole in raising his campaign money, which allowed him to spend more money on media buys.

Unchallenged within his party, the president could use his "primary election" money to boost his image and to attack Bob Dole once Dole's nomination was assured. The party continued its soft money spending on issue ads for Clinton throughout 1996. Thus Clinton had a formidable financial advantage over Dole: All of his primary election money went to the general election, whereas Dole had to spend his money fending off Gramm, Buchanan, and Forbes, and Clinton could count on party soft money eighteen months before the election—something that became available to Dole only after he clinched the nomination.

Clinton's early fund-raising is unusual among sitting presidents. Table 3.5 shows the dynamics of fund-raising over time for all nomination campaigns since 1980. Jimmy Carter in 1980, Ronald Reagan in 1984, and George Bush in 1992 all started their fund-raising later in the election cycle, despite the fact that both Carter and Bush faced intraparty challenges. Whether Clinton's quick start was an idiosyncratic result of his electoral insecurity following the 1994 elections or another sign of the historic pressure to raise money earlier in the election cycle remains to be seen.

Table 3.5

**Presidential Prenomination Campaigns: The Dynamics of Funds Raised, 1980–1996** (in million $)

|  | Sept. | Dec. | Jan. | Feb. | Mar. | Apr. | May |
|---|---|---|---|---|---|---|---|
| **1996** | | | | | | | |
| Clinton | 25.64 | 31.50 | 32.12 | 34.66 | 39.06 | 40.43 | 40.42 |
| | | | | | | | |
| Alexander | 11.52 | 12.54 | 15.53 | 16.04 | 16.88 | 17.58 | 17.57 |
| Buchanan | 7.22 | 10.73 | 14.52 | 17.43 | 20.02 | 21.80 | 21.79 |
| Dole | 24.62 | 31.98 | 33.99 | 38.90 | 41.96 | 43.15 | 43.15 |
| Forbes | 17.97 | 25.44 | 32.73 | 37.69 | 40.57 | 42.10 | 42.10 |
| Gramm | 20.76 | 25.72 | 27.86 | 27.86 | 28.72 | 28.79 | 28.78 |
| Keyes | 1.70 | 2.08 | 2.45 | 2.81 | 3.23 | 3.55 | 3.54 |
| Lugar | 5.90 | 7.37 | 7.77 | 7.58 | 7.71 | 7.74 | 7.73 |
| Specter | 3.02 | 3.20 | 3.20 | 3.23 | 3.23 | 3.49 | 3.49 |
| Wilson | 5.35 | 6.35 | 6.47 | 6.90 | 6.90 | 7.33 | 7.33 |
| **1992** | | | | | | | |
| Brown | 0.05 | 0.52 | 0.94 | 1.46 | 3.41 | 6.02 | 6.02 |
| Clinton | 0.20 | 3.29 | 5.47 | 8.61 | 12.87 | 16.64 | 20.33 |
| Harkin | 0.71 | 2.17 | 3.56 | 4.61 | 4.75 | 4.85 | 4.85 |
| Kerrey | 0.22 | 1.91 | 3.26 | 4.92 | 5.26 | 5.40 | 5.53 |
| Tsongas | 0.79 | 1.31 | 1.88 | 3.75 | 6.23 | 6.67 | 6.77 |
| | | | | | | | |
| Buchanan | 0 | 0.71 | 1.72 | 4.22 | 6.16 | 7.05 | 7.77 |
| Bush | 0 | 9.96 | 14.17 | 18.97 | 23.63 | 27.08 | 30.95 |
| **1988** | | | | | | | |
| Babbitt | 1.92 | 2.45 | 3.57 | 3.93 | 4.01 | 4.11 | 4.24 |
| Dukakis | 7.74 | 10.37 | 14.69 | 17.56 | 20.99 | 4.43 | 27.89 |
| Gephardt | 3.46 | 5.90 | 8.08 | 9.57 | 11.66 | 12.16 | 12.30 |
| Gore | 2.70 | 3.94 | 5.99 | 7.53 | 10.94 | 12.37 | 12.83 |
| Jackson | 1.04 | 1.40 | 2.68 | 4.15 | 7.42 | 12.28 | 16.93 |
| Simon | 2.04 | 6.06 | 9.00 | 10.68 | 11.62 | 11.92 | 12.21 |
| | | | | | | | |
| Bush | 12.73 | 19.06 | 26.29 | 27.75 | 29.92 | 32.06 | 32.58 |
| Dole | 7.96 | 14.32 | 21.09 | 23.12 | 25.52 | 26.88 | 27.31 |
| du Pont | 3.43 | 5.54 | 8.23 | 8.68 | 8.81 | 9.09 | 9.11 |
| Kemp | 6.30 | 10.21 | 15.93 | 17.55 | 18.20 | 18.99 | 19.44 |
| Robertson | 11.74 | 16.41 | 29.70 | 34.69 | 37.01 | 38.10 | 38.60 |
| **1984** | | | | | | | |
| Glenn | 4.25 | 6.42 | 9.01 | 12.45 | 13.15 | 13.36 | 13.47 |
| Hart | 1.55 | 1.88 | 2.83 | 3.82 | 12.05 | 16.41 | 19.92 |
| Jackson | 0 | 0.35 | 0.76 | 1.57 | 1.94 | 3.61 | 5.55 |
| Mondale | 6.95 | 11.45 | 16.48 | 18.25 | 23.01 | 25.92 | 29.82 |
| | | | | | | | |
| Reagan | 0 | 3.77 | 4.81 | 10.85 | 16.43 | 23.17 | 26.25 |

| 1980 | | | | | | | |
|---|---|---|---|---|---|---|---|
| Carter | 2.42 | 5.75 | 8.53 | 11.13 | 12.98 | 14.71 | 16.46 |
| Kennedy | 0 | 3.89 | 6.11 | 7.67 | 9.49 | 11.06 | 13.62 |
| | | | | | | | |
| Anderson | 0.29 | 0.51 | 0.66 | 1.58 | 4.52 | 6.87 | 6.96 |
| Bush | 2.43 | 4.46 | 6.56 | 9.41 | 14.47 | 18.68 | 20.51 |
| Connally | 4.30 | 9.16 | 10.01 | 11.64 | 12.66 | 12.85 | 12.99 |
| Crane | 2.94 | 3.27 | 4.11 | 4.51 | 4.95 | 5.19 | 5.22 |
| Dole | 0.51 | 0.78 | 1.27 | 1.35 | 1.43 | 1.43 | 1.47 |
| Reagan | 2.79 | 7.21 | 12.02 | 16.36 | 18.91 | 21.55 | 24.49 |

*Source:* FEC Reports of Financial Activity: Final Presidential Reports 1980, 1984, 1988, and monthly press releases for 1991 and 1992.

*Note:* Figures represent total cumulative receipts of campaign committees for each reporting period.

## The Republicans

Overall, the Republican contenders continued a trend toward earlier fund-raising that was briefly interrupted by the late start to the 1992 campaign. The early frontrunner in the dollar dash was Senator Phil Gramm of Texas, who kicked off his campaign with a fund-raising dinner in Dallas that raised more than $4 million (Verhovek 1996), where he told a cheering throng, "I have the most reliable friend that you can have in American politics, and that is ready money" (Fritsch 1995a). Gramm also transferred almost $5 million from his Senate account, giving him a substantial amount of early money. Gramm spent heavily early in 1995 on building campaign organizations and events, spending nearly $9.5 million by the end of June. Gramm invested heavily in 1995 on a series of straw polls, hoping that his strong showing would make him an acceptable alternative to Dole. But Gramm's fund-raising foundered in the third quarter of 1995, as his networks failed to expand much beyond his Texas base. The problems were the same as those that doomed his candidacy: He was not a personally attractive candidate, and his issue positions did not appeal to a distinctive party constituency. His defeats in Louisiana and Iowa led him to drop out early, despite having spent more than $27 million.

By the third quarter of 1995, Senator Bob Dole led the GOP fund-raising race. Dole tapped his preexisting networks of personal solicitors among lobbyists and corporate executives, and even raised a sizable amount from PACs. Dole's fund-raising skills and donor lists were honed by House and Senate races, two previous presidential bids, a leadership PAC, and two foundations that he had sponsored. By one estimate, Dole had raised $100 million through these various entities over the course of his career (Babcock and Marcus 1996). Dole had used his PAC, Campaign America, to develop a list of reliable donors of smaller amounts, who would respond to mail solicitations. The PAC also paid for Dole's travels to stump for GOP candidates, enabling Dole to develop a large donor base as well. By 1994, Campaign America led all leadership PACs in fund-raising. Dole's Better America Foundation, aimed at promoting GOP goals using Dole as a spokesman, also helped him cultivate his financial constituency and build political IOUs. Dole disbanded the foundation during the campaign under strong criticism that it was a mechanism for excessive spending.

The Dole plan was to raise nearly $16 million through the mail (some of which would be in the form of large contributions), $10 million at events, $7 million through solicitations by the candidate and the network, and $2 million from PACs. By the end of December, he had raised nearly $25 million, more than any candidate in any past campaign. This qualified Dole for more than $9 million in matching funds, which meant that nearly all of Dole's hard money fund-raising was completed before the campaign began. Unlike Clinton, however, Dole was not an automatic party nominee, and so he could not rely on issue ads from party soft money until after he had cinched the nomination. Moreover, because the federal fund did not have enough money to cover all required payouts in January, Dole and others had to borrow money from banks against a federal guarantee. The matching funds were not all paid to the Dole campaign until April.

Dole's advantage over Gramm was even larger than the fund-raising totals suggest, for he had more available cash than Gramm. Table 3.6 shows the cash on hand and debts of major campaigns in 1996 at different time periods. In December and January, Dole had an approximately 4–1 advantage over Gramm in available cash. Note, however, the huge sums sitting in the Clinton campaign bank account during this period.

Dole's other centrist opponents were Lamar Alexander and Senator Richard Lugar of Indiana. Alexander's flannel shirts belied an image of an insider politician who raised significant sums in the Washington lobbying community. Alexander raised significant sums in 1995, but as his candidacy never found a niche, and as his fortunes sagged, his fund-raising dried up. Senator Lugar's campaign, which stressed foreign policy and threats of international terrorism, barely registered

Table 3.6

**Presidential Prenomination Campaigns: Cash on Hand and Debt of Major Candidates, 1996, by Period** (in million $)

|  | 12/95 | 1/96 | 2/96 | 3/96 | 4/96 | 5/96 | 6/96 | 7/96 |
|---|---|---|---|---|---|---|---|---|
| **Clinton** | | | | | | | | |
| Cash | 13.44 | 17.86 | 16.76 | 15.60 | 19.34 | 18.03 | 17.10 | 17.65 |
| Debt | 0.39 | 0.67 | 0.62 | 0.65 | 0.62 | 0.63 | 0.61 | 0.61 |
| **Alexander** | | | | | | | | |
| Cash | 0.61 | 0.43 | 0.72 | 0.11 | 0.67 | 1.24 | 1.18 | 1.17 |
| Debt | 1.59 | 0.09 | 1.44 | 0.50 | 0.02 | 0.00 | 0.00 | 0.00 |
| **Buchanan** | | | | | | | | |
| Cash | 0.11 | 0.10 | 0.26 | 0.08 | 0.13 | 0.99 | 0.22 | 0.21 |
| Debt | 1.44 | 1.39 | 3.08 | 2.89 | 2.89 | 2.14 | 1.65 | 1.82 |
| **Dole** | | | | | | | | |
| Cash | 4.35 | 4.84 | 0.57 | 0.72 | 1.90 | 3.24 | 2.50 | 2.43 |
| Debt | 0.76 | 5.45 | 6.71 | 4.63 | 1.10 | 0.94 | 1.07 | 0.11 |
| **Forbes** | | | | | | | | |
| Cash | 0.04 | 0.30 | 0.10 | 0.17 | 0.09 | 0.30 | 0.47 | 0.24 |
| Debt | 16.81 | 23.65 | 30.70 | 36.81 | 37.68 | 37.96 | 37.94 | 37.89 |
| **Gramm** | | | | | | | | |
| Cash | 1.18 | 1.52 | 1.66 | 0.60 | 0.70 | 0.74 | 0.70 | 0.66 |
| Debt | 0.91 | 1.78 | 2.94 | 1.93 | 0.21 | 0.01 | 0.00 | 0.00 |

*Source:* Federal Election Commission.

with the public. Table 3.4 shows that Lugar never extended his fund-raising network much beyond his home-state constituency.

Patrick Buchanan once again raised money in small contributions through direct-mail solicitations and drew attention with his populist crusade. With a stronger economy in 1996, Buchanan sounded more cultural themes: His "lock and load" theme excited NRA supporters, and his talk of "culture wars" appealed to moral conservatives. Buchanan raised far more money in 1996 than he had in 1992: Table 3.5 shows that he had raised more than $7 million by December of 1995, compared with only $700,000 in 1991. He ultimately raised more than $20 million, nearly three times his 1992 totals. His strong showing in New Hampshire worried the conservative core of the party, who feared that if Buchanan was the nominee, the party would lose control of

Congress. But although Buchanan remained a thorn in Dole's side, his campaign did not become the rallying point for the Christian Right wing of the GOP. This may have been because his Catholicism was unattractive to Evangelical Protestants or because pragmatic Christian Right leaders such as Ralph Reed worked hard to deliver the nomination to Dole (Drew 1997). Dole's other conservative challengers— Alan Keyes and Bob Dornan—raised little money and were not a factor in the race.

Dole also faced two challenges from his left—Governor Pete Wilson from California and Senator Alan Specter from Pennsylvania. Neither campaign took off—and in the case of Wilson this surprised many observers. Generally, sitting governors can mobilize significant resources for presidential campaigns, and California's recovering economy would seem to be a substantial base to launch any campaign. By the end of 1995, Wilson had raised only $5 million, significantly less than Lamar Alexander, a former governor of Tennessee, a much smaller state. Wilson had promised many of his core contributors that he would not seek the presidency when he had sought their financial help for his gubernatorial reelection campaign, and the fact that a President Wilson would leave California with a Democratic governor did not sit well with that state's wealthiest contributors. Moreover, neither Wilson nor Specter could find many early states where the party electorate would favor their moderate positions on social issues, and thus their campaigns died on the vine.

Dole's most serious challenge came from millionaire Steve Forbes, who spent nearly $18 million in the second half of 1995—$14 million of it in the fourth quarter—in a media campaign that aimed squarely at Dole. Most of this money went into media buys, where Forbes ripped Dole for his record on taxes and spending. Where most candidates spent time and money raising campaign funds, Forbes simply wrote another check to the campaign and devoted his time and money to advertising. When Forbes spent an additional $7 million in January, the other candidates began to pay serious attention (Corrado 1997a). Forbes's spending got him significant media attention and propelled his rise in the polls, but he was unable to overcome Dole's organizational advantage in key states. In Arizona, Forbes won by spending more than $4 million, perhaps a record amount for that state, but Dole won handily in South Carolina, swept the South, and the race was over. Dole had spent years cultivating party officials and activists in every state of the union, and when the race narrowed, he could count on their support.

With Maury Taylor spending nearly $6 million and Ross Perot $8 million, Forbes might initially seem to be just another millionaire out on a lark to buy an expensive toy—the presidency. But Forbes showed considerable determination and is running for the 2000 race, having adjusted his positions on social issues to appeal to the Christian Right. His 1996 campaign was mostly focused on a single issue—the flat tax. Such a tax would have benefited Forbes personally: Citizens for Tax Justice, a liberal policy group that ferrets out information on tax breaks for the rich, estimated that it would save Forbes more than $1.9 billion in taxes over his lifetime, partially by easing a tax burden on his inheritance. If this figure is true, then Forbes's $37 million might be thought a shrewd investment. Forbes sold the plan as tax "simplification" on the campaign trail and downplayed the obvious redistributive aspects of the proposal. Although Forbes could never beat Dole in the critical states, his flat tax did attract enormous attention and eventually was trumpeted by conservative House Republicans. Indeed, even Dole eventually began to promote a "flatter" tax system. Richard Lugar, whose campaign never got off the ground, argued that "the reason the flat tax is generally more popular is that it's been marketed with extraordinary multiples of any other policy than I have seen in the campaign" (Holmes 1996).

The ultimate effect of Forbes's spending was to drive Dole to spend almost the legal limit during the primaries, leaving him legally unable to raise and spend money from late March until the convention in July. By the New York primary, Dole was forced to recycle older, generic ads and broadcast them exclusively on cable TV in an effort to stay within the spending limits.

## The Reform Party

For most of the period leading up to the presidential nomination contests, Reform Party founder Ross Perot was coy about the prospects of his candidacy. Although Perot conceded that he would run if drafted by his party, he insisted that he was looking for someone else to head the ticket. On July 9, 1996, a former Colorado governor, Richard Lamm, announced his candidacy for the Reform Party nomination. Lamm, who was a Democratic governor, stressed many of Perot's original issues—a balanced budget and the need to plan for the retirement of the baby-boom generation. Two days later, Perot announced that he would himself run for the nomination.

Perot financed the Reform Party himself, paying for its ballot access petitions, its eighty-four full-time workers, and more than $700,000 per month in operating costs. Moreover, it was clear that Perot was qualified to receive some $32 million in federal campaign funds if he accepted overall spending limits and limits on his own contributions to the campaign, but there was some question whether Lamm would qualify for those funds.

The Reform Party used a complicated system for selecting its presidential nominee, involving mailed ballots to party members and those who had signed ballot access petitions, followed by a convention at which both candidates spoke, and then a runoff election (by telephone, mail, and electronic balloting) between the two candidates. There were a number of irregularities in the balloting: Many Lamm supporters and even Lamm himself had difficulties receiving ballots, while other Reform Party members received multiple ballots. Only a tiny percentage of available ballots were returned. The convention itself was run by Perot, and Lamm supporters were unable to show their signs on the floor because they were apparently six inches longer than regulation. Perot reported contributing more than $8 million of his own money to the nomination process and raising more than $80,000 in individual contributions. Lamm contributed $5,000 of his own money and raised $224,000 in individual donations. The outcome was never in doubt, and the public was not especially interested. After the contest, Lamm complained about the process and praised but did not endorse Perot.

**Postprimary Spending**

After Dole secured the nomination, he had spent almost the legal limit for the primary election period and was therefore officially unable to spend real money on the campaign until the convention, when he would accept the federal grant. In May, Dole had between $1 million and $2 million of spending authority left, while Clinton had more than $20 million (Marcus 1996a).

Clinton used this time quite profitably, pounding Dole in advertising and further lowering Dole's ratings. Into the brink stepped the Republican National Committee, with party issue advertising designed to boost

Dole's chances. The FEC preliminary audit determined that this spending was general election advocacy of Dole's campaign and suggested a $17.7 million payback to the federal fund. The FEC ruled that no money was owed, as it did for the Clinton campaign. The GOP also paid for Dole's travel costs after he won the nomination, but Dole still faced a severe financial disadvantage. After struggling to win his party's nomination while Clinton spent millions boosting his own image and attacking Dole, Dole was unable to mount a massive spending campaign to gain momentum going into the fall. In the end, it probably did not matter—Dole stood little chance of winning in 1996 no matter how much he spent. But the systematic advantage of incumbent presidents who do not face an internal party challenge is something that reformers may wish to consider as they begin to draw plans for a new regulatory regime.

## Creative Campaigning

Every successive presidential nomination contest brings new challenges to the existing FECA regulations. In 1984 Walter Mondale, up against a spending limit and fighting off a strong challenge from Senator Gary Hart, encouraged his potential delegates to form committees of their own and to accept money from labor and other interests to fund their campaigns to win election as delegates to the convention. After the campaign, the Mondale campaign paid a fine.

During the 1988 campaign and those after, many candidates formed leadership PACs, which helped their campaigns in several ways. First, candidate PACs could hire and pay for the candidate's main consultants in the months before any official declaration of candidacy. Second, the PAC could raise money and give it to federal, state, and local party candidates, creating a web of political debts. In the process, the PAC could pay for the candidate's travel across the country to speak on behalf of these candidates, and coincidentally build a political network. A candidate's strongest supporters could give $5,000 to the PAC and an additional $1,000 to the campaign, thereby easing the burdens of the contribution limits. Perhaps the most significant advantage of candidate PACs, however, was in the development and honing of various types of donor lists, which could later be solicited by the campaign (Wilcox 1991; Corrado 1993).

By the early 1990s, many candidates were forming foundations, which often performed the same functions as leadership PACs. Yet foundations had two obvious advantages over candidate PACs. First, foundations could raise the money in unlimited amounts, since they were not obviously involved in electoral activity and were not bound by FECA contribution limits. Second, there need be no disclosure of the contributors to the foundation or of the foundation's spending.

An example of such a foundation in 1996 was American Cause, associated with Patrick Buchanan. The foundation enabled Pat to travel, to research issues, and to develop a stronger political base. Similarly, donors who wanted to assist Senator Bob Dole's presidential prospects gave over $4 million to the Better America Foundation. The Associated Press reported that the tax-exempt "conservative think tank" spent $1.5 million on a poll, a TV ad that included Dole, and other efforts that could have helped a Dole nomination campaign. Under pressure from the press and Democrats, Dole dissolved the foundation in June 1995, released the donor list, and returned $2.5 million to eighty-six individual and corporate donors, including such major contributors as T. Boone Pickens and billionaire Ronald O. Perelman, who gave $250,000.

Nine days after President Bush's defeat in 1992, Lamar Alexander returned to Tennessee to begin his bid for the 1996 Republican presidential nomination. As part of the effort, he founded the Republican Exchange Satellite Network (RESN), a tax-exempt group that broadcast monthly television messages from Alexander to the homes of party activists. The network beamed Alexander's phone-in show to more than 3,000 sites in all fifty states, and also provided the funds to hire an organizer in Iowa. Alexander credited the network with helping him develop the fund-raising base and organization for his presidential campaign. The network raised more than $4.5 million before it was disbanded, including eleven individuals and three corporations that gave more than $100,000.

"Raising money for the network helped Alexander introduce himself to wealthy donors who subsequently both gave money to his presidential campaign and agreed to help Alexander raise funds through their established networks" (Marcus and Babcock 1995). A number of contributors to RESN later hosted fund-raisers for Alexander. Alexander himself noted, "Of all the things it did for me, I'd say it was probably the financial network that was most important. It turned out to be a lot better than a PAC" (cited in Marcus and Babcock 1995).

Alexander also formed a PAC, Republicans for the 1990s, which raised more than $430,000 in two years, but the PAC could only accept contributions in amounts of $5,000 or less and had to report the names of its donors. Alexander kept the donors to his network secret until pressured to reveal them during the campaign.

The staff of RESN largely became the staff of the Alexander campaign; thus the network allowed Alexander to pay his staff and some consultants before the campaign began. It paid for Alexander's travel across the country, paid for staff to research issues that he used during the campaign, and helped him stay visible in early states such as Iowa. The network mailed a newsletter monthly to some 15,000 GOP activists and officeholders.

### The Last Regulated Campaign?

By far the most important new development in the 1996 prenomination campaign was issue advocacy spending. A series of decisions by federal courts have allowed advertising that raises policy issues and may even use the picture of a candidate, so long as that advertisement does not expressly call for the election of a specific candidate. Some of the Democratic Party issue ads that helped Bill Clinton in 1995 used the same film clips and some of the same voiceovers as the Clinton campaign ads—indeed, they were distinguishable only by their failure to call explicitly for the president's reelection.

When the FEC ignored the advice of its auditors and lawyers and accepted this activity at the end of the 1996 campaign, they opened the door to significant extra spending and essentially eliminated spending limits in presidential campaigns. By some estimates the Democratic issue ads for Bill Clinton through the end of the primary elections totaled more than Clinton was legally allowed to spend—and Clinton spent $37 million of "primary" campaign money as well. For an incumbent president, there is now no barrier to raising unlimited soft money and spending it in carefully crafted advertising designed to bolster his or her image. Moreover, challengers can also ignore the spending limits once they have clinched the nomination.

Soft money is raised in a very different way from the money accepted by candidate campaign committees. Contributions need not come from individuals or PACs; they can come from corporate, labor union, or other group treasuries, and they can come in unlimited amounts. Such contributions raise potentially troubling issues about corruption and the appearance of corruption. When individuals give $1,000 to a presidential candidate, they cannot expect much in return, but a contribution of $500,000 or an industrywide contribution of $4 million is perhaps a different matter. Issue advertising need not come from political parties; it can come from individuals or interest groups as well. During the Iowa caucuses, some real estate interests spent money on advertisements that argued against the flat tax, which would have ended the mortgage interest tax deduction and therefore perhaps lowered the value of homes.

In the 2000 campaign, it is quite possible that soft-money–financed issue advocacy campaigns will be waged by candidate foundations that raise money in unlimited amounts from large donors and spend it to advocate the issues for which a candidate stands. Such a development would herald the effective end of the FECA, and pre-FECA rules would again apply: large donations from wealthy individuals and interest groups, collected and spent in secret. Indeed, it might even be possible for wealthy candidates to spend their own money on issue ads while raising and spending money under the FECA guidelines, thereby accepting federal matching funds.

Whatever happens in 2000, it seems likely that 1996 will be the last campaign governed by the FECA regulations. It is ironic that the FEC commissioners, selected to uphold the FECA system, ultimately chose to undermine it instead. In the next election, it is likely to be much harder to "follow the money," and there will surely be much more money to follow.

## 4

ANTHONY CORRADO

# Financing the 1996 Presidential General Election

The 1996 race for the presidency offered the electorate little drama and little reason for change. A robust economy and peaceful conditions abroad defined the political landscape, all to the benefit of the incumbent President William Clinton, whose popularity held steady throughout the election year. The Republican nominee, Senator Robert Dole, faced an uphill climb from the start and failed to reduce the president's sizable lead until the last days before the election. Indeed, the fall campaign seemed to matter hardly at all as voters followed the pattern of similar recent elections, sticking with the status quo because of good times and a popular incumbent.

On election day, Clinton became the first Democrat since Franklin Roosevelt and only the fourth candidate of his party (Andrew Jackson and Woodrow Wilson were the others) to win two consecutive presidential elections. Clinton captured 379 electoral college votes to Dole's 159. The president increased the share of the vote he received in 1992 in every state of the Union, but he did not receive a popular majority. Clinton garnered 49 percent of the popular vote, compared to 41 percent for Dole and about 8 percent for Reform Party candidate Ross Perot. In 1992, Clinton won with 43 percent. He was thus the first president since Wilson to win two elections without receiving a majority of the popular vote.

Although his share of the popular vote was greater than in 1992, Clinton's electoral coalition proved to be fairly stable. His 54.7 percent share of the two-party vote in 1996 was essentially the same as the 53.5 percent he received in 1992 (Pomper 1997, 182). In the electoral college balloting, Clinton won two states he had lost four years earlier

(Florida and Arizona) and lost three states (Colorado, Georgia, and Montana) he had previously won by narrow margins. And even though the final vote margin was smaller than that predicted by most preelection polls, the outcome of the race seemed to be determined long before the ballots were cast.

When placed in the context of recent elections, the 1996 contest was most reminiscent of 1984 (see chapter 3; Herrnson and Wilcox 1997, 138; Sabato 1997, 145). In both of these races, a popular incumbent president, running in the midst of a strong economy and peace abroad, was reelected. The incumbent chose to focus on the economy and the improvements in the state of the nation that had occurred during his first four years, while the challenger failed to develop an effective message or pursue strategies that could overcome the external factors that determined the dynamics of the race. Moreover, in both cases, the challenger was perceived as a representative of a style and approach to politics whose time had passed.

From a campaign finance perspective, however, the election differed greatly from 1984. The financial patterns exhibited by the candidates demonstrated how presidential campaigns have adapted to the constraints imposed by the Federal Election Campaign Act (FECA), first operative in 1976, taking advantage of the opportunities afforded under the law to make the most of their campaign dollars. More importantly, the election highlighted the issues raised by new forms of funding. When Ronald Reagan was seeking reelection in 1984, parties were just beginning to discover the value of soft money, and issue advocacy advertising had not yet become a matter of public debate. By 1996, these unlimited kinds of funding were integral parts of the electoral strategies in both parties (see chapters 7 and 8), and they spurred a controversy over fund-raising practices in the final weeks of the campaign. Thus, 1996 was the first election since the FECA was adopted in which fund-raising became a major issue in the presidential campaign. It is unlikely to be the last.

**The General Election Campaign**

As early as October 1995, more than a year before the election, President Clinton led prospective challenger Senator Robert Dole by a margin of 48 to 35 percent in national opinion polls (Pomper 1997, 186). Little changed over the course of the next year. By the traditional start of the general election campaign on Labor Day, Dole's internal polling of likely voters showed Clinton with a thirteen-point lead. A Gallup poll of registered voters found Clinton to be ahead by twenty-one points, the largest Labor Day lead of any presidential candidate since 1972 (Kranish 1996b, A5). No candidate had ever overcome such a large lead since polls became a popular means of tracking public opinion in the 1940s. Even Harry Truman, who staged the best-known comeback, managed only a thirteen-point turnaround in 1948, starting eight points back and winning by five (Kranish 1996b, A5). Dole faced an uphill battle from the start.

As these survey results suggest, the political contours of the election were established well before the fall campaign began. Although Clinton appeared to be vulnerable after the Republican victory in the 1994 midterm elections, by 1996 his political fortunes had completely reversed. His adept handling of the 1995 budget crisis and government shutdown, along with a robust economy, had increased the president's job approval rating to 60 percent by the beginning of September, a four-year high (Kranish 1996b, A5). Moreover, generally positive perceptions of the state of the nation helped Clinton overcome lingering doubts about his character and trustworthiness. For the first time in years, more Americans believed that the nation was headed in the right direction than in the wrong direction, an attitude that clearly benefited the incumbent (Sabato 1997, 150).

Clinton also had the advantage of an unopposed nomination contest, which left him with millions of dollars to spend during the summer months (see chapter 2). In contrast, Dole was financially weak, having essentially reached the legal spending limit by the end of the primaries. He therefore lacked the ability to respond to the president's attacks. The Republican National Committee tried to assist Dole by running issue ads during the summer designed to favor his candidacy (Republican National Committee 1996, 1; Common Cause 1996, 7), but they were not as effective as the president's targeted assault in key electoral states, which included $4 million in advertising just before the Democratic National Convention (Herrnson and Wilcox 1997, 128). Clinton capitalized on his financial advantage by broadcasting ads that targeted traditional Democratic constituencies and independents. These commercials associated Dole with Newt Gingrich and the unpopular Republican Congress, portraying them as extremists who would cut popular programs such as Medicare and Social Security, reduce Head

Start funding, and promote "risky" tax policies that would undermine the economic recovery.

Thus, by early September, Clinton had established the basic framework of the message he would advance throughout the campaign. This message heralded the strength of the economy and highlighted the accomplishments of his administration, especially with respect to the balanced budget and welfare reform. It also contrasted his agenda, which he claimed would preserve Social Security and Medicare, improve education, and protect the environment, with the "conservative" agenda of Dole and Gingrich. This platform was framed under the broad thematic structure of "Building a Bridge to the Twenty-First Century." Clinton thus asked voters to look back on the previous four years, but with an eye toward the future.

While Clinton presented a clear message that resonated with Democrats and attracted the support of moderates and independents, Dole struggled to find a major theme or issue salient to voters. In August, he sought to bolster his campaign by announcing a bold economic plan based on a program of tax reductions that included a 15 percent across-the-board tax cut, a $500-per-child tax credit, and a 50 percent reduction in the capital gains tax rate. The plan was designed to link Dole with economic growth, challenge Clinton on the economy, and energize traditional Republicans (Ceaser and Busch 1997, 102–3). But the plan was greeted with skepticism, as Dole, a traditional deficit hawk, appeared to be embracing this approach for purely political purposes. The Clinton campaign immediately responded by attacking the plan, highlighting the projected revenue loss and its effect on the prospects for a balanced budget (Berke 1996).

When it became clear that the economic plan was not significantly improving Dole's standing in the polls, the challenger shifted to other messages. He also changed his media team. In early September, less than nine weeks before Election Day, the campaign replaced media strategists Don Sipple and Mike Murphy, who had been hired as replacements in February, when Dole dismissed his original media strategists after his disappointing performance at the start of the primaries. The new team consisted of three veteran Republican media consultants—Alex Castellanos, Greg Stevens, and Chris Mottola—who were brought into the campaign to develop advertisements that would better present the tax-cutting plan and draw sharper contrasts between Dole and Clinton (Seelye 1996; Balz and Kurtz 1996).

The Dole campaign continued to advance its economic plan into October, but also altered its message to highlight "character" issues that were designed to draw a sharper contrast with Clinton. The result was a disconnected series of issues and messages, beginning with drug policy and extending to immigration policy, affirmative action, education, and claims that Clinton was a "closet liberal" (Ceaser and Busch 1997, 153). Most of the electorate, however, was already aware of the questions concerning Clinton's character, and Dole offered no significant new information that would give substantial numbers of voters a reason to reassess their decision. As a result, by the time of the presidential debates, Dole still trailed Clinton by double-digit margins in the polls.

### *The Perot Campaign*

While Dole was trying to narrow Clinton's lead, Perot was trying to jump-start a moribund campaign. Unlike 1992, when his unorthodox insurgent candidacy captured national attention, Perot played a minor role in the 1996 contest. Although he had polled between 15 and 20 percent earlier in the election year, by September his support had declined to about 5 percent (Thomas et al. 1996, 105). By this time, Perot's image had dulled. His highly publicized "debate" over the North American Free Trade Agreement with Vice President Al Gore in 1993 and his subsequent policy pronouncements had led to the perception that he lacked a detailed understanding of key issues. His Reform Party was still trying to develop a nationwide organizational framework and finding it difficult to build a broader movement out of its core base of supporters. There were also doubts about the viability of his candidacy. In July 1996, only 7 percent of the electorate believed that he could win (Herrnson and Wilcox 1997, 130).

Another important difference between Perot's 1992 bid for office and his 1996 effort was the financing of his campaign. In 1992 Perot ran as an independent and relied on his personal fortune to pay for his campaign, spending over $60 million out of his own pocket. In 1996 he chose a different approach. Instead of relying on his own funds or the contributions of supporters, Perot decided to seek public financing. In April, Perot sought an advisory opinion from the FEC as to whether the Reform Party would qualify as a minor party under the law and be eligible for a preelection public subsidy based on Perot's share of the 1992 vote, since in that election he had run as an independent in forty-three states and as a candidate of a new party in seven others. The FEC ruled that he would be eligible for $29.1 million in public funds, or 47 percent of the major party subsidy, based on his 19 percent share of the vote in the previous election (Federal Election Commission 1996c, 1996b, 3).

When Perot received the Reform Party presidential nomination, he decided to accept the public subsidy and agreed to limit his own contributions to $50,000 and his aggregate spending to $61.8 million. He thus became the first minor-party candidate to receive preelection public funding since the beginning of the program in 1976. (The only other non-major-party candidate to receive public money, independent presidential candidate John Anderson, received $4.2 million in postelection funding in 1980 by winning more than 5 percent of the general election vote.) This decision may have alienated some of Perot's supporters, but it was considered an important step toward institutionalizing the new party and reducing its dependence on Perot (Hall 1996, 4A). If Perot again received more than 5 percent of the vote, as was expected by most of his staff, the Reform Party would be eligible for public funding again in 2000. The nominee in 2000 would thus have a guaranteed financial base that would supplement private contributions.

The decision to accept public funding meant that Perot would begin the general election campaign with less than one-half of the resources of his opponents. If he wanted to match the major-party contenders, he would have to raise another $32 million in individual contributions of no more than $1,000 in less than three months. In any circumstance, this would be a daunting task. It proved particularly difficult for Perot, since his low standings in the polls and lack of a national donor base were not conducive to an effective broad-based fund-raising effort. While the Perot campaign did engage in private fund-raising to supplement its public resources, the results were not very encouraging. By mid-October, the campaign had raised only $625,000.

Perot hoped to capitalize on half-hour infomercials, a hallmark of his 1992 campaign, to generate attention to his candidacy and momentum for his campaign. He aired his first such ad on September 10 and used it to introduce his vice-presidential nominee, Pat Choate. But the paid announcement drew low ratings, and thereafter network executives showed little interest in selling Perot such large blocs of time, forcing him to shift to a more traditional media strategy based on 15-

or 30-second spot advertisements. Beyond this advertising, Perot hardly engaged in the campaign. He gave only occasional speeches and had little direct contact with voters. Instead, he looked for another way to generate some enthusiasm for his campaign. He hoped the debates would afford such an opportunity. But 1996 was a different election from that of 1992.

## The Debates

In 1996, as in each election since 1988, the Commission on Presidential Debates (CPD) sponsored general election debates between the candidates. The CPD recommended four ninety-minute debates, three for the presidential candidates and one for the vice-presidential candidates, to take place on consecutive Wednesdays between September 25 and October 16 (Commission on Presidential Debates 1995). But, as in previous elections, the candidates did not adopt the CPD's proposal; instead, they took it as a starting point for private negotiations among themselves.

Clinton and Dole staff members began to negotiate a debate agreement in mid-September. In these sessions, Dole argued that Perot should be excluded, since he feared that Perot would use the forum to discredit the Republican tax plan (Kranish 1996a). But even before the candidates reached a final agreement, the CPD determined that Perot should not be invited to participate. Relying on criteria established before the 1992 election, the CPD decided that Perot did not qualify because he did not have a "realistic" or "more than theoretical" chance of winning the election (Kranish 1996a; Lewis 1996a). At the time, polls showed that a majority of the public would like Perot to be included (Adams 1996). Nevertheless, Clinton and Dole also agreed to exclude Perot and decided to meet in two presidential debates on October 6 and October 16, with a vice-presidential debate on October 9.

Perot responded to this decision by filing a suit in federal district court, as did another minor-party challenger, John Hagelin, the presidential candidate of the Natural Law Party. Perot complained that the criteria used by the CPD went beyond FEC regulations and that the FEC had improperly delegated its power to a private group with respect to debate participation. He further claimed that the exclusion violated his constitutional right of free speech and denied him an equal opportunity to participate in the political process. But the court rejected

Perot's contentions, claiming that it was a matter to be resolved by the FEC, not the courts. The court also noted that the CPD was not an arm of the government, as Perot had asserted, and that such discrimination with respect to participation would only be constitutional if committed by a government organ (Lewis 1996b). Perot also filed a complaint with the Federal Communications Commission (FCC) in an attempt to force major television networks to sell him time for his infomercials. But the FCC also failed to side with Perot, since in their view he had been given ample access to the airwaves, albeit not in the blocs of time that he had requested (Lewis 1996b).

Beyond the decision to exclude Perot, the debates produced little drama. Although they drew sizable audiences, the viewership was much smaller than that of four years earlier. In 1992 the audience for the first debate was 20 percent larger than in 1988, and viewer interest rose during the course of the debates, with more than 90 million viewers watching the final forum (Twentieth Century Fund Task Force 1995, 85). In 1996 the viewership for the first debate was significantly lower than in 1992, encompassing only about one-third of television households, or about 30.6 million homes (Lowry 1996). The audience for the second debate represented a decline of 44 percent as compared to the audience for the second debate in 1992, while the viewership for the vice-presidential debate dropped by 45 percent (Associated Press 1996). Moreover, there were no significant defining moments or major gaffes during the debates that might have changed the dynamics of the race or allowed Dole to make up a sizable share of the president's lead. Instead, polls showed that the public considered Clinton the winner of both debates by significant margins, and judged Gore the victor over Dole's running mate, Jack Kemp. By the end of the debate period, Dole had made up little ground and lagged far behind in the prospective electoral college vote.

### The Campaign Finance Controversy

While the debates did not immediately improve Dole's prospects, they did provide him with an opportunity to draw increased attention to the controversial fund-raising practices of the Democratic Party and Clinton's role in them. The controversy, which was gaining increased press attention during the debate period, was elevated to center stage by Dole in the debates, and became a central issue in the final weeks of the campaign.

The controversy swirled around the fund-raising practices the Democrats had used to raise soft money for their issue advertising and other election-related operations. The debate specifically centered on the role of John Huang, a Democratic National Committee (DNC) fund-raiser, who had served in the U.S. Department of Commerce under Clinton. At issue was whether the Democrats had received large contributions from foreign sources and provided major donors with privileged access to White House officials, including the president and vice president, in exchange for these gifts. These questions led to a broad media investigation of White House and DNC fund-raising, which raised troubling questions about the influence of soft money donations in the political process.

The story took a relatively long time to develop into a major scandal. It had begun in 1993 and 1994, when Tim Mann, a reporter for the *Los Angeles Times,* uncovered questionable connections among the Clinton administration, John Huang, and James Riady. Riady was the son of Mochtar Riady, the founder and chairman of the multibillion-dollar, Indonesian-based conglomerate, Lippo Group. Huang was an ex-Lippo Group employee who had raised money for the Democrats in 1992 and was then appointed to a position in the Department of Commerce. Mann was investigating the relationship between the administration and the Lippo Group, and even interviewed top White House officials about the apparent connections. But his story was never published; in fact, his editors killed the story twice (Kurtz 1996, C1).

The administration's ties to the Lippo Group were not raised again until August 1996, when the *Philadelphia Inquirer* ran a story about a large soft money contribution from an Indonesian landscaper, Arief Wiriandinata, that raised the possibility that contributions from the Lippo Group or Riady were being laundered and donated to the DNC (Goldstein and Greve 1996, A6). Arief and Soraya Wiriandinata were relatives of a former executive of the Lippo Group and were legally residing in Virginia. The Wiriandinatas had donated $425,000 to the DNC, reportedly in appreciation for a get-well card that President Clinton had sent to Soraya's father, Hashim Ning, a co-founder and major shareholder of the Lippo Group, who had fallen ill on a trip to Washington (Waldman 1996). This contribution (and an additional contribution of $25,000 revealed in October) raised questions as to how they had afforded such a gift and whether the money had been illegally funneled to the DNC from a foreign source, namely Mochtar Riady and the Lippo Group. The disclosure of the contribution thus raised troubling issues: Was the DNC accepting foreign contributions? If so, how might these contributions be influencing administration decision making?

Despite the potential significance of the Indonesian contribution, the *Inquirer* report did not garner national attention, and the story withered again. Other reports of illegal fund-raising also failed to capture public attention. For example, in September, the *Los Angeles Times* reported that the DNC had received another questionable soft money contribution. In this instance, the donation came from Cheong Am America, Inc., a subsidiary of the Korean-based Cheong Am Business Group, an electronics company located in Seoul. The chairman of the group, John H.K. Lee, had attended a DNC fund-raiser in April, where he met President Clinton, DNC Chairman Don Fowler, and DNC General Chairman Christopher Dodd. Thereafter Cheong Am America donated $250,000 to the DNC (Miller 1996, A16). Cheong Am America, however, was little more than a U.S. bank account of the Korean company, and federal law required that any contributions by foreign corporations must come from the revenues generated by a U.S. subsidiary. Since the funds did not come from a U.S. subsidiary, the contribution was illegal. In response to the report, the DNC returned the money (Jackson 1997, 246).

The storm finally broke in October, after the *Wall Street Journal* began investigating the Indonesian connection and revealed that John Huang was the key link between the Clinton White House and Asian business interests (Simpson and Abramson 1996). Huang had raised the contribution from the Wiriandinatas as well as the contribution from Cheong Am America. His involvement suggested a link between these gifts and the president. This implication led to a feeding frenzy of media speculation and within days DNC fund-raising was a subject of intense investigation. These investigations revealed other questionable contributions raised by Huang. For example, Huang was linked to a $140,000 fund raiser held at a Buddhist temple in California in conjunction with an appearance by Vice President Al Gore. This event raised additional questions about the legality of DNC fund-raising, since the monks and nuns listed as donors had taken vows of poverty, and at least one nun reported receiving cash and being asked to donate it at the event (Fineman and Hosenball 1996, 26–27; Gerth and Labaton 1996, A20). Reports also revealed Huang's frequent trips to the White House while serving in the Department of Commerce (seventy-eight visits in fifteen months), which prompted questions about the influence of foreign donors and concerns about the interaction between the party fund-raisers and the government. By mid-October, the DNC and the White House were under intense public scrutiny.

Clinton's opponents seized on the campaign finance issue to highlight the character and trust issues that continued to be the president's major weakness. In the final two weeks of the campaign, Dole hammered away at the president on the fund-raising issue, contending that the Democrats were running a "money laundry," observing that Clinton was building "a bridge to wealthy political donors," and calling on the president to "come clean" (Nagourney 1996b, A8). Dole also offered a campaign finance reform plan to heighten the contrast between himself and the president (Nagourney 1996a, A2). The controversy also revived Perot, who predicted that Clinton's second term would be filled with investigations and scandal. In his view, the nation was headed for another Watergate and a constitutional crisis (Jackson 1997, 247).

Clinton responded to the criticism by trying to disregard the inquiries. But his campaign released an ad that decried Dole's "desperate attacks" and charged that the Republicans were also receiving contributions from foreign sources (Harris 1996). Meanwhile, the DNC claimed that the problems resulted from mistakes and oversights and continued to return the monies raised from illegal or suspect contributions. Between September 20 and election day, the DNC returned $762,000 in contributions, $590,000 of which had been solicited by John Huang (Jackson 1997, 247).

Although it is difficult to assess the influence of the fund-raising controversy on the final outcome of the election, it appears that it did have some effect. Clinton won by eight percentage points, about one-half of his margin in most polls over the final ten days. Both Dole and Perot gained support during this final stretch, and Dole actually received the largest share of those voters who decided in the last week. But only one out of six voters, about 17 percent, waited until this point to make up their minds (Ceaser and Busch 1997, 154). The true beneficiary of the fund-raising controversy may have been Perot. He picked up significant support in the final weekend of the campaign and finished with 8.5 percent of the vote. While well below his vote share in 1992, it was enough to ensure that a Reform Party nominee in 2000 would be eligible for a proportionate share of the public funding subsidy. What is clear, however, is that the questions about Democratic fund-raising and the lingering concerns with respect to Clinton's trust-worthiness and character were not enough to overcome the strong support the president had from the majority of voters who thought the economy was strong and the country was headed in the right direction.

## Sources of Funding: An Overview

As in every presidential election conducted under the FECA, public financing was the principal source of candidate funding in the 1996 presidential general election. But as in previous contests financed with public money, the revenues provided by this program were not the sole source of support available to candidates. The FECA allows candidates to raise private contributions during the general election period to finance the legal and accounting costs incurred to comply with the law. It also allows party organizations to spend a limited sum on behalf of a presidential ticket in coordination with the nominees. Party organizations, as well as individuals and groups, may also spend monies independently in support of the presidential nominees. As a result, the amount spent on a general election campaign is significantly greater than the expenditure ceiling attached to the public subsidy. *And this accounting includes only monies that are regulated under federal law.* It does not include the tens of millions of dollars of soft money spent on issue advocacy advertising and voter contact programs designed to influence the outcome of the presidential race (see chapters 7 and 8).

As noted in Table 4.1, a total of approximately $192 million in federally regulated monies was raised or spent on the presidential general election contest, including almost $153 million in public subsidies. The major-party candidates each received $61.8 million in public money and raised an additional $13.6 million in general election legal and accounting compliance (GELAC) funds. Perot received a proportionate share of public money, $29.1 million, and raised an additional $975,000 in contributions from supporters, $345,000 of which was received in the last two weeks of the campaign after Perot began criticizing Clinton's fund-raising. Thirty other minor-party candidates raised a total of $3.3 million. Most of this amount was raised by Harry Browne, the Libertarian Party nominee, who received over $1.4 million in contributions, and John Hagelin of the Natural Law Party, who received over $1.3 million.

Table 4.1

**Presidential General Election Funding, 1996** (in million $)

| Source | Total | Clinton | Dole | Perot | Others |
|---|---|---|---|---|---|
| Candidates | | | | | |
| Public funding | $152.7 | $61.8 | $61.8 | $29.1 | $0.0 |
| Private contributions | 4.3 | 0.0 | 0.0 | 1.0 | 3.3 |
| GELAC funding | 13.6 | 8.0 | 5.6 | 0.0 | 0.0 |
| Subtotal | $170.6 | $69.8 | $67.4 | $30.1 | $3.3 |
| Noncandidate sources | | | | | |
| Party-coordinated expenditures | 18.3 | 6.7 | 11.6 | 0.0 | 0.0 |
| Independent expenditures | 0.9 | 0.1 | 0.7 | 0.1 | 0.0 |
| Partisan communications | 2.7 | 2.7 | 0.0 | 0.0 | 0.0 |
| Totals | $192.5 | $79.3 | $79.7 | $30.2 | $3.3 |

*Source:* Based on data reported by the Federal Election Commission.

## GELAC Funds

A notable aspect of the candidates' finances in 1996 is the amount raised by both Clinton and Dole in GELAC funds. Federal law allows publicly funded campaigns to raise private contributions in amounts of up to $1,000 per individual donor to pay for legal and accounting expenses, as long as these funds are maintained in a separate account from other campaign monies. These funds are subject to full public disclosure but are exempt from candidate spending limits on the theory that the regulations governing campaigns should not impose an inordinate burden on limited campaign funds.

In 1996, the major-party candidates raised a total of $13.6 million in GELAC funds. Most of this sum was raised by the Clinton campaign, which solicited $8 million in compliance contributions, as compared to $5.6 million for Dole. According to the FEC audit reports released well after the election, the Clinton GELAC fund disclosed approximately 173,000 contributions from individuals, which totaled more than $6.4 million (Federal Election Commission 1998a, 2). The Dole campaign disclosed about 32,000 individual contributions, which provided about $3.4 million in revenue, as well as ninety contributions from PAC and party committees that generated about $184,000 (Federal Election Commission 1998b, 2).

The amount of GELAC money raised in 1996 represented a substantial increase over previous elections. In 1992, Clinton and then President George Bush raised a total of $10.3 million in GELAC funds, approximately 30 percent less than the sums solicited in 1996 (Alexander and Corrado 1995, 115). In 1988, Bush and Democrat Michael Dukakis raised $6.5 million, less than one-half the 1996 amount (Alexander and Bauer 1991, 41).

Presidential campaigns have placed greater emphasis on the solicitation of GELAC contributions, primarily because these funds have proven to be a valuable means of supplementing the limited public subsidies that they receive from taxpayer funding. The basic purpose of these funds is to finance legal and accounting expenses, the costs of soliciting GELAC contributions, the expenses incurred in "winding down" the campaign, and any repayments for violations of public funding regulations. But the definition of compliance costs and the purposes for which they can be used has been significantly broadened beyond these basic purposes. For example, under federal guidelines (see 11 C.F.R. § 9003.3), a campaign can accept a reimbursement of 10 percent of payroll expenses (including payroll taxes) and overhead expenditures for national and state campaign headquarters from GELAC funds on the theory that this portion of salaries and overhead are related to compliance activities. Such overhead costs include rent, utilities, office equipment, furniture, supplies, and all telephone charges except for those related to special uses such as voter registration and get-out-the-vote efforts. A candidate may also use GELAC funds to reimburse 50 percent of the costs associated with computer services, including rental and maintenance of computer equipment, nonstaff data entry services, and related supplies. The way the process works is simple: A candidate pays these costs out of his or her federal funding and then submits the appropriate documentation for GELAC reimbursement. Monies are then transferred from the GELAC fund to the candidate's campaign account.

GELAC funds can thus be an important means of defraying campaign costs, which in turn frees up limited campaign dollars for use on television and other campaign activities. They can also be a valuable tool for managing a campaign's cash flow. For example, GELAC funds can be used as a loan mechanism for financing some of the costs of preparing for the general election prior to the receipt of the general election subsidy. Candidates can borrow GELAC funds to finance portions of staff salaries or overhead, travel, and planning costs, as long as the costs are solely associated with the general election campaign, and then reimburse the GELAC fund when the public subsidy is received for any noncompliance related expenses. Similarly, a campaign may borrow funds from a GELAC fund to gain access to cash owed to the campaign. The FEC sanctioned such activity in 1992, when it allowed the Clinton campaign, which was running out of its $55 million in public funds, to borrow from its GELAC fund after the election in anticipation of a $1.2 million reimbursement from the Secret Service for the costs associated with the travel of Clinton's security contingent (Alexander and Corrado 1995, 126).

These advantages of GELAC funding were demonstrated by the financial activity in 1996. The Clinton campaign spent over $5.3 million in GELAC funds, including $1.8 million in reimbursements to the campaign for exempt legal and accounting costs. The campaign also borrowed almost $2.5 million from its GELAC fund to finance general election expenses incurred prior to August 30, 1996. In addition, GELAC monies were used to pay approximately $1.2 million in "winding down" expenses incurred as of June 1998, with an additional $800,000 in such costs anticipated through 1999 (Federal Election Commission 1998a, 2 and 58). The Dole campaign spent about $5 million in GELAC funds. In the summer of 1996, when Dole had essentially reached the limit on primary spending, his campaign borrowed $1.5 million in GELAC funds to finance expenses incurred prior to receiving the general election subsidy (Federal Election Commission 1998b, 2). In its audit of the Dole committee, the FEC auditors determined that approximately $377,000 that came from the GELAC account was used for expenses that were actual primary campaign expenditures and therefore violated the rules governing GELAC funds (Federal Election Commission 1998b, 17). In addition, Dole paid $2.1 million in "winding down" expenses, at least 50 percent of which were reimbursable by the GELAC fund (Federal Election Commission 1998b, 63).

Given the financial benefits of GELAC funds, it is not surprising that candidates have begun to place increased emphasis on this kind of fund-raising. What is surprising is how early in the election cycle they begin to raise these funds. In the 1992 cycle, President Bush established his GELAC fund in October 1991, while Clinton did not register his account until May 1992. In the 1996 election cycle, both of the general election candidates registered their GELAC accounts with the FEC more than a year before the election, and well before they had respectively clinched their respective parties' nominations. Dole registered his GELAC account with the FEC on February 15, 1995, while Clinton registered his account on September 7, 1995. One of the reasons why GELAC funding has increased, therefore, is that candidates spend a greater amount of time raising these funds.

Candidates establish GELAC accounts as early as possible in order to take advantage of primary campaign fund-raising efforts. Under the contribution regulations, candidates can raise up to $1,000 from an individual donor for the primary campaign and an additional $1,000 for the GELAC account. Candidates can also redesignate contributions in excess of the $1,000 primary limit to a GELAC fund, as long as a donor has given permission to do so. As a result, campaigns can achieve economies of scale in fund-raising by raising GELAC funds simultaneously with primary monies or by relying on fund-raising lists developed during the primaries for direct mail solicitations for compliance donations. They can also share the costs of fund-raisers that jointly solicit campaign and GELAC monies. By adopting this approach, campaigns can reduce the costs of GELAC fund-raising and also take advantage of the fund-raising staffs on the primary campaign payroll. For example, Dole raised about $700,000 in GELAC funds by the end of 1995, spending only $20,000 in GELAC money to do so. Clinton also raised GELAC money during the primaries, but he concentrated his fund-raising efforts in the general election period, raising about $6.7 million of his $8 million total between August and November of the election year.

The growth of GELAC funds has served to undermine one of the objectives of the public funding program, which was to eliminate the need for private fund-raising in the presidential general election. The expanding role of these funds raises the question of whether the legal and accounting exemption needs to be more narrowly drawn in order to ensure that candidates do not use these funds in ways that allow them to use creative accounting to circumvent the spending limits. Recognizing this concern, the FEC in 1995 took a first step toward tightening the rules on GELAC funds by promulgating new regulations that better define the circumstances under which GELAC funds may be used to pay expenses prior to the start of the general election campaign. The new rules presume that any expenditure made before the party nominates its candidate is a primary expenditure, unless a campaign can demonstrate that the expense was exclusively related to the general election (see 11 C.F.R. § 9034.4[e]; 60 Fed. Reg. 31855–857 [June 16, 1995]). Further changes may be needed, however, if the role of GELAC funds continues to expand. As former FEC Commissioner Trevor Potter has noted: "The legal and accounting fund, a creation of the Commission, has grown far beyond its intended bounds. As a result, it presents the spectacle of high profile private fund-raising by a presidential campaign which has forsworn this very activity. This can only sow confusion about the public funding system" (cited in Alexander and Corrado 1995, 126).

## Noncandidate Funding

Parties and organized groups are also important sources of funding in presidential elections. Under the provisions of the FECA, these organizations are allowed to spend monies expressly to advocate the election or defeat of a presidential candidate, provided that the monies used for this purpose are raised in accordance with federal contribution limits. A national party committee can spend a limited amount of money on behalf of its presidential ticket in coordination with the presidential campaign. In 1996 the amount each party was allowed to spend in this manner was $12.1 million. Organized groups and individuals can spend unlimited amounts of money in support of a presidential candidate, as long as the group or individual does so independently, without any coordination with the candidate or members of his or her campaign staff.

### Party Coordinated Expenditures

In 1996 the Democratic and Republican national party committees spent a combined $18.3 million in coordinated expenditures. According to the reports filed with the FEC, the major part of this amount was disbursed by Republicans, who spent $11.6 million on behalf of Dole, which was less than the $12.1 million allowed by the law. In the past, the Republicans had always spent the maximum allowable amount. Of this $11.6 million, approximately $8.5 million, or about 73 percent of the total, was spent on media advertising and related costs. Almost one-half of this media money was expended in July and August. This included $250,000 in media costs in July and $350,000 in production expenses and about $3.2 million in media costs in August, including a $737,000 media buy in the days before the Democratic National Convention. The remaining share of the $8.5 million was disbursed in the first two weeks of October, during which the Republican National Committee spent $4.7 million on media.

The Democrats spent significantly less than the Republicans in coordinated funds, disbursing about $6.7 million, or slightly more than one-half of the amount allowed under the law. Like the Republicans, the Democrats devoted most of their expenditures to the costs of media advertising. The party spent $5.4 million on coordinated media expenses, about 81 percent of their total. These expenditures were made in two waves: The party disbursed $2.7 million in the week before the Democratic National Convention in August and another $2.7 million in the last week of the campaign. The 1996 election was thus the first since 1984 in which the party did not take advantage of the full allocation.

That the parties failed to maximize their coordinated spending suggests the declining importance of these funds in an era of unlimited soft money and issue advocacy. While coordinated expenditures are supposed to be the principal means by which parties participate in presidential campaigns, the reality in 1996 was that they played a relatively minor role in the funding of the presidential campaigns. Prior to the general election, the DNC spent at least $46 million on issue ads designed to benefit Clinton's candidacy by highlighting the president's accomplishments and criticizing the "Gingrich-Dole" agenda (Federal Election Commission 1998a, 30). The RNC spent at least $12 million on issue ads in support of Dole (Federal Election Commission 1998b, 25–26). These ads were financed through a combination of hard and soft money in accordance with allocation formulas established by the FEC (Corrado 1997b, 173–77; Federal Election Commission 1995). But because they did not advocate the election or defeat of a candidate, the monies spent on them were not subject to the coordinated spending limits or candidate spending limits, even though the FEC's audit division felt that there was reason to believe that they should be.

Similarly, party committees can spend unlimited amounts of money on election-related generic party activities such as voter registration and identification, volunteer recruitment and organization, and direct-mail and get-out-the-vote programs. These efforts are usually designed to help all party candidates by encouraging party supporters to go to the polls. In doing so, they benefit the presidential candidates as well as those seeking other offices. In 1996, the national party committees spent substantial amounts on such activities. The Democratic national party committees disbursed an estimated $40 million in hard and soft money on state and local party building and voter outreach efforts. The DNC alone spent approximately $20 million to contact over 14 million prospective voters through direct mail and 11 million through telemarketing calls. The national Republican Party committees spent a record $48 million to post over 84 million pieces of targeted political mail and make over 14 million voter identification or get-out-the-vote telephone calls (Herrnson 1998a, 94–95).

As long as parties can spend unlimited amounts on ads or other activities that serve essentially the same purpose as coordinated media, the relative value of limited coordinated expenses is significantly diminished. Even though issue ads may not expressly advocate the election or defeat of a candidate, as may coordinated ads, in 1996 the parties demonstrated a preference for issue ads because a major portion of the costs of these communications can be paid for with unrestricted soft money funds. By engaging in issue advocacy advertising rather than coordinated spending, parties can make their limited hard dollars go further; that is, they can get more advertising bang for the buck. Put another way, parties can purchase more advertising time and broadcast more spots if they use their hard-dollar resources for issue ads instead of coordinated communications. As a result, in 1996, coordinated expenditures were not the primary means by which party organizations assisted their candidates. Instead, coordinated expenditures were used to supplement activities financed with soft money and conducted outside of the spending limits.

### *Independent Expenditures and Partisan Communication Costs*

Organized groups devoted relatively small amounts of money to independent expenditures in connection with the presidential race. According to FEC disclosure filings, PACs and other political committees spent slightly more than $800,000 in independent expenditures, most of which was spent to help elect Bob Dole (see Table 4.2). Independent groups spent about $312,000 in support of Dole and $411,000 against Clinton. In comparison, only $68,500 was spent in support of

Table 4.2

**Presidential General Election, Independent Expenditures and Communication Costs** (in thousand $)

|  | Clinton | | Dole | |
|---|---|---|---|---|
|  | For Clinton | Against Dole | For Dole | Against Clinton |
| Independent expenditures | 68.5 | 4.3 | 311.8 | 411.3 |
| Communication costs | 2,415.8 | 261.1 | 12.8 | 0.0 |

*Source:* Based on data reported by the Federal Election Commission.

Clinton and $4,300 against Dole. Some Reform Party supporters spent funds in support of Perot, which totaled about $12,000.

Most of the expenditures in support of Dole came from pro-life groups. The major share of these expenditures were made by the National Right to Life Committee, with smaller amounts spent by pro-life PACs in Michigan and Illinois, and even smaller sums by committees in nine other states. The bulk of the money spent against Clinton came from nonconnected conservative PACs, led by the Conservative Trust, East Coast Conservative PAC, and Mid-America Conservative PAC. As for the monies spent in support of Clinton, almost two-thirds came from two labor organizations: The Union of Needletrades, Industrial, and Textile Employees Campaign Committee spent about $32,700, and the New York Teachers VOTE/COPE committee disbursed around $10,700.

Labor unions can also participate in the financing of presidential campaigns by spending funds to communicate internally with their members. The FECA exempts the monies spent by labor unions to communicate with their members from the law's contribution and spending restrictions. Labor unions can therefore spend unlimited amounts in this regard, including partisan communications that endorse or oppose a specific candidate. Trade associations and corporations are granted a similar exemption for partisan communications with their members. The law requires, however, that any expenditures over $2,000 per election that expressly advocate the election or defeat of a candidate be reported to the FEC.

As in other recent presidential campaigns, most of the partisan communication costs reported to the FEC consisted of expenditures made by labor unions in support of the Democratic nominee. In 1996, approximately $2.7 million in communication costs were disclosed, less than $13,000 of which was spent in support of Dole. About $2.4 million was spent in support of Clinton and another $261,000 spent to advocate the defeat of Dole. Almost half of the expenditures made in support of Clinton were the result of spending by the Communication Workers of America, who reported a total of more than $1.1 million. Other major spenders included the United Auto Workers ($516,000), the AFL-CIO ($315,000), and the American Federation of Teachers ($189,000). The amounts spent by labor unions advocating the president's reelection thus dwarfed the amounts spent independently by ideological groups in support of Dole.

## Candidate Spending Patterns: The Media Campaign

### *Media Expenditures*

Presidential campaigns are driven by the desire of the candidates to share their message with as large a portion of the electorate as possible. Modern presidential campaigns are therefore largely media campaigns in which the candidates rely heavily on paid advertising to broadcast their views. In this respect, the 1996 election was no exception.

According to an analysis of campaign spending conducted by the independent nonpartisan Campaign Study Group (CSG), both Clinton and Dole spent the major share of their general election monies on television and radio advertising (Chinoy 1997b, A19). CSG studied all of the reports filed with the FEC by Clinton and Dole as of December 31, 1996, including GELAC accounts, as well as the coordinated expenditure reports filed by the respective national party committees, and constructed an itemized catalogue of all the disbursements. This compilation revealed that the candidates each spent more than 60 percent of his general election funds on media advertising (see Table 4.3). Dole and the RNC spent about $47 million on advertising, or 61 percent of their total, while Clinton and the DNC spent slightly less, $46.1 million, which represented 63 percent of their total.

Although the CSG findings clearly document the emphasis presidential campaigns place on media spending in waging their campaigns, it is important to note that these data actually underestimate the share

Table 4.3

**Presidential General Election Expenditures, Clinton and Dole, 1996**

| | Clinton | | Dole | | Totals | |
|---|---|---|---|---|---|---|
| Item | Amount (in thousands $) | % of Clinton's total | Amount (in thousand $) | % of Dole's total | Combined total (in thousand $) | % of total |
| Advertising | | | | | | |
| Electronic media | 46,057.9 | 62.6 | 46,874.4 | 61.2 | 92,932.3 | 61.9 |
| Other media | 60.1 | 0.1 | 158.3 | 0.2 | 218.4 | 0.1 |
| Total | 46,118.0 | 62.7 | 47,032.7 | 61.4 | 93,150.7 | 62.0 |
| Overhead | | | | | | |
| Salaries/taxes | 4,926.3 | 7.0 | 5,014.4 | 6.5 | 9,940.7 | 6.6 |
| Travel | 5,515.4 | 7.5 | 1,572.7 | 2.0 | 7,088.1 | 4.7 |
| Telephone | 2,238.3 | 3.0 | 1,486.0 | 1.9 | 3,724.3 | 2.5 |
| Computers/office equipment | 1,501.8 | 2.0 | 2,828.1 | 3.7 | 4,329.9 | 2.9 |
| Office furniture/supplies | 748.5 | 1.0 | 1,024.8 | 1.3 | 1,773.3 | 1.2 |
| Lawyers/accountants | 305.7 | 0.4 | 179.6 | 0.2 | 485.3 | 0.3 |
| Rent/utilities | 388.5 | 0.5 | 741.8 | 1.0 | 1,130.3 | 0.8 |
| Bank/investment fees | 17.3 | 0.1 | 229.9 | 0.3 | 247.2 | 0.2 |
| Food/meetings | 60.7 | 0.1 | 56.0 | 0.1 | 116.7 | 0.1 |
| Total | 15,702.5 | 21.6 | 13,133.3 | 17.0 | 28,835.8 | 19.2 |
| Other campaign activity | | | | | | |
| Events | 8,058.4 | 11.0 | 13,481.0 | 17.6 | 21,539.4 | 14.3 |
| Persuasion mail/brochures | 0.0 | 0.0 | 1,033.8 | 1.3 | 1,033.8 | 0.7 |
| Staff/volunteers | 37.8 | 0.1 | 17.5 | 0.1 | 55.3 | 0.1 |
| Total | 8,096.2 | 11.1 | 14,532.3 | 19.0 | 22,628.5 | 15.1 |

| | | | | | | |
|---|---|---|---|---|---|---|
| Fund-raising | | | | | | |
| Direct mail | 2,285.1 | 3.1 | 875.4 | 1.1 | 3,160.5 | 2.1 |
| Events | 24.7 | 0.1 | 69.5 | 0.1 | 94.2 | 0.1 |
| Telemarketing | 235.6 | 0.3 | 23.0 | 0.1 | 258.6 | 0.2 |
| Total | 2,545.4 | 3.5 | 967.9 | 1.3 | 3,513.3 | 2.3 |
| Polling | 909.7 | 1.2 | 939.8 | 1.2 | 1,849.5 | 1.2 |
| Other expenses | | | | | | |
| Gifts/entertainment | 0.0 | 0.0 | 8.4 | 0.1 | 8.4 | 0.1 |
| Donations to parties | 0.3 | 0.1 | 0.0 | 0.0 | 0.3 | 0.1 |
| Nonitemized expenses | 135.8 | 0.2 | 40.3 | 0.1 | 176.1 | 0.1 |
| Total | 136.1 | 0.3 | 48.7 | 0.2 | 184.8 | 0.1 |
| Total | 73,507.9 | | 76,654.7 | | 150,162.6 | |

*Source:* Based on data developed by the Campaign Study Group as reported in the *Washington Post*, March 31, 1997, A19.

*Note:* Percentages may not sum to 100 percent as a result of rounding.

of resources devoted to advertising by the two campaigns. The CSG study includes GELAC funds in its analysis in order to give an accurate portrayal of the total funding and expenditures in the general election campaign. But GELAC funds may not be used to pay for general election advertising. If these funds are excluded and only those funds that could be used for media are considered (the public subsidy received by the candidate and the party-coordinated expenditures), then the share of funds devoted to advertising increases to around 67 percent for Clinton and almost 64 percent for Dole. Even if the party-coordinated expenditures are excluded and only the $61.8 million public grant provided to each candidate is considered, Clinton's estimated media allocation was slightly more than $40 million and Dole's just under $39 million. In other words, almost $2 out of every $3 that could be used for media spending was allocated to costs related to media advertising.

Perot devoted an even larger share of his budget to media advertising. Perot's effort to reach voters largely consisted of televised advertisements; he rarely traveled out on the stump and did not develop an extensive field operation to develop grassroots mobilization efforts in many states. As a result, most of his campaign monies were spent to produce ads and purchase broadcast time. Based on the data disclosed in FEC reports, Perot spent approximately $690,500 on production costs and about $20.5 million on media buys for a total of about $21.2 million in electronic media expenses. This sum represented 76 percent of his total campaign spending. Most of this amount, including more than $660,000 in production expenses and $13.2 million in broadcast time, was disbursed after October 14 for the final push toward the election.

The amounts spent on media in the general election contest were significantly higher than the allocations in the primary campaign. During the primaries, Clinton spent an estimated $13.1 million on media, which represented about 32 percent of his total prenomination spending. Dole spent around $7.2 million on media, or about 18 percent of his total (Chinoy 1997b, A19). One reason for this difference in candidate allocations is the lack of fund-raising expenses in the general election period. Fund-raising costs usually consume, on average, 10 to 20 percent of a candidate's budget (Fritz and Morris 1992; Morris and Gamache 1994). But in the general election candidates receive public funding, so they have no fund-raising expenses. The only expenses of this type incurred in the fall campaign are those associated with GELAC funds, and these costs can be paid out of GELAC receipts. In addition, these costs can be minimized by capitalizing on primary fund-raising efforts, as noted above.

Another reason for the difference is party soft money spending. Because parties have assumed a major role in identifying partisan supporters and turning out the general election vote, presidential campaigns can allocate less money to these activities. Instead of mounting extensive voter mobilization programs of their own, the candidates can rely on national and state party efforts. This, in effect, frees up millions of dollars in regulated funds that can then be used for media advertising.

### Media Targeting

How much candidates spend on media is important, but even more important is how they use the funds. Media campaigns are based on a complex set of decisions that must weigh the candidates' individual electoral college strategies, polling information, the relative value of broad-based network advertising versus less expensive local media buys, the specific markets to be targeted, the timing of ads, the content of the communications, and the need to respond to an opponent's message. At the center of this decision making is the desire to advance the most effective message strategy at the most efficient cost. How well a campaign executes these decisions is often the key to winning the "air wars" that have come to dominate presidential contests.

In 1996, the Clinton and Dole campaigns pursued the most sophisticated advertising strategies yet seen in a national election. New technologies allowed the candidates to target markets and messages more precisely than ever before, and dramatically expanded the speed with which they could respond to an opponent's message or change their media buys. The most important new technology was the advertisement detector service, known as the "Polaris Ad Detector," that was originally developed by Competitive Media Reporting (CMR) for use in monitoring advertisements sponsored by its corporate clients. The system basically monitors the satellite transmissions of the national television networks (ABC, CBS, NBC, and Fox), as well as twenty-five national cable networks. It also monitors all advertising in the nation's top seventy-five media markets, which cover over 80 percent of the country's population (Goldstein 1997, 5–6). The system allows users to determine when an ad is aired, the market and day and time of broadcast, the program and demographics of the program on which it was broadcast, and the content of the ad. In brief, it allows the user to know exactly where and when a specific message was broadcast and the audience it was intended to reach. In 1996, the CMR system tracked over 93 million commercials, including over 750,000 political spots (Goldstein 1997, 6).

Both presidential committees made use of this new technology. The Republican media firm, National Media Incorporated, and the Democratic firm, Squier, Knapp, and Ochs, contracted with CMR early in 1996 to track commercials during the 1996 campaign. These services allowed the Dole and Clinton campaigns to review media buys around the country on a daily basis and thereby take into account the advertising decisions of the rival campaign in determining their own media purchases. The CMR data also made it more difficult for campaigns to air messages in a way that was either undetected or broadcast without a response by the rival campaign. Further, it allowed one candidate to determine when his opponent was shifting his media targeting or giving up on a particular state, which made it easier to shift his own media purchases more precisely in response to changes (Novotny 1997, 20).

The information garnered from advertising detector services was particularly effective as a result of the synergies that were possible with other campaign technologies. A campaign organization could receive the content of an ad and convert it into digital format and distribute it by computer through the Internet to pollsters and other campaign strategists for focus-group testing and review. A response ad could then be developed and be placed on the air within the next day or two. The Clinton campaign proved to be especially efficient at the new technique. By October, the campaign could identify new Dole or RNC spots and distribute them via computer to twenty-six suburban shopping malls around the country where campaign polling analysts were set up to field-test public response to the ads. This information, combined with the media buy data, would then be factored into the creation of a response ad, and a new Clinton spot would be sent to stations, sometimes less than twenty-four hours after the Dole spot began airing, and in some cases, by the evening of the same day (Novotny 1997, 20; Mundy 1996).

These new technologies allowed the presidential contenders to make greater use of less expensive, more effectively targeted local media markets. In fact, "the 1996 election is likely to be remembered as the year when local markets truly displaced the networks in terms of the allocation of financial expenditures by the major candidates" (Novotny 1997, 19). For the first time, neither of the major-party candidates placed much emphasis on network advertising broadcasts. The Clinton campaign, especially, "determinedly avoided advertisements on the networks" (Novotny 1997, 15). Instead, the campaigns chose to purchase time in selected local media markets, which is less expensive than network time and offers a better ability to focus ads in time slots likely to be seen by particular groups of voters. In this way, the campaigns were able to purchase more time with their limited campaign dollars and at the same time enhance the potential effectiveness of their communications.

## The Contours of the Media Campaign

The extent of the candidates' reliance on local media buys can be discerned from the data gathered by the CMR monitoring system. According to an analysis of these data by political scientist Kenneth Goldstein, the candidates and their parties broadcast a total of close to 164,000 spots on local television in the top seventy-five media markets between April and November of 1996 (Goldstein 1997, 9; all of the data that follow is based on Goldstein's analysis, unless otherwise noted). Of these, about 91,000 spots were paid for by Clinton or the DNC, and close to 73,000 by Dole or the RNC. By contrast, the Clinton campaign and DNC aired only 12 spots on network television and 214 spots on national cable networks. The Dole campaign and RNC aired 102 spots on network television and 1,622 on national cable networks. The Republicans made more use of national distribution networks because throughout most of the campaign Dole was well behind in the polls in a majority of the states and needed to reach large numbers of voters. Even so, his use of network broadcasting was relatively insignificant compared to candidates in previous elections, especially given his position throughout the fall race.

Overall, as the above data suggest, the Democrats broadcast a substantially greater number of ads than did the Republicans in the period from April to November. Much of this advantage was achieved in the spring and summer of 1996, when Clinton still had plenty of money left to spend from his prenomination campaign and Dole had to rely on

RNC spending because his campaign had essentially reached the primary campaign spending limit. During these months before the start of the traditional general election period, Clinton and the DNC broadcast almost twice as many spots, approximately 17,000 more, than Dole and the Republicans. More than one-half of these advertisements (9,905) were paid for by the Clinton campaign out of remaining primary funds. Although the RNC came to Dole's aid by financing a number of issue advocacy ads, the Republican effort failed to match the DNC's spending. In all, the DNC financed 31,847 spots from April through election day, or about 34 percent of the Democratic total. The RNC financed 26,245 spots, or about 36 percent of the Republican total. From September to the end of the campaign, the two candidates broadcast roughly the same number of spots and spent relatively equal amounts of money on advertising. But this relative equity in the final stage of the election was not enough to overcome the substantial advantage Clinton and the Democrats had achieved before the nominating conventions had even begun to convene.

Dole's strategic problems were further complicated by his prospective electoral college position at the start of the fall campaign. Clinton held substantial leads in most of the key electoral states, including California, Ohio, Michigan, New York, New Jersey, and Pennsylvania, as well as in most of the South. He held narrower leads in the traditionally Republican states of Florida, Arizona, and Virginia (Herrnson and Wilcox 1997, 131). There were few states, other than the most staunch Republican strongholds, that Dole could count on. Consequently, Dole had to expend valuable resources attempting to shore up his support in traditionally Republican states, while Clinton had the opportunity to challenge Dole in some Republican states and focus more of his resources on key electoral battlegrounds. Dole's need to adopt a more scattershot approach in advertising was made more difficult by the conflicts over the campaign's message and media management, since shifting issues and changing personnel did not make for an efficient decision-making structure. As a result, Clinton was able to broadcast more spots in most of the electorally important top markets than Dole, and in some cases, out-advertised Dole by sizable margins.

In general, Dole and Clinton, along with their party committees, targeted roughly the same media markets. Of the top seventy-five markets, thirty-four essentially experienced the same level of advertising, including twenty-two where relatively few spots were aired. Of the remaining forty-one, Clinton gained an advantage in at least thirty-four, including seven markets where the margin between the two camps was more than 1,000 spots (Grand Rapids, Green Bay, Harrisburg, Hartford, Milwaukee, Minneapolis, and Portland) and three others in Ohio where the margin was close to 1,000 spots. Both sides heavily targeted Albuquerque (the only market to cover New Mexico), Cincinnati, Cleveland, Denver, Sacramento, and Tampa. Dole's top ten also included Los Angeles, San Diego, Las Vegas, and Nashville, while Clinton's top ten added Detroit, Flint, Lexington, and Louisville. Dole's greatest marginal advantage over Clinton in a heavily contested market was in the highly costly Los Angeles market, where Dole aired 3,500 spots, as compared to only 2,100 for Clinton. These data alone reflect Dole's electoral college problem. While Clinton was airing large numbers of spots in Midwestern markets and Florida, Dole was making significant media buys in California, where he trailed badly, in an effort to break Clinton's electoral lock.

California was not the only state where Dole spent significant sums to no avail. He also expended large sums in New York ($2.7 million), Pennsylvania ($2.2 million), and Connecticut ($900,000), but as election day neared, he failed to reduce Clinton's lead significantly (Bennet 1996, D20). By mid-October, Dole and the RNC had only $14 million left to spend in public monies and coordinated funds, while Clinton and the Democrats had $25 million remaining (Chinoy 1997b, A19). Thus, in the last few weeks of the contest, Dole was forced to reduce his advertising frequency in a number of markets, while shifting resources to the more expensive markets in California. During this period, Dole financed only token levels of advertising in Chicago, St. Louis, and some of the Michigan and Ohio markets, while increasing his advertising in Los Angeles (Goldstein 1997, 15). Clinton maintained his broad-based attack, spending $17 million on advertising over the final twenty days of the campaign (Chinoy 1997b, A19). The final component of Clinton's victory was thus complete. He had won the "air war."

## Conclusion

If there is a maxim applicable to presidential elections, it is that popular incumbents running with a strong economy are usually reelected. Indeed, this thesis is so accepted that many political scientists have developed models of presidential voting behavior based on economic forces and presidential popularity. In 1996, most of these models predicted a Clinton victory. On election day, the voters fulfilled these predictions.

A strong economy, peaceful conditions abroad, and the lack of a challenge to his renomination placed Clinton in a strong position from the start of the general election campaign. In such a circumstance, only a dramatic event or major controversy that unsettled the electorate could have altered the dynamics of the race. But the 1996 election offered little drama. Dole attempted a variety of approaches and messages in challenging the president, but in the end even a major controversy over illegal contributions and the president's dubious role in party fund-raising failed to overcome the more powerful forces that defined the political landscape. The 1996 election thus provided new evidence for an old thesis.

Even though the outcome seemed predetermined, the election offered much that was new, especially in the context of the financing of the campaigns. The campaign highlighted the financial and technological innovations that will characterize elections in the next century. The candidates relied on new technologies that were unheard of only a decade ago and demonstrated how these innovative tools can change the strategic tactics employed in a national race. These technologies played an important role in facilitating campaign resource decisions and signaled the beginning of a new era in media campaigns. Broad-based network advertising and weekly reviews of media purchases may now be a thing of the past. As the experience of 1996 indicates, the future may be found in highly localized media buying, digital transmissions, day-by-day media strategies, and the Internet.

What was most notable about the 1996 campaign, however, was that it drew into high relief the flaws in the current scheme of campaign finance. The 1996 election made obvious to the public what many observers have known for a long time: the financing of presidential general election campaigns consists of much more than the expenditure of the public subsidy provided to each campaign. Presidential campaigns continue to push the limits of the law, finding new and creative means of gathering additional resources for their campaigns. They continue to adapt their own patterns of spending to conform to new forms of finance, especially the growth of soft money and the rise of issue advocacy advertising. Consequently, they continue to undermine the objectives of the current regulations, which have essentially been rendered meaningless as a result of continued abuse.

No event in recent years demonstrated the problems in the current system more clearly or boldly than the fund-raising controversy that dominated the final weeks of the presidential campaign. The allegations that the president and his party sold access to the White House and the documentation of illegal or suspect contributions resurrected memories of the Watergate scandal and of the abuses that plagued the system in the years before the adoption of the FECA. The revelations made clear that reform is long overdue and that the need for congressional action is urgent.

Clinton promised to build "a bridge to the twenty-first century." The 1996 election was that bridge. In its financing and tactics, it offered a model for how to conduct campaigns in an era of expanding communications technology and how to take advantage of the campaign finance rules to pay for such campaigns. What remains to be seen is whether future elections will be based on the pragmatic bridge that Clinton built during his campaign, or the ideological bridge that he proclaimed with its promise of a new start for the next millennium.

## Acknowledgment

The author would like to acknowledge the assistance of Alexander Quigley and Philip Russell in the preparation of this chapter.

## 5

PAUL S. HERRNSON

# Financing the 1996 Congressional Elections

The 1996 elections were the first to occur after the Republicans' historic takeover of Congress in 1994. Given that the GOP had majorities in both the House and Senate for the first time in four decades, the time was ripe for change in the flow of money in congressional campaigns. Nevertheless, the 1996 contests for the House and Senate were marked by both continuities and changes in campaign fund-raising and spending. Some of these were predictable; some were not. One area of continuity was that congressional candidates once again set new records for campaign financing, raising a total of $790.5 million and spending $765.3 million. Another predictable pattern was that incumbents and members of the majority party continued to raise and spend more money than challengers and members of the congressional minority. Among the predictable changes was that for the first time Republican congressional candidates outspent their Democratic opponents. Among the unpredictable changes was the unprecedented number of supposedly independent political communications that parties and interest groups made to improve their preferred candidates' election prospects.

This chapter examines the financing of the 1996 congressional elections. The first section discusses the setting for those contests, highlighting the climate in which campaign contributors and fund-raisers operated. The next two sections analyze how parties, PACs, and individuals distributed their campaign contributions and the impact that their decisions had on the resources available to different types of candidates. This analysis is followed by a discussion of two controversial kinds of campaign expenditures that reached significant proportions in the 1996 congressional elections: independent and issue advocacy spending.

## The Setting for the 1996 Congressional Elections

The GOP's ascendance in the 104th Congress turned the established order on Capitol Hill on its head. With the exception of Representative Newt Gingrich (R-Ga.), Republican of Georgia, virtually no one anticipated that the Republicans would wrest control of the House or the Senate from the Democrats. Democrats had been the majority party in the House for so long that only one House Member in the 104th Congress, Representative Sidney Yates (D-Ill.), had served during a period of Republican control. Members of both parties and their interest-group allies, many of which routinely made campaign contributions, had become accustomed to Democrats occupying the leadership positions and sitting in the committee chairs that controlled the flow of business in the House. The flow of campaign money reflected that reality. In every election held between 1978 and 1994, Democratic candidates collected a majority of the campaign money raised in House elections (see Figure 5.1). It was not until after House Republicans had won control of the chamber that they collected more campaign cash than did House Democrats.

The situation in the Senate was somewhat different. While the Democrats had possessed a majority of Senate seats for most of recent history, their procedural control over the upper chamber was neither uninterrupted nor unchallenged. The Republicans won a majority of Senate seats in 1980 and were able to hold that majority for six consecutive years. Moreover, holding a majority of Senate seats does not enable a party to dominate the upper chamber in the same way that holding a majority of House seats enables it to dominate the lower chamber. The ability of any one senator to use the filibuster to obstruct the Senate from conducting its business and the sixty-vote requirement for cloture make it difficult for the majority party to impose its will unless it possesses sixty seats. As a result, senators of both parties have had significant influence over how the Senate conducted its business prior and after 1994, and neither party's candidates consistently raised more money during this period. Democratic Senate candidates raised the most money during the 1978 and 1980 elections, when their party had a majority of seats, and Republicans enjoyed a fund-raising

Figure 5.1. **Congressional Candidates' Campaign Receipts, 1978–1996**

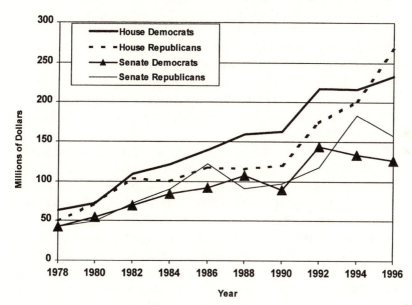

*Source:* Federal Election Commission.

advantage in the three elections between 1982 and 1986, when they controlled the chamber. Then the partisan advantage in fund-raising flipped back and forth, with Democrats enjoying a financial advantage in 1988 and 1992 and Republicans enjoying the upper hand in 1994 and 1996.

The Republican takeover gave GOP candidates and party committees an opportunity to increase their campaign receipts, but one of the big questions on the minds of many political operatives and scholars was how big that increase would be. Would individuals and PACs that had formerly contributed primarily to Democratic candidates abandon them in favor of the Republicans, once the Democrats no longer occupied Congress's committee and subcommittee chairs and other major leadership posts, or would these donors continue to provide some support for the Democrats? It would have made sense for business and trade association PACs and individual contributors who were ideologically attuned to the Republican's policy positions and had routinely contributed large sums to Democratic incumbents to switch their contributions once the GOP had won majorities in both chambers. But it was also plausible to expect these donors to react with caution and continue to donate some of their funds to Democrats, given that Republicans enjoyed only slim majorities in both chambers. The GOP's small majorities, and the fact that a Democrat occupied the White House, meant that Democrats would continue to exercise some influence over the legislative process in the 104th Congress. The thinness of the Republicans' majorities also meant that it was well within reach for the Democrats to regain their majority status when the 105th Congress convened.

The performance of the 104th Congress added to the uncertainty surrounding the 1996 elections. Public hostility toward the federal government was instrumental in helping the Republicans win control of Congress in 1994, and it injected a great deal of uncertainty into their prospects for maintaining control in 1996. Political scandal, the federal deficit, and government gridlock drove public approval of Congress downward in the early 1990s to where roughly three out of every four Americans disapproved of Congress's performance prior to the 1994 elections (Magleby, Patterson, and Wirls 1994). As the party in control of both Congress and the White House, Democrats were in position to feel the brunt of the voters' anger. President Clinton's early missteps on health care reform and gays in the military, his failure to enact a promised middle-class tax cut, and allegations of ethical misconduct by the president and members of his administration fanned the flames of hostility that voters had vented on congressional Democrats. The Republicans capitalized on voter hostility by waging a two-pronged nationalized campaign. The first prong presented a negative message that linked congressional Democrats to the president and blamed both for the perceived shortcomings of the Washington establishment. The second prong provided a positive message that was communicated through the House Republicans' Contract with America, a ten-point, market-tested, election manifesto that included many popular Republican ideas (Gimpel 1995; Koopman 1996). The Republicans' strategy had its intended effect of energizing Republican candidates and their supporters, while demoralizing Democrats and their allies.

Following their capturing control of Congress, House Republicans passed nine out of ten elements of the Contract, but major pieces of the legislation failed to win the support of the Senate or were vetoed by the president. The public was sharply divided over the Contract. Most voters supported congressional reform, crime reduction, welfare reform, the balanced budget amendment, and other measures designed to reduce the size and costs of government. Most opposed GOP legislation that proposed to give $240 billion in tax cuts to the wealthiest Americans while reducing future Medicare funding by $270 billion and cutting federal appropriations for Medicaid, environmental protections, and education. Disagreements over the budget between the president and the Republican Congress led to two federal government shutdowns, which were largely blamed on the GOP. Democrats sought to capitalize on the public's hostility toward the Republicans by mounting a national campaign against what they labeled "the extremist Republican Congress" and offering a modest, alternative agenda designed to appeal to middle-income and working families. However, the 1996 election did not become fully nationalized because conditions of divided government—a GOP-controlled Congress and a Democratic-controlled executive branch—made it difficult for either party to take full credit or place full blame for the government's performance on its opponent. Late deal making by the president and Republican congressional leaders also blurred lines of accountability when the Republicans accepted the president's compromise budget and the president signed the GOP's welfare bill. Events leading up to the 1996 elections injected much uncertainty into the outcomes of many House and Senate races, as well as the critical issue of which party would maintain control over the House (Herrnson 1998a).

## Campaign Contributors

Political parties, PACs, and individuals make campaign contributions for a variety of reasons. Democratic and Republican Party committees and some PACs and individuals contribute to influence the outcomes of elections. Some PACs and individuals view contributions mainly as investments that are useful in gaining access to influential members of Congress. Some individuals also contribute because they get a sense of satisfaction from rubbing shoulders with politicians and the other well-connected individuals who routinely attend fund-raising events.

### *Political Parties*

American political parties are known for being more pragmatic than ideological. Party strategies are first and foremost designed to win control of governmental offices, not restructure society along some grand vision (Epstein 1986). Both parties seek to win as many House and Senate seats as possible. This strategic imperative encourages them to become heavily involved in competitive elections, where their efforts have the potential to make the difference between victory and defeat, and to virtually ignore most other contests.

The Democratic Congressional Campaign Committee (DCCC) and the National Republican Congressional Committee (NRCC) play the lead role in devising the parties' national strategies in House elections. They account for the lion's share of spending in House races. They also take the lead in advising House candidates on campaign strategy and in providing candidates with campaign services ranging from assistance in hiring campaign consultants to producing television ads to raising large contributions from PACs and individuals. The Democratic Senatorial Campaign Committee (DSCC) and the National Republican Senatorial Committee (NRSC) perform similar roles in Senate elections (Herrnson 1998a).

The overall competitiveness of the 1996 elections made it possible for both parties, including the four congressional and senatorial campaign committees, to raise record sums of money. Interest groups and individuals donated large and small contributions in order to try to influence which party would control Congress. The DCCC raised slightly less than $39 million, the NRCC about $92.8 million, the DSCC approximately $45 million, and the NRSC $93.9. The advantages the Republicans enjoyed in fund-raising in 1996 are not unusual. The GOP congressional, senatorial, national, and state and local campaign committees have consistently raised more money than their Democratic counterparts since at least the mid-1970s, when the Federal Election Commission (FEC) first began disclosing such information.

These funds include so-called hard money, which is regulated by the Federal Election Campaign Act of 1974 and its amendments (collectively referred to as the FECA) and soft money, which is not.[1] Hard money, which is subject to federal contribution and spending limits, can be directly spent to advocate the election or defeat of individual House and Senate candidates. It includes direct contributions and coordinated expenditures. National, congressional, and state party committees can each contribute $5,000 to a House candidate in the general election.[2] The parties' national and senatorial campaign committees can contribute a combined total of $17,500 to a Senate candidate, and state party committees can contribute an additional $5,000. The limits for party coordinated expenditures in House general elections were originally set in 1974 at $10,000 for all national party organizations and are adjusted for inflation. They reached $30,910 in the 1996 elections.[3] The limits for national party coordinated expenditures in Senate elections vary by state population and are also indexed for inflation. They ranged from $61,820 in the smallest states to $823,690 in Texas in 1996. If an election had been held in California that year, the coordinated expenditure limit would have been $1,409,249. State party committees are authorized to spend the same amounts in coordinated expenditures in House and Senate elections as the parties' national organizations.

Soft money is not subject to federal limits, but it can be spent to organize voter registration and get-out-the-vote drives, sponsor slate cards, and distribute other materials that bear the names of federal or nonfederal candidates. Soft money has also traditionally been used to fund campaign ads that communicate an overall party message designed to influence the national political agenda. During the 1996 elections, both parties expanded the uses of soft money to include so-called issue advocacy ads—television and radio ads designed to influence the outcome of individual House and Senate elections without expressly advocating the candidates' election or defeat.

During the 1996 elections, Democratic Party organizations directly contributed more than $1.5 million to their party's House candidates and spent nearly $6.8 million in coordinated expenditures on their candidates' behalf. Coordinated expenditures typically consist of polls, television and radio ads, issue and opposition research, and other campaign activities over which both the candidate and party exercise some control. Parties distribute more in coordinated expenditures than direct contributions because the limits for coordinated expenditures are substantially higher. The Democrats also contributed $690,000 to their Senate candidates and spent almost $9.1 million on their behalf. The major beneficiary of Democratic Party contributions and coordinated expenditures in the 1996 House elections was Bill Yellowtail, who ran for Montana's at-large seat, which became open when Representative Pat Williams decided to retire. Yellowtail received $128,229 in contributions and coordinated expenditures.[4] Richard Durbin, who gave up his Illinois House seat to run for the Senate, was the major beneficiary of Democratic spending in the 1996 Senate elections. He received $1,064,256 in party contributions and coordinated expenditures.

Republican Party committees spent significantly more in 1996 than the Democrats, reflecting their greater wealth. The GOP contributed more than $2.6 million to its House candidates and made $8.2 million in coordinated expenditures on their behalf. It contributed slightly in excess of $1 million to its Senate candidates and spent more than $11 million on their behalf. Rick Hill, Yellowtail's opponent in the Montana race, was the major beneficiary of Republican spending in House contests. He received $172,617 in GOP contributions and coordinated expenditures.[5] Senator Phil Gramm of Texas, who received $1,148,975 in Republican Party contributions and coordinated expenditures, topped the list of Senate beneficiaries of GOP money. Although Republican candidates traditionally receive more party support than do their Democratic opponents, the gap between the two parties has narrowed during the last few years.

Party spending in House campaigns was well targeted in 1996. Both parties distributed most of their hard money to candidates involved in competitive contests. The Democrats distributed 77 percent of their funds to candidates involved in elections decided by 20 percent or less of the two-party vote (see Table 5.1). The Republicans delivered 86 percent of their funds to GOP candidates in these same contests. Republican Party spending favored House incumbents, who received 39 percent of all party funds. Republican challengers and open-seat candidates received less, reflecting the fact that the GOP needed to focus its resource on incumbents in jeopardy, which included many first-term members. Democratic Party spending, on the other hand, was heavily skewed toward challengers, followed by open-seat candidates. The Democrats' aggressive allocation patterns are typical of a minority party that believes it is favored by the immediate political climate, whereas the Republicans' expenditures are typical of a majority party that senses that political conditions threatens its continued control over the chamber (Herrnson 1998a).

Party spending in the 1996 Senate races was very well targeted and also responsive to the political environment. Both parties spent well over 90 percent of their funds in competitive races. Democratic Party committees followed a moderately aggressive strategy, investing more money on challengers than incumbents. Their Republican counterparts followed a defensive strategy that favored incumbents over challengers. Both parties spent large sums in the unusually large number of open-seat contests.

Table 5.1

**The Distribution of Party Contributions in the 1996 House and Senate Elections**

| | House | | Senate | |
|---|---|---|---|---|
| | Democrats | Republicans | Democrats | Republicans |
| Incumbents | | | | |
| In jeopardy | 17% | 37% | 16% | 34% |
| | (44) | (75) | (5) | (9) |
| Shoo-ins | 6 | 2 | — | 3 |
| | (112) | (125) | (2) | (4) |
| Challengers | | | | |
| Hopefuls | 40% | 26% | 27% | 19% |
| | (75) | (44) | (9) | (5) |
| Likely losers | 13 | 6 | 1 | 1 |
| | (125) | (112) | (4) | (2) |
| Open-seat candidates | | | | |
| Prospects | 20% | 23% | 52% | 41% |
| | (32) | (32) | (12) | (12) |
| Long shots | 4 | 6 | 4 | 2 |
| | (18) | (18) | (2) | (2) |
| Total (in thousand $) | $7,860 | $9,987 | $9,246 | $11,513 |
| (*N*) | (406) | (406) | (34) | (34) |

*Source:* Paul S. Herrnson, *Congressional Elections: Campaigning at Home and in Washington* (Washington, D.C.: CQ Press, 1998). Reprinted with permission.

*Notes:* Incumbents in jeopardy are defined as those who lost or who won by 20 percent or less of the two-party vote. Shoo-ins are incumbents who won by more than 20 percent of the two-party vote. Hopeful challengers are those who won or who lost by 20 percent or less of the two-party vote. Likely loser challengers are those who lost by more than 20 percent of the two-party vote. Open-seat prospects are those whose election was decided by 20 percent or less of the two-party vote. Open-seat long shots in one-party districts are those whose election was decided by more than 20 percent of the two party vote. Figures include contributions and coordinated expenditures by all party committees to general election candidates in major-party contested races, excluding a small number of atypical races that were decided in runoffs or won by independents. They do not include soft money expenditures. Some columns do not add to 100 percent because of rounding. The numbers of candidates are in parentheses. Dash = less than 0.5 percent.

Congressional party leaders also succeeded in convincing many of their fellow incumbents and former members of Congress to contribute significant sums from their campaign accounts and leadership PACs to other candidates in 1996. Democratic officeholders (and former officeholders) redistributed more than $2.8 million to their party's House candidates and almost $389,000 to its Senate candidates. The Republicans redistributed significantly more funds, almost $5.8 million, to GOP candidates for the lower chamber and more than $1.8 million to candidates for the upper chamber. Most of the Democratic and Republican Party connected contributions flowed to the same House and Senate candidates who received the largest donations from formal party organizations: candidates competing in close contests. Democratic officeholders' contributions favored challengers over incumbents. Republican officeholders favored incumbents over challengers, and both parties' officeholders also contributed large sums to candidates for Senate open seats. The major difference between the distribution of party-connected donations made by members of Congress and actual party contributions is that more of the party-connected donations were given to incumbents (Herrnson 1998a).

### Political Action Committees

More than 4,500 PACs were registered with the FEC during the 1996 elections, and these groups contributed a record $200.7 million to congressional candidates. Although they represent diverse interests, not all elements of American society are represented in the PAC community. More than 64 percent of all PACs were sponsored by business interests, such as corporations, corporations without stock, cooperatives, and trade, membership, and health associations. Labor PACs constituted approximately 8 percent of the PAC community, and nonconnected PACs, sometimes called ideological committees, made up the final 28 percent. One would be hard pressed to find a PAC sponsored by the homeless or formed to represent the interests of the poor.

A relatively small group of organizations account for most PAC contributions. A mere 10 percent of all PACs made 76 percent of all PAC contributions to congressional candidates in 1996. PACs sponsored by business interests contributed more money than any other group. Corporate and trade association PACs made 36 percent and 28 percent of these contributions, respectively. PACs sponsored by corporations without stock and cooperatives accounted for another 4 percent. Labor PACs contributed 22 percent and ideological PACs another 11 percent of all PACs dollars.

Most PACs use ideological, access-oriented, or mixed strategies when making contributions to House and Senate candidates (e.g.,

Eismeier and Pollock 1988; Humphries 1991; Sorauf 1992). PACs that use ideological strategies are similar to political parties in that they primarily seek to influence the political process through elections. Most ideological PACs make contributions in order to maximize the number of House members who share their policy views, often on such salient issues as abortion rights and the environment. These PACs distribute most of their resources to candidates involved in competitive contests, but they occasionally make contributions to encourage the careers of promising politicians. Ideological PACs rarely make contributions for the purposes of gaining access to legislators because these PACs seek to advance issues that are linked to fundamental values that officeholders are rarely willing to compromise.

Access-oriented PACs view elections pragmatically. They make contributions mainly for the purpose of gaining access to members of Congress who are in a position to influence regulations, appropriations, or treaties that effect the environment in which the PAC's industry or workforce operates. These groups consider campaign contributions an important tool for reaffirming or strengthening their relationships with influential lawmakers. They recognize that contributions can create good will with representatives and senators, thereby making it easier for the group's lobbyists to influence the legislative process.

PACs that follow access strategies are likely to contribute most of their money to incumbents. Members of the House and Senate who occupy party leadership posts, chair or are members of important committees or subcommittees, or are recognized leaders in specific policy areas are likely to receive the most access-oriented PAC money. Because these PACs are interested in influencing congressional policy decisions more than election outcomes, they are not overly concerned with whether the incumbents to whom they contribute are involved in competitive elections. In fact, some of the recipients of the PACs' dollars do not even have any election opponents.

The last group of PACs follows mixed strategies. These PACs give some contributions to candidates who share their group's views and other contributions to incumbents with whom they wish to maintain access. Most of the contributions that are motivated by the former goal are given to candidates in close races, and most of those motivated by the latter goal are given to powerful incumbents. In elections where PAC decision makers are cross-pressured because the incumbent is in a position to influence the group's legislative priorities and the challenger is more supportive of the group's interests, most PACs that follow mixed strategies contribute solely to the incumbent, but a few also contribute to the challenger.

The Republican takeover of Congress had a major impact on the distribution of PAC contributions to House candidates. Business-oriented committees responded most strongly to the switch in partisan control. In 1994, corporate PACs made 57 percent of their contributions to candidates in contested House elections to Democrats and 43 percent to Republicans (see Table 5.2). Two years later, they more than reversed the partisan balance of their contributions, donating a mere 30 percent of their funds to Democrats and 70 percent to Republicans. Trade association PACs made a similar reversal in their contributing patterns. Even labor union PACs, which have been Democratic congressional candidates' most loyal supporters, responded to the changing climate in Congress. The percentage of the contributions they gave to House Democratic candidates fell from 97 percent to 93 percent, as labor attempted to respond to the new order on Capitol Hill. The contribution patterns of nonconnected PACs also changed, but not because these groups shifted the partisanship of their contributions. Instead, conservative PACs raised more money than their liberal rivals, which worked to the advantage of GOP candidates.

It is difficult to assess the effect of the shift in partisan control of the Senate on PAC contributions because different Senate seats are up for election every two years and the idiosyncrasies of the candidates and states involved can have a major impact on the flow of PAC money. Nevertheless, the evidence suggests that the PAC community responded to the partisan change in both the upper and lower chambers of Congress in similar ways. Corporate and trade association PACs, many of which had already backed GOP Senate candidates, increased their support for Republicans substantially once the they took charge of the chamber (see Table 5.3). Labor PACs continued to give most of their funds to Democrats, but the rock-solid support they had given to Democratic candidates in previous years eroded somewhat. Conservative ideological PACs increased their contributions to Republican candidates, while liberal PAC contributions to Democrats decreased.

Despite the fact that many PACs began to favor Republican candidates over Democrats during the 1996 elections, they did not totally abandon the Democrats, nor did they abandon their previous contribution strategies. Corporate PACs continued to use the vast majority of

Table 5.2

**The Partisan Distribution of PAC Contributions in the 1994 and 1996 House Elections** (in percentages)

| | Corporate | | Trade Association | | Labor | | Nonconnected | |
|---|---|---|---|---|---|---|---|---|
| | 1994 | 1996 | 1994 | 1996 | 1994 | 1996 | 1994 | 1996 |
| Democrats | 57 | 30 | 59 | 37 | 97 | 93 | 64 | 43 |
| Republicans | 43 | 70 | 41 | 63 | 3 | 7 | 35 | 57 |
| Total (in thousand $) | $38,213 | $46,118 | $34,411 | $40,054 | $30,110 | $35,781 | $10,520 | $13,718 |

*Source:* Compiled from Federal Election Commission data.

*Notes:* Figures comprise PAC contributions to general election candidates in two-party contested elections. Some columns do not add to 100 percent because of rounding.

Table 5.3

**The Partisan Distribution of PAC Contributions in the 1994 and 1996 Senate Elections** (in percentages)

| | Corporate | | Trade Association | | Labor | | Nonconnected | |
|---|---|---|---|---|---|---|---|---|
| | 1994 | 1996 | 1994 | 1996 | 1994 | 1996 | 1994 | 1996 |
| Democrats | 42 | 20 | 43 | 28 | 96 | 94 | 56 | 33 |
| Republicans | 59 | 81 | 56 | 71 | 3 | 5 | 44 | 66 |
| Total | $17,864 | $16,547 | $10,362 | $10,982 | $6,611 | $6,316 | $5,170 | $6,292 |

*Source:* Compiled from Federal Election Commission data.

*Notes:* Figures comprise PAC contributions to general election candidates in two-party contested elections. Some columns do not add up to 100 percent because of rounding.

Table 5.4

**The Distribution of PAC Contributions in the 1996 House Elections**
(in percentages)

|  | Corporate | Trade, membership, and health | Labor | Non-connected |
|---|---|---|---|---|
| **Democrats** |  |  |  |  |
| Incumbents |  |  |  |  |
| In jeopardy | 11 | 12 | 22 | 12 |
| Shoo-ins | 16 | 16 | 27 | 11 |
| Challengers |  |  |  |  |
| Hopefuls | 1 | 4 | 25 | 13 |
| Likely losers | — | — | 6 | 2 |
| Open-seat candidates |  |  |  |  |
| Prospects | 1 | 3 | 10 | 4 |
| Long shots | 1 | 2 | 3 | 1 |
| **Republicans** |  |  |  |  |
| Incumbents |  |  |  |  |
| In jeopardy | 25 | 24 | 3 | 24 |
| Shoo-ins | 36 | 29 | 4 | 15 |
| Challengers |  |  |  |  |
| Hopefuls | 2 | 3 | — | 7 |
| Likely losers | — | 1 | — | 1 |
| Open-seat candidates |  |  |  |  |
| Prospects | 5 | 5 | — | 8 |
| Long shots | 2 | 2 | — | 2 |
| **Total (in thousands $)** | $46,118 | $40,054 | $35,781 | $3,718 |

*Source:* Paul S. Herrnson, *Congressional Elections: Campaigning at Home and in Washington* (Washington, D.C.: CQ Press, 1998). Reprinted with permission.
*Notes:* Figures are for general election candidates in major-party contested races, excluding a small number of atypical races that were decided in runoffs or won by independents. Dashes = less than 0.5 percent. The categories and numbers of candidates are the same as those in Table 5.2. Some columns do not add to 100 percent because of rounding.

their funds to court incumbents. They allocated 88 percent of their House contributions to incumbents, 9 percent to open-seat candidates, and a mere 3 percent to challengers (see Table 5.4). Moreover, corporate PACs gave little consideration to the closeness of the incumbent races, distributing 52 percent of their House contributions to shoo-ins, who won by more than 20 percent of the two-party vote. The contribution patterns for trade PACs are very similar, except these committees invested slightly more money in challenger and open-seat contests.

Labor PAC contributions to 1996 House candidates continued to reflect their inclination to follow mixed strategies. These committees donated virtually all of their money to Democrats, with whom they share ideological goals. Nevertheless, they distributed more than one-half of the contributions they made to Democratic House candidates to incumbents who were best positioned to influence legislation of importance to the labor movement. Indeed, shoo-ins received more labor dollars than any other group of Democratic candidates.

Nonconnected PACs also followed the usual pattern of giving most of their House contributions to candidates in close elections in 1996. They contributed more than 29 percent of their funds to Democrats involved in competitive contests and 39 percent of their funds to their Republican opponents. These PACs also distributed 38 percent of their House contributions to challengers and open-seat contestants.

PAC contributions to Senate candidates also exhibited predictable patterns during the 1996 elections (see Table 5.5). Corporate and trade PACs invested significant sums in pursuit of access; however, the unusually large number of open seats (fourteen out of thirty-four) and incumbents in jeopardy (seventeen) skewed significant portions of their resources toward candidates in those elections. Both sets of PACs were more generous to candidates who belong to the majority than the minority party.

Labor and nonconnected PACs were also heavily influenced by the structure of competition in Senate races. Labor invested slightly less than one-fourth of its contributions on behalf of Democratic incumbents, pumping the vast majority of the remainder into the campaigns of competitive Democratic challengers and open-seat contestants. Nonconnected PACs invested 84 percent of their funds in competitive elections, with Republican candidates benefiting the most from ideologically motivated contributions.

### Individuals

Individuals constitute the largest source of campaign money in congressional elections, having contributed approximately $444 million to all primary and general election candidates in the 1996 House and Senate elections. They spend money in politics for a variety of reasons, making their contributing behavior somewhat more difficult to categorize than that of parties and PACs. Some individuals view campaign

Table 5.5

**The Distribution of PAC Contributions in the 1996 Senate Elections** (in percentages)

| | Corporate | Trade, membership, and health | Labor | Non-connected |
|---|---|---|---|---|
| Democrats | | | | |
| Incumbents | | | | |
|   In jeopardy | 6 | 8 | 19 | 11 |
|   Shoo-ins | 2 | 2 | 4 | 2 |
| Challengers | | | | |
|   Hopefuls | 1 | 3 | 15 | 5 |
|   Likely losers | — | — | 2 | — |
| Open-seat candidates | | | | |
|   Prospects | 9 | 12 | 47 | 13 |
|   Long shots | 2 | 3 | 7 | 2 |
| Republicans | | | | |
| Incumbents | | | | |
|   In jeopardy | 32 | 28 | 2 | 24 |
|   Shoo-ins | 13 | 10 | 2 | 8 |
| Challengers | | | | |
|   Hopefuls | 9 | 7 | — | 8 |
|   Likely losers | — | — | — | — |
| Open-seat candidates | | | | |
|   Prospects | 23 | 22 | 1 | 23 |
|   Long shots | 4 | 4 | — | 3 |
| Total (in thousand $) | $16,547 | $10,982 | $6,316 | $6,292 |

*Source:* Paul S. Herrnson, *Congressional Elections: Campaigning at Home and in Washington* (Washington, D.C.: CQ Press, 1998). Reprinted with permission.

*Notes:* Figures are for general election candidates in major-party contested races. Dashes = less than 0.5 percent. The categories and numbers of candidates are the same as those in Table 5.2. Some columns do not add to 100 percent because of rounding.

contributions as little more than a routine part of doing business. They consider contributions an investment that helps them gain access to members of Congress who approve the regulations, appropriations, and trade agreements that affect their business activities. These "investors" are believed to behave in ways that are similar to those of access-oriented PACs, contributing to incumbents who occupy leadership positions and rarely supporting challengers. Many of these individuals make large contributions (see chapter 6 in this volume for more information on individuals who make large contributions).

Another group of individual contributors, referred to as "ideologues," are primarily motivated by a few salient issues or some general beliefs about the structure of society or the role of government. Like ideological PACs, individual ideologues view elections—not lobbying—as their primary means for influencing public policy. As such, they give most of their contributions to candidates in competitive contests, including challengers and open-seat candidates, but are willing to support a few budding politicians involved in races that are not highly competitive.

A third group of individual donors, referred to as "intimates," emphasizes the importance of personal contact and local ties when contributing to candidates for the House and Senate. Some of these individuals contribute because of the sense of satisfaction they get from supporting local politicians. Others make donations because they get a sense of satisfaction from rubbing shoulders with politicians and the other well-connected individuals who routinely attend fund-raising events.

Regardless of their motives, individual contributors apparently respond to major changes in the political climate. The Republican takeover had a significant impact on the flow of individual contributions of all sizes. Between the 1994 and the 1996 elections, individual contributions to Democratic general election candidates for the House fell, while contributions to Republicans experienced a corresponding increase (see Table 5.6). The switch in giving patterns was greatest for large contributions, more of which are presumably given as investments. Democratic House candidates raised one-half of all individual contributions of between $750 and $1,000 in 1994 and only 41 percent of these contributions in 1996. The dropoff in Democratic contributions of under $200 was much smaller: from 43 percent in 1994 and 41 percent in 1996.

Individual contributors also react to incumbency and electoral competitiveness when making contributions to House candidates. During the 1996 elections, individuals gave the majority of their contributions to incumbents, especially those belonging to the Republican Party. This generalization holds for contributions of all sizes, including those given in amounts of less than $200 and those ranging between $750 and $1,000 (see Table 5.7). Individual contributors did not pay too much attention to the competitiveness of the election when contributing to incumbents, reflecting their investment motives. This is especially the case for individuals who made contributions of $500. They

Table 5.6

**The Partisan Distribution of Individual Contributions in the 1994 and 1996 House Elections** (in percentages)

| | Less than $200 | | $200–$499 | | $500–$749 | | $750–$1,000 | |
|---|---|---|---|---|---|---|---|---|
| | 1994 | 1996 | 1994 | 1996 | 1994 | 1996 | 1994 | 1996 |
| Democrats | 43 | 41 | 48 | 43 | 49 | 43 | 50 | 41 |
| Republicans | 57 | 59 | 52 | 57 | 51 | 57 | 50 | 59 |
| Total (in thousand $) | $63,085 | $83,145 | $25,564 | $33,252 | $30,975 | $40,070 | $53,255 | $75,720 |

*Source:* Compiled from Federal Election Commission data.

*Notes:* Figures comprise individual contributions to general election candidates in two-party contested elections. Some columns do not add to 100 percent because of rounding.

Table 5.7

**The Distribution of Individual Contributions in the 1996 House Elections**
(in percentages)

|  | Less than $200 | $200–$499 | $500–$749 | $750–$1,000 |
|---|---|---|---|---|
| Democrats |  |  |  |  |
| Incumbents |  |  |  |  |
| In jeopardy | 9 | 9 | 8 | 7 |
| Shoo-ins | 9 | 12 | 14 | 15 |
| Challengers |  |  |  |  |
| Hopefuls | 13 | 12 | 10 | 9 |
| Likely losers | 3 | 3 | 2 | 2 |
| Open seats |  |  |  |  |
| Prospects | 5 | 6 | 6 | 6 |
| Long shots | 2 | 2 | 2 | 2 |
| Republicans |  |  |  |  |
| Incumbents |  |  |  |  |
| In jeopardy | 23 | 21 | 20 | 22 |
| Shoo-ins | 18 | 18 | 21 | 18 |
| Challengers |  |  |  |  |
| Hopefuls | 7 | 6 | 6 | 7 |
| Likely losers | 3 | 3 | 2 | 2 |
| Open seats |  |  |  |  |
| Prospects | 6 | 6 | 6 | 7 |
| Long shots | 2 | 2 | 2 | 3 |
| Total (in thousand $) | $63,085 | $25,564 | $30,975 | $53,255 |

*Source:* Compiled from Federal Election Commission data.

*Notes:* Figures comprise individual contributions to general election candidates in two-party contested elections. Some columns do not add to 100 percent because of rounding.

gave more than one-third of their donations to incumbents who were shoo-ins.

Individual contributions to Senate general election candidates also shifted between 1994 and 1996. But the change in giving patterns differs from the change that occurred in elections for the House. The Democratic Senate candidates' share of large contributions fell, as many investment-oriented contributors switched their contributions to support Republicans, who had almost twice as many incumbents up for reelection than did the Democrats (see Table 5.8). The Democrats' share of small individual contributions, in contrast, grew substantially.

Table 5.8

**The Partisan Distribution of Individual Contributions in the 1994 and 1996 Senate Elections** (in percentages)

| | Less than $200 | | $200–$499 | | $500–$749 | | $750–$1,000 | |
|---|---|---|---|---|---|---|---|---|
| | 1994 | 1996 | 1994 | 1996 | 1994 | 1996 | 1994 | 1996 |
| Democrats | 33 | 52 | 41 | 51 | 50 | 48 | 52 | 46 |
| Republicans | 67 | 48 | 59 | 49 | 50 | 52 | 48 | 54 |
| Total (in thousand $) | $57,187 | $46,768 | $15,238 | $13,298 | $23,532 | $20,456 | $60,834 | $60,027 |

*Source*: Compiled from Federal Election Commission data.

*Notes*: Figures comprise individual contributions to general election candidates in two-party contested elections. Some columns do not add to 100 percent because of rounding.

The fact that total contributions to all Senate general election candidates fell between 1994 and 1996, while the total for House candidates increased, suggests that some of the switch in giving patterns may be due to a reorientation in the contribution activities of Republican donors, not a switch in their loyalties. GOP small and moderate contributors, including ideological donors, may have shifted some of their contributions from Republican Senate to Republican House candidates because the real battleground in the 1996 elections was over control of the House, not the Senate.

Individuals responded to factors besides partisanship when making contributions to 1996 Senate candidates. They donated almost one-half of their small contributions to incumbents, and most of these were given to incumbents in jeopardy (see Table 5.9). They gave slightly more of their midsize contributions to open-seat candidates than to incumbents, and they gave substantially more of their large contributions to open-seat candidates than to incumbents. The fact that more midsize and large contributions than small ones were given to safe incumbents and open-seat prospects suggests that those who make larger contributions are motivated somewhat more by access and those who make small contributions respond more to electoral competitiveness.

### The Money Chase

Candidates are not passive spectators in the financing of congressional elections. Instead, many play active roles in the money chase, developing sophisticated strategies for campaigning for money and other election resources. They target their fund-raising appeals to individuals who are most likely to respond to them, including contributors who helped finance their previous campaigns. Candidates who can afford to, mainly incumbents and nonincumbents in competitive races, hire professional fund-raising consultants to assist them with raising money (Herrnson 1998a). They use direct mail, telemarketing, receptions, and other fund-raising events to collect money from individuals, parties, and PACs. Most candidates often hold backyard barbecues, coffee klatches, and cocktail parties to raise small and moderate contributions in their districts or states. Incumbents and the small number of competitive nonincumbents who have national fund-raising constituencies also hold "high-dollar" receptions, often costing $250 or more per individual and $500 or more per PAC, in Washington, D.C., New York City, Hollywood, and other wealthy cities across the country.

Table 5.9

## The Distribution of Individual Contributions in the 1996 Senate Elections
(in percentages)

| | Less than $200 | $200– $499 | $500– $749 | $750– $1,000 |
|---|---|---|---|---|
| Democrats | | | | |
| Incumbents | | | | |
| In jeopardy | 25 | 16 | 14 | 11 |
| Shoo-ins | 1 | 2 | 3 | 3 |
| Challengers | | | | |
| Hopefuls | 15 | 13 | 11 | 9 |
| Likely losers | 0 | 1 | 1 | 1 |
| Open seats | | | | |
| Prospects | 9 | 17 | 18 | 21 |
| Long shots | 1 | 2 | 2 | 1 |
| | | | | |
| Republicans | | | | |
| Incumbents | | | | |
| In jeopardy | 17 | 15 | 15 | 15 |
| Shoo-ins | 4 | 6 | 5 | 5 |
| Challengers | | | | |
| Hopefuls | 9 | 8 | 10 | 14 |
| Likely losers | 0 | 1 | 1 | 1 |
| Open seats | | | | |
| Prospects | 16 | 19 | 19 | 18 |
| Long shots | 1 | 2 | 1 | 1 |
| | | | | |
| Total (in thousand $) | $46,768 | $13,298 | $20,456 | $60,027 |

*Source:* Compiled from Federal Election Commission data.

*Notes:* Figures comprise individual contributions to general election candidates in two-party contested elections. Some columns do not add to 100 percent because of rounding.

The fund-raising efforts of House and Senate primary and general election candidates resulted in their raising record sums in the 1996 contests (see Table 5.10). Republican incumbents in both chambers raised and spent considerably more than their Democratic counterparts, reflecting both their greater numbers and the fund-raising advantages associated with holding congressional office. Democratic challengers, however, outfinanced Republican challengers. Democratic House challengers did especially well, raising $27.1 million more than their GOP counterparts. The financing of open-seat campaigns in the House was fairly competitive, with Democrat candidates raising slightly more than

Table 5.10

**Campaign Receipts and Expenditures of All 1996 Major-Party Primary and General Election Candidates** (in million $)

|  | House | | Senate | |
|---|---|---|---|---|
|  | Receipts | Expenditures | Receipts | Expenditures |
| Democrats |  |  |  |  |
|   Incumbents | $107.5 | $97.5 | $ 35.1 | $ 36.1 |
|   Challengers | 73.1 | 71.7 | 40.5 | 40.4 |
|   Open seats | 52.5 | 51.6 | 50.9 | 50.6 |
| Total | $233.1 | $221.2 | $126.5 | $127.4 |
| Republicans |  |  |  |  |
|   Incumbents | $172.3 | $158.2 | $ 46.7 | $ 49.1 |
|   Challengers | 46.0 | 45.5 | 38.0 | 37.8 |
|   Open seats | 48.7 | 47.7 | 73.0 | 72.3 |
| Total | $267.0 | $251.4 | $157.7 | $159.2 |
| All major-party candidates | $500.1 | $472.6 | $284.2 | $286.6 |

*Source:* Federal Election Commission.

the Republicans. The Senate elections, which featured numerous hotly contested open-seat primary and general election contests, presented a different pattern. Republicans involved in those contests raised about $22 million more than did the Democrats.

The fund-raising advantages incumbents enjoy over their general election opponents were highly visible during the 1996 contests. The typical House incumbent collected 2.7 times more money than the typical challenger, reflecting the lopsided nature of most incumbent-challenger races. Incumbents usually rely on a different mix of sources than challengers (see Table 5.11). Incumbents depend more on PAC money and individual large contributions, whereas challengers depend more on small individual contributions, party committees, and money that they donate or loan to their own campaigns. Open-seat House candidates raise somewhat less than incumbents but more than twice as much as challengers, reflecting the fact that open-seat races tend to be among the most competitive. Open-seat campaigns resemble challenger campaigns in their reliance on party funds and candidate resources.

Table 5.11

**The Sources of House Candidates' Campaign Resources** (in percentages)

|  | Incumbents | Challengers | Open seats |
|---|---|---|---|
| Individual contributions under $200 | 18 ($138,688) | 22 ($ 61,784) | 17 ($117,770) |
| Individual contributions between $200 and $1,000 | 35 ($259,590) | 32 ($ 88,712) | 36 ($248,984) |
| PACs | 39 ($294,792) | 19 ($ 53,556) | 24 ($163,745) |
| Parties | 2 ($ 15,812) | 7 ($ 20,772) | 7 ($ 48,230) |
| Candidates | 1 ($ 6,328) | 16 ($ 4,222) | 13 ($ 91,091) |
| Miscellaneous | 5 ($ 34,702) | 3 ($ 9,473) | 3 ($ 20,505) |
| Total resources | $749,913 | $278,519 | $690,326 |

*Source:* Compiled from Federal Election Commission data.

*Notes:* Party figures include contributions and coordinated expenditures. Candidate contributions include contributions and loans from the candidate. Miscellaneous includes interests from savings accounts and revenues from investments. All figures are for contributions to general election candidates in two-party contested elections.

Senators also enjoy important fund-raising advantages over challengers, but these are not nearly as substantial as those enjoyed by House members. During the 1996 elections, the typical Senate incumbent raised one and one-half times more funds than did his or her opponent (see Table 5.12). Senators depended more on PAC contributions than did their challengers, but members of the upper chamber did not rely on PACs nearly as much as did their House counterparts. Another major difference between the campaigns of Senate incumbents and Senate challengers is that the former contribute relatively little to their own campaigns, whereas the latter dig relatively deeply into their own pockets. Finally, Senate candidates for open seats raise substantially more than challengers and less than do incumbents.

Table 5.12

## The Sources of Senate Candidates' Campaign Resources (in percentages)

|  | Incumbents | Challengers | Open seats |
|---|---|---|---|
| Individual contributions under $200 | 26 ($1,100,730) | 21 ($    591,046) | 13 ($    461,884) |
| Individual contributions between $200 and $1,000 | 39 ($1,668,077) | 39 ($1,111,201) | 39 ($1,364,110) |
| PACs | 22 ($    959,284) | 9 ($    247,886) | 18 ($    621,501) |
| Parties | 7 ($    287,472) | 9 ($    243,411) | 10 ($    362,207) |
| Candidates | 3 ($    135,784) | 23 ($    644,808) | 13 ($    468,615) |
| Miscellaneous | 4 ($    152,537) | — ($        204) | 6 ($    223,246) |
| Total resources | $4,303,877 | $2,838,557 | $3,501,563 |

*Source:* Compiled from Federal Election Commission data.

*Notes:* Party figures include contributions and coordinated expenditures. Candidate contributions include contributions and loans from the candidate. Miscellaneous includes interests from savings accounts and revenues from investments. All figures are for contributions to general election candidates in two-party contested elections.

## "Independent" Political Communications

The 1996 elections were distinguished by the rise of what some maintain are independent political communications made by political parties and interest groups. A series of court decisions, including one that was handed down in the middle of the 1996 campaign season, allowed political parties and interest groups to greatly increase their election-related political advertising. The Supreme Court's ruling in *Colorado Republican Federal Campaign Committee et al.* v. *FEC* allowed parties for the first time to make independent expenditures in federal elections (518 U.S. 604 [1996]). The ruling stated that parties had the right to spend unlimited amounts of hard money *expressly to* advocate the election or defeat of individual federal candidates—a privilege previously reserved for PACs. Court rulings in *FEC* v. *Massachusetts Citizens for Life, Inc.* and related cases permitted political parties and interest groups to spend unlimited amounts of soft money on so-called issue advocacy advertisements (479 U.S. 248 [1986]).[6] Parties and interest groups can use issue advocacy ads to communicate directly with voters about candidates and issues as long as the ads do *not expressly* call for a candidate's election or defeat and were produced without the candidate's cooperation. In reality, there is often little difference between the campaign ads that candidates broadcast and the independent expenditure and issue advocacy ads broadcast by parties and interest groups (Herrnson and Dwyre 1999).

Party and interest-group independent expenditures and issue advocacy ads are supposed to be made independently of federal candidates' campaigns. Nevertheless, there is evidence that some coordination did indeed take place. In some cases, the same party aides, interest-group officials, and consultants who helped a candidate devise a campaign strategy early in the election season later designed issue advocacy communications or independent expenditures intended to help that candidate.

Political parties and interest groups spent an estimated $135 million to $150 million on independent political communications during the 1996 elections (Beck et al. 1997). Some independent expenditure ads and issue advocacy ads were aired in the election season in order to influence either the national political agenda or the agendas of individual congressional elections. Later ads were used to supplement candidates' media campaigns or attack their opponents.

Most party independent expenditures in 1996 were made by the parties' senatorial campaign committees to influence the outcomes of Senate elections. The GOP greatly outspent the Democrats, committing approximately $4.7 million to advocate the election of fifteen Republican Senate candidates and another $5.3 million to attack fourteen Democratic candidates. The Democrats spent a mere $50,000 to advocate the election of three Democrats and slightly less than $1.4 million to call for the defeat of six Republicans. Virtually all of these expenditures were made in elections decided by twenty points or less.

The two parties made less than $68,000 in independent expenditures in the 1996 House races. Neither party's congressional campaign committee was responsible for any of these expenditures. Party officials stated that their staffs were too involved in their candidates' campaigns for their expenditures to have been considered independent and that they were unprepared to hire new personnel to carry out these expenditures. Instead, they opted to use issue advocacy as their vehicle for independent political communications.

Both parties' national, senatorial, congressional, and state party campaign committees aired issue advocacy ads during the 1996 elections. The Democratic National Committee (DNC) spent $42.4 million on issue advocacy, and the party's congressional and senatorial campaign committees spent $8.5 million and $10 million, respectively. The DNC began televising issue advocacy ads in mid-October 1995 to boost President Clinton's standing in the polls, characterize congressional Republicans as right-wing extremists who wanted to help wealthy individuals and corporations at the expense of working people, and set a political agenda favorable to Democratic candidates. Later in the campaign season, the DCCC and DSCC supplemented these ads with television and radio commercials designed to help Democratic candidates in sixty marginal congressional districts and fourteen marginal Senate seats (Herrnson 1998a).

The Republicans waited until Bob Dole clinched the primary to begin airing issue advocacy ads. The RNC spent $20 million between March and its August national convention to boost Dole's and congressional Republicans' election prospects. The NRCC and the RNC spent $27 million on six ads that were aired in fifty-eight congressional districts. These ads were intended to clarify the GOP's positions on welfare reform, congressional reform, and Medicare; point out the policy failures of the Clinton administration; and discourage voters from reelecting the president and reinstalling a Democratic majority in Congress. The NRSC spent a mere $2 million on issue advocacy ads in five states, having committed a large portion of its communications budget to independent expenditures. Most of these ads focused on welfare reform, Republican plans to balance the budget, Republican spending priorities, and the vulnerabilities of specific Democrat candidates (Herrnson 1998a).

Interest groups also spent huge amounts on independent election-related communications in 1996. PACs spent $8.8 million on independent expenditures to influence the outcomes of House and Senate elections in marginal districts. Nonconnected PACs were responsible for about 90 percent of these expenditures, most of which were designed to work to the advantage of Republican candidates.

Labor groups spent the most on issue advocacy ads, with the American Federation of Labor-Congress of Industrial Organizations (AFL-CIO) and affiliated unions spending $35 million on television ads, video guides, and election pamphlets designed to help the Democrats reclaim their congressional majorities. Most of labor's issue advocacy ads were broadcast in the 114 closest House contests and 15 closest Senate races. Business groups, most notably the National Federation of Independent Businesses (NFIB), attempted to counter labor's issue advocacy campaigning. The NFIB assembled a coalition of business organizations that spent $5 million to air television and radio spots and mailed 2 million letters to small business owners advocating the reelection of GOP members of Congress. Most of their activity was focused on 133 close House and Senate contests. Several noneconomic groups, including the National Rifle Association, the Sierra Club, and the National Abortion and Reproductive Rights League, also carried out issue advocacy campaigns in selected states and congressional districts (Herrnson 1998a; Beck et al. 1997).

**Winners and Losers**

What impact did campaign spending have on the outcomes of the 1996 congressional elections? As is usually the case, most of the candidates who raised and spent the most money won, and most of these candidates were incumbents (see, e.g., Jacobson 1980). Because most members of Congress have political clout and a high probability of electoral success, they are able to amass huge war chests, which they use to deter strong challenges and defeat those opponents who run against them. Nevertheless, not every incumbent was successful in 1996. Two House incumbents, Republican Greg Laughlin of Texas and Democrat Barbara-Rose Collins of Michigan, were defeated in primaries, and another twenty House members were defeated in the general election. One Senator, Sheila Frahm (R-Kans.) lost her primary. Another, Senator Larry Pressler (R-S. Dak.), was defeated by Democratic Tim Johnson, who had previously occupied South Dakota's at-large House seat.

Was money the major determinant of the outcomes of these contests? Probably not. In the cases of Laughlin, Collins, and Frahm other forces were at work. Laughlin, who was first elected to Congress in 1988 as a Democrat, had switched parties following the Republican takeover of the House and was defeated in a primary runoff by Ron

Paul, a former conservative GOP House member who campaigned as the "real Republican" in the contest. Laughlin was unsuccessful despite the fact that he outspent Paul $361,057 to $294,581. Carolyn Cheeks Kilpatrick, a seventeen-year veteran of the Michigan statehouse, was able to capitalize on allegations that Collins had engaged in ethical and financial misconduct, even though Collins outspent her by $83,975 to $48,980. Frahm, who had been appointed to fill Bob Dole's seat when he resigned from the Senate to run for president, was defeated by Representative Sam Brownback, a leading conservative from the House freshman class of 1994, despite the fact that she outspent him $725,890 to $400,390. And Pressler lost to Johnson even though he enjoyed a spending advantage of $4.1 million to $2.9 million. Factors other than money played a major role in these contests.

Money was important in the nineteen major-party contested House races in which challengers defeated incumbents. The challengers spent an average of $1,075,007 in these contests, a mere $8,346 less than their opponents. Nine of the challengers who won actually spent more than did their opponents. Among these were California Democrat Ellen Tauscher and Utah Republican Christopher Cannon, who outspent their opponents by more than $1 million. The remaining ten challengers were outspent by sums ranging from less than $20,000 to more than $1 million. These results demonstrate that not every congressional challenger needs to outspend the incumbent in order to win. Once a challenger's spending reaches the threshold level, that candidate becomes visible among voters and is able to disseminate a campaign message—both of which are necessary to wage a viable campaign.

## Conclusion

The 1996 congressional elections took place in a political environment that was very different from those that had preceded them. The Republicans' historic takeover of Congress encouraged many campaign contributors to adjust their giving patterns. Nevertheless, most campaign money flowed in predictable ways. Party committees and PACs, which are strongly committed to electing candidates who share their partisan affiliations or policy views, continued to focus most of their resources in close elections. Access-oriented PACs and individuals contributed to favor congressional incumbents and members of the majority party. Money also continued to play a role in influencing election outcomes. As is usually the case, most incumbents raised and spent more funds than did their opponents, and most incumbents won. Nevertheless, not every incumbent outspent his or her challenger, and not every incumbent won. Indeed, several challengers were able to spend enough funds to deliver their messages successfully and win congressional seats.

The growth in independent political expenditures by parties and interest groups was an unanticipated aspect of the financing of the 1996 congressional elections. Given that control of Congress was at stake, it came as little surprise that most political organizations would raise and spend record sums in their efforts to influence election outcomes. When the courts gave their assent to party independent expenditures and party and interest-group issue advocacy spending, however, they effectively removed the ceilings on these organizations' political expenditures, encouraging them to raise and spend record sums on campaign-related activities. Parties and interest groups spent more on issue advocacy than they did on independent expenditures during the 1996 elections—a pattern that will probably be repeated in future elections because only issue advocacy ads can be financed with soft money. The introduction of these new vehicles for campaign spending has the potential to increase greatly the roles of organized groups in congressional elections and to challenge the abilities of candidates to dominate the political communications intended to influence their elections.

## Notes

1. The term soft money was coined by Elizabeth Drew (1983, 15). See also Alexander and Corrado (1995) and Biersack (1996).

2. Party committees can also contribute $5,000 to candidates in primaries and runoffs, but they rarely contribute money until after a candidate has received the nomination.

3. Parties can only make coordinated expenditures for general election candidates. The limits for coordinated expenditures in states that have only one House member are twice the level as those for states with two or more House members.

4. See note 3.

5. See note 3.

6. However, the ratio of soft to hard money that a national party organization can spend in a state, including funds spent on issue advocacy, is determined by the number of state and federal elections held in the state in a given election year (Dwyre 1996, 411).

## 6

PETER L. FRANCIA, RACHEL E. GOLDBERG,
JOHN C. GREEN, PAUL S. HERRNSON, AND
CLYDE WILCOX

# Individual Donors in the 1996 Federal Elections

Individual campaign contributors were the most important source of funds in the 1996 federal elections, despite record soft money expenditures by political parties and interest groups (see chapters 7 and 8). According to the Federal Election Commission (FEC), individual contributors provided some $1.5 billion in federally regulated donations. This figure included $126 million given directly to presidential nomination campaigns (which enabled those campaigns to obtain an additional $56 million in public matching funds); $444 million given directly to Senate and House candidates; $401 million to PACs, and $533 million to the Republican and Democratic Party committees.

Campaign contributing is a form of political participation that requires financial resources that are not available to all citizens (Verba, Schlozman, and Brady 1995). Contributions can provide donors with a disproportionate voice in policymaking, distort the democratic process, and create a corrupting influence on politics. It is for this reason that federal law limits the amounts that individuals can give in an election. The Federal Election Campaign Act (FECA) allows individuals to give up to $1,000 to any single candidate per election, which could translate into as much as $3,000 for a candidate who runs in a primary, runoff, and general election. Individuals can give up to $5,000 to any single PAC and up to $20,000 to all party committees in a calender year. Individual contributions are subject to an overall limit of $25,000 per year for all FECA-regulated contributions, including candidates, parties, and PACs. In addition to these limited hard money donations, the law also permits individuals to give unlimited amounts of soft money to party committees and interest groups for a variety of activities, including party building, voter mobilization, and issue advocacy.

Despite the importance of individual donors, relatively little is known about them. In contrast to the countless studies of federal PACs and party committees, there have been just a few studies of individual contributors (Brown, Powell, and Wilcox 1995; Green and Guth 1986). One reason is the difficulty of studying donors from FEC records, which do not list contributors individually, but instead list contributions reported by the receiving candidate or committee. A donor might appear with several variations in the spelling of his or her name, city, zip code, or occupation. In fact, one single donor appeared in the FEC records under twenty variations of name and address in 1990 (Wilcox, Biersack, Herrnson, and Joe 1998). The required information on occupation and employer is often missing, vague, or misleading. Thus, the best information on individual donors comes from survey data.

In this chapter, we study donors with data from four surveys. First, we rely on two studies of major donors in the 1995–96 election cycle: a survey of individuals who made at least one hard money contribution of more than $200 to a presidential nomination campaign, and a separate survey of individual contributors who made equivalent donations to House and Senate candidates. Because the presidential candidate pool in 1996 contained only one centrist Democrat, President Bill Clinton, we also make reference to a survey of 1988 presidential donors, who contributed in a year in which many Democrats sought their party's nomination (Brown, Powell, and Wilcox 1995). In addition, we use the 1996 National Election Study, a national survey of the general public, to put donors in perspective.[1]

We begin by comparing the social and political characteristics of campaign contributors to the general public, with an emphasis on major donors. We next describe the motives of major contributors and the ways candidates solicit them. Then we investigate differences among the major donors to the 1996 presidential and congressional campaigns. Our analysis demonstrates that individual contributors, and especially major donors, were not representative of the public at large. But major donors were not monolithic either. There were significant differences among them, reflecting the mix of candidates and the way the candidates raised funds. In 1996, these factors produced significant differences between and among donors to Democratic and Republican candidates. The Democratic presidential and congressional donors were far more united than their Republican counterparts. Factional divisions were especially severe among the financiers of GOP presidential contenders.

## Who Gives and Why

Campaign contributing is a relatively rare form of political participation. For example, the 1996 National Election Study asked the general public about donations to candidates, political parties, and interest groups, and 88 percent reported no contributions at all. About 8 percent claimed to have given to one of these recipients and only 3 percent to more than one. In contrast, approximately 25 percent of the public claimed to have been active in the campaign and 77 percent reported voting. These figures are no doubt inflated, so contributing may be even less common than reported.

Table 6.1 compares the demographic characteristics of our samples of *major donors* (presidential and congressional contributors) to three groups of citizens: *general donors* (all three kinds of contributions), *voters*, and *nonvoters* (excluding donors in both cases). The bulk of general donors are probably givers of small contributions; one study found that more than 80 percent of all campaign contributors gave less than $250 annually to all sources combined (Verba, Schlozman, and Brady 1995, 78). Thus, the majority of *individual contributors* are small givers, but the majority of the *money contributed* comes from a small number of citizens who make many large donations. Indeed, 10 percent of all donations to House and Senate candidates in 1990 came from only 4,288 contributors who either contributed $4,000 to these candidates or contributed lesser amounts to four different candidates; many also gave to parties and PACs (Wilcox, Biersack, Herrnson, and Joe 1998). The major presidential and congressional donors in 1996 fell between these extremes: Most gave a few hundred dollars to a single candidate, but some made many contributions that total to sizable sums.

As one might expect, campaign contributors were wealthier than the general public. In 1996, 66 percent of the presidential donors and 82 percent of congressional donors reported family incomes of more than $100,000 per year, compared to 16 percent of general donors, 6 per-

Table 6.1

**Demography of the Donor Pool and General Public in 1996**
(in percentages)

| | Major donors | | General public | | |
|---|---|---|---|---|---|
| | Presi-dential | Congres-sional | All donors | Voters | Non-voters |
| Income | | | | | |
| Less than $50,000 | 19[a] | 4 | 38 | 62 | 85 |
| $50,000–$99,999 | 25 | 14 | 46 | 32 | 14 |
| $100,000–$249,999 | 32 | 36 | 16[b] | 6[b] | 1[b] |
| $250,000+ | 24 | 46 | | | |
| Education | | | | | |
| Less than college | 27 | 17 | 49 | 68 | 87 |
| College degree | 23 | 27 | 30 | 21 | 9 |
| Postgraduate | 50 | 56 | 21 | 11 | 4 |
| Male | 72 | 81 | 59 | 46 | 45 |
| White | 96 | 95 | 94 | 86 | 83 |
| Age | | | | | |
| Under 35 years | 7 | 3 | 18 | 24 | 43 |
| 35–50 years | 30 | 28 | 36 | 38 | 32 |
| 51–65 years | 25 | 41 | 27 | 20 | 14 |
| 66+ years | 37 | 29 | 20 | 18 | 11 |
| Religious tradition | | | | | |
| Mainline Protestant | 37 | 41 | 19 | 20 | 12 |
| Evangelical Protestant | 18 | 11 | 25 | 25 | 27 |
| Catholic | 23 | 22 | 27 | 27 | 20 |
| Jew | 6 | 12 | 3 | 2 | 1 |
| Secular | 10 | 8 | 17 | 15 | 29 |
| All others | 6 | 6 | 9 | 11 | 11 |
| Region | | | | | |
| Northeast | 22 | 25 | 24 | 23 | 18 |
| Midwest | 28 | 20 | 19 | 25 | 23 |
| West | 18 | 21 | 29 | 20 | 21 |
| South | 33 | 35 | 29 | 32 | 38 |

*Source:* Surveys by authors and the 1996 National Election Study.
[a]Columns may not add to 100 percent due to rounding.
[b]Figures include all persons with incomes greater than $100,000.

cent of voters, and only 1 percent of nonvoters (see Table 6.1). The presidential donors were somewhat less affluent than their congressional counterparts: About one-quarter of the former had incomes of more than $250,000 compared to nearly one-half of the latter. This

Table 6.2

**The Political Identifications of the Donor Pool and the General Public in 1996** (in percentages)

| | Major donors | | General public | | |
| --- | --- | --- | --- | --- | --- |
| | Presi-<br>dential | Congres-<br>sional | All<br>donors | Voters | Non-<br>voters |
| Partisanship | | | | | |
| Strong Democrat | 11 | 12 | 21 | 21 | 10 |
| Democrat | 14 | 18 | 22 | 31 | 45 |
| Independent | 12 | 21 | 6 | 6 | 16 |
| Republican | 33 | 31 | 23 | 28 | 27 |
| Strong Republican | 30 | 18 | 28 | 14 | 2 |
| Ideology | | | | | |
| Extremely liberal | 2 | 3 | 2 | 1 | 2 |
| Liberal | 14 | 27 | 29 | 23 | 22 |
| Moderate | 17 | 19 | 15 | 30 | 47 |
| Conservative | 47 | 43 | 48 | 43 | 28 |
| Extremely conservative | 20 | 10 | 5 | 3 | 1 |

*Source:* Surveys by authors and 1996 National Election Study.
*Note:* Columns may not add to 100 percent due to rounding.

difference results from the fact that some presidential candidates, such as Pat Buchanan, appealed to less affluent donors for small contributions.

Donors differed from the public in other important ways. More than one-half of the major donors had postgraduate training, compared with fewer than one-fifth of general donors and fewer than one-eighth of voters. Most major donors were male, white, and middle-aged, presenting a contrast with voters and nonvoters. In addition, mainline Protestants and Jews were overrepresented among the major donors compared to the general public, while Evangelical Protestants, Catholics, and seculars were all underrepresented. However, there were no significant regional differences between the major donors and the general public.

As one might expect from their high social status, most major donors were Republicans (Table 6.2). Some 63 percent of the presidential contributors identified as Republicans or strong Republicans, compared to 49 percent of the congressional donors, 42 percent of voters, and 28 percent of nonvoters. This large proportion of Republican presidential donors reflects the fact that only Clinton ran for the Democratic presidential nomination in 1996. In 1988, when a large Democratic primary field produced more Democratic donors, 59 percent claimed to be Republicans or strong Republicans, and 35 to be Democrats or strong Democrats.

In 1996, 67 percent of all presidential donors claimed to be conservative or extremely conservative compared to 53 percent of the congressional donors, 46 percent of voters, and 29 percent of nonvoters. As with partisanship, the strong conservatism of the presidential donors reflects the special circumstances of the 1996 presidential primaries. In 1988, when the campaigns of liberal Democrats such as Jesse Jackson and Paul Simon produced more ideological diversity, 57 percent of presidential donors claimed to be conservative or extremely conservative, and 33 percent identified as liberal or extremely liberal. It is worth noting that general donors closely resembled the congressional donors in partisanship and ideology.

Major donors were more active politically than the general public in other ways as well. For example, two-thirds of the 1996 congressional donors reported contacting at least one member of Congress in the previous two years and one-sixth reported six or more such contacts. In contrast, less than one-third of general donors, one-seventh of voters, and one-twentieth of nonvoters reported a contact of any kind with a member of Congress (data not shown).

Major donors routinely contribute to a variety of candidates and committees. As Table 6.3 shows, two-thirds of 1988 presidential and three-quarters of 1996 congressional contributors reported regular and extensive giving. These numbers were smaller for presidential donors in 1988 because Pat Robertson's presidential campaign brought a new group of Evangelical Protestants into the contributor pool. The Robertson mobilization is not unique in American politics. The pool of contributors routinely expands as candidates' appeal to new demographic and issue groups. Jesse Jackson brought increased numbers of African Americans into the presidential pool in 1984, and women candidates for Congress have inspired more female contributions in the 1990s. Many of the newly mobilized contributors continue to give once their favored candidate has ceased to run. For instance, two-thirds of Robertson's new 1988 contributors gave again in 1992, splitting their support between Pat Buchanan and George Bush (Brown, Powell, and Wilcox 1995).

What motivates individuals to engage regularly in the unusual act of

Table 6.3

**The Frequency and Type of Contributions Made by Major Donors**
(in percentages)

|  | 1988 presidential donors | 1996 congressional donors |
|---|---|---|
| Give in "most" elections to[a] |  |  |
| Presidential candidates | 50 | 45 |
| Senate candidates | 38 | 47 |
| House candidates | 36 | 54 |
| State and local candidates | 39 | 50 |
| Political parties | 39 | 37 |
| PACs | 26 | 29 |
| Give in "most" elections to |  |  |
| No type of candidate/committee | 35 | 27 |
| 1–3 | 35 | 35 |
| 4–5 | 19 | 27 |
| All 6 | 11 | 11 |

*Source:* Surveys by authors.

[a]Percentage of respondents to both surveys falling into each category. Other options for questions included "some elections" and "never."

making a campaign contribution? Scholars have found that political activists of all sorts, including donors, are motivated by three kinds of incentives (Wilson 1995). Contributors with *purposive* motives seek the adoption of their preferred policies in one or more areas, while those with *material* motives seek tangible benefits that will increase their financial well-being. Donors with *solidary* motives enjoy social interaction with politicians and other contributors.

Most major donors in congressional and presidential elections cite purposive goals as their reason for giving, such as "influence public policy" or "help win elections" (Table 6.4). A much smaller number of donors admit to being motivated by material incentives, such as giving for "business/employment reasons" or because it is "expected" as part of their job. Slightly fewer report solidary motives, including social contacts and personal recognition.

Interestingly, purposive responses were more common among the 1996 presidential and congressional donors than among the 1988 presidential donors. This difference probably reflects the circumstances of each campaign. The donors to Bob Dole in 1988 and 1996 provide a

Table 6.4

**The Motives for Giving of Major Donors** (in percentages)

| Percentage "very important" | Presidential | | Congressional |
|---|---|---|---|
| | 1996 | 1988 | 1996 |
| Influence policy/government | 76 | 46 | 66 |
| Help win elections | 74 | 46 | 66 |
| Business/employment | 15 | 13 | 9 |
| Expected of me | 11 | 10 | 5 |
| Social contacts, friends/associates | 10 | 7 | 3 |
| Recognition | 9 | 6 | 2 |

*Source:* Surveys by authors.

case study of shifting donor motives. In 1988, 36 percent of Dole's donors said that influencing the outcome of an election was very important; in 1996, the figure rose to 70 percent. In 1988, the Republican nomination contest was mainly fought between two moderates, and Dole was a leader in the Senate with the ability to help contributors even if he failed to win the presidential nomination. In 1996, Dole faced a stiff challenge from the party's right wing, and Republican donors felt a special urgency to defeat Bill Clinton. Similarly, it could be that the close contest for control of the Congress in 1996 heightened the purposive motivations of access-oriented donors.

Candidates attempt to appeal to these diverse motives of donors to raise funds. First, candidates assess their resources for fund-raising. Contributors who are unusually high in purposive motives are much more likely to be extremely liberal or extremely conservative and are thus likely to respond to strong appeals from candidates from the ideological wing of their party. Candidates who take moderate positions have little chance of appealing to those contributors. In contrast, candidates who control the government agenda, such as party leaders, committee chairs, sitting governors, and presidents, can distribute tangible benefits, and they are in a good position to appeal to materially motivated donors. Finally, almost any candidate, particularly presidential contestants, can distribute solidary benefits by greeting guests or providing them with photo opportunities at fund-raising events.

Table 6.5

**The Motives for Giving by Type of Candidates, 1996 Presidential Election**

| Candidate | Material | Solidary | Purposive |
|-----------|----------|----------|-----------|
| Clinton | 0.140[a] | 0.008 | −0.001 |
| Dole | 0.005 | 0.008 | −0.190 |
| Moderates | 0.230 | 0.001 | 0.005 |
| Conservatives | −0.005 | −0.120 | 0.001 |
| Buchanan | −0.450 | −0.100 | 0.240 |
| Moralists | −0.370 | −0.210 | 0.270 |

*Source:* Surveys by authors.

[a]Figures are mean factor scores of motives; see text for details.

*Key: Moderates:* Alexander and Lugar; *Conservatives:* Gramm and Forbes; *Moralists:* Keyes and Dornan.

In 1996 the presidential nomination attracted donors with different motives for giving. Table 6.5 reports mean scores on measures of material, solidary, and purposive motives to various types of candidates.[2] Donors to President Clinton and to "moderate" Republican candidates (Governor Lamar Alexander of Tennessee and Senator Richard Lugar of Indiana) were motivated mainly by material goals. In contrast, those who gave to Pat Buchanan and to "moralist" candidates (Ambassador Allan Keyes of Maryland and Representative Robert Dornan of California) were much more likely to be motivated by purposive goals. Dole's financial constituency was distinctive only in the relatively low levels of purposive motives compared to other candidates' donors. Individuals who gave to other "conservative" GOP candidates (Senator Phil Gramm of Texas and millionaire Steve Forbes) were distinctive only in their low levels of solidary motives. Gramm was by far the most prominent of these candidates, and perhaps meeting him was not a top priority for donors.

Once candidates have assessed their resources and targeted their base in the contributor pool, they solicit contributions using appropriate methods. For individuals with purposive motives, candidates frequently use impersonal solicitations that stress ideological messages, such as direct mail or telemarketing. For donors with material or solidary motives, candidates often personally solicit contributions or establish a network of fund-raisers to do it for them. In some cases, the contribution is made because the donor has difficulty saying no to the solicitor; in others because the individual is a staunch supporter of the candidate (Brown, Powell, and Wilcox 1995). Members of congressional committees may ask a lobbyist to help them raise money from a particular industry, and the lobbyist may then solicit contributions on behalf of the candidate (Herrnson 1998a). Contributors motivated by solidary motives are usually invited to fund-raising dinners, intimate White House coffees, or just backyard barbecues. Generally, the candidate attends these events, mingles with the contributors, and personally greets as many as he or she can.

In sum, campaign contributors and especially major donors are unrepresentative of the general public; they enjoy higher social status and engage in more political activities. Nonetheless, the exact character of the donors in a given election varies with the mix of candidates, the ways they seek funds, and the offices sought.

### Presidential Donors in 1996: United Democrats, Divided Republicans

In 1996 Democratic candidate Bill Clinton had a relatively easy time raising the maximum allowable funds for his nomination campaign in hard money and millions of additional soft money contributions for his party (Corrado 1997a). Clinton was a centrist who had no primary challenger, and he quickly raised the legal maximum in campaign funds (see chapter 2). Having no need to appeal to a wide variety of donors in Democratic circles, his backers were fairly homogeneous.

In contrast, Republican presidential candidates sought to mobilize long-standing factions within the party and appealed to specific GOP constituencies, resulting in a more diverse group of donors than their Democratic counterparts. The most important factional fight in the GOP was between Christian conservatives and party moderates, but there are many other GOP factions as well (Rozell and Wilcox 1995; Green and Guth 1993).

Table 6.6 reports on the demographic characteristics of the presidential donors.[3] Compared with Dole's donors and the other Republican candidates, Clinton's contributors tended to be wealthier, better educated, and younger. They also contained far more Jewish, secular, and northeastern donors. Gender differences were quite large: Nearly

Table 6.6

**The Demography of Presidential Donors in 1996** (in percentages)

|  | Clinton | Dole | Moder-ates | Conserv-atives | Buchanan | Moralists |
|---|---|---|---|---|---|---|
| Income |  |  |  |  |  |  |
| Less than $100,000 | 24 | 53 | 36 | 40 | 71 | 61 |
| More than $250,000 | 34 | 18 | 13 | 12 | 17 | 6 |
| Education |  |  |  |  |  |  |
| Less than college | 14 | 35 | 25 | 26 | 44 | 11 |
| Postgraduate | 70 | 41 | 57 | 42 | 32 | 66 |
| Age |  |  |  |  |  |  |
| Less than 50 years | 58 | 26 | 24 | 39 | 29 | 52 |
| More than 65 years | 13 | 55 | 43 | 30 | 50 | 18 |
| Male | 61 | 77 | 75 | 73 | 76 | 64 |
| White | 93 | 95 | 98 | 98 | 99 | 97 |
| Denomination |  |  |  |  |  |  |
| Mainline | 29 | 45 | 55 | 38 | 20 | 27 |
| Evangelical | 8 | 20 | 10 | 25 | 30 | 44 |
| Catholic | 18 | 22 | 18 | 27 | 39 | 27 |
| Jewish | 19 | 4 | 3 | 1 | 1 | 0 |
| Secular | 18 | 6 | 13 | 9 | 5 | 0 |
| Region |  |  |  |  |  |  |
| South | 28 | 33 | 34 | 42 | 34 | 35 |
| Northeast | 30 | 20 | 20 | 14 | 19 | 6 |

*Source:* Surveys by authors.

*Note:* Data coded as in Table 6.1; only relevant categories included for ease of presentation, so columns do not add to 100 percent.

40 percent of Clinton's financial supporters were women, compared to roughly one-quarter of most of the GOP candidates' backers.

Compared with other GOP contributors, Dole's donors were only notable for their age—well over one-half were more than sixty-five years old. Most were well-educated mainline Protestants, a traditional Republican constituency. The lack of distinctiveness of the Dole constituency reflects Dole's front-runner status in the primary contest and his ability to attract a wide diversity of donors seeking to back a winner.

In contrast, supporters of Dole's moderate rivals were even better educated, somewhat more likely to be mainline Protestants, and much

more likely to have secular backgrounds. Dole's conservative opponents raised more money from younger, less wealthy individuals who
were more likely to be Evangelical Protestants or Catholics. Interestingly, all these donors were markedly less affluent than their counterparts in the Clinton campaign.

The biggest contrast was between Dole's backers and the supporters
of Buchanan and the moralist candidates. These candidates sought the
same socially conservative constituency by means of direct-mail solicitation, which accounts for the higher proportion of middle-income people and Evangelical Protestants among their donors. However, there
were some important differences between these candidates' constituencies. Buchanan's donors were less educated, older, and more likely to
be Catholic (reflecting Buchanan's own religious background). The
supporters of the moralist candidates were better educated, younger,
and had a higher proportion of women—nearly as many as the Clinton
campaign. The South was important to all GOP candidates, accounting
for one-third or more of their contributors.

As Table 6.7 shows, the presidential candidates drew virtually all of
their donations from individuals who identified with their party. Clinton donors were almost all Democrats; only 6 percent were independents and 8 percent identified with the GOP. Donors to Republican
candidates were overwhelmingly Republican, but with some variation
in their intensity. For instance, the Dole and Buchanan campaigns
contained a number of independents, and backers of both moderate and
moralists candidates had fewer strong Republicans.

The presidential candidates also raised most of their funds from
donors who shared their ideological perspective. The Clinton donors
were predominantly liberal, with few extreme liberals, many moderates, and some conservatives. In contrast, the Republican donors were
overwhelmingly conservative. Dole's donors and those of his moderate
rivals contained large minorities of both extreme conservatives and
moderates, but very few liberals of any kind. Buchanan's contributors
were the farthest to the right, with more than one-half describing themselves as "extremely conservative." Interestingly, the moralist contributors were less likely to accept the extreme label, and resembled the
self-reported ideology of donors to other conservative candidates
rather than Buchanan.

The presidential donors were also divided in their support for a
variety of issues (Table 6.8). Compared to the Republicans, Clinton's

Table 6.7

**The Political Identifications of Presidential Donors in 1996**
(in percentages)

|  | Clinton | Dole | Moder-ates | Conserv-atives | Buchanan | Moralists |
|---|---|---|---|---|---|---|
| Partisanship |  |  |  |  |  |  |
| Strong Democrat | 42 | 2 | 0 | 2 | 1 | 10 |
| Democrat | 45 | 5 | 5 | 3 | 0 | 0 |
| Independent | 6 | 17 | 19 | 12 | 21 | 14 |
| Republican | 5 | 40 | 53 | 35 | 45 | 49 |
| Strong Republican | 3 | 47 | 24 | 48 | 33 | 37 |
| Ideology |  |  |  |  |  |  |
| Extremely liberal | 6 | 1 | 1 | 0 | 0 | 0 |
| Liberal | 54 | 3 | 3 | 0 | 0 | 0 |
| Moderate | 30 | 22 | 25 | 9 | 1 | 0 |
| Conservative | 10 | 54 | 58 | 61 | 46 | 62 |
| Extremely conservative | 0 | 20 | 10 | 30 | 52 | 38 |

*Source:* Surveys by authors.
*Note:* Columns may not add to 100 percent due to rounding.

donors were strong supporters of national health insurance, increased spending on environmental protection, and decreased funding for defense. They were also opposed to tax cuts, restricting abortion, and school vouchers. Nevertheless, they agreed with many Republican donors in supporting free trade and opposing stricter regulation of pornography. Interestingly, the Clinton donors were the least likely to favor cutting government aid to business.[4]

The Republican donors favored tax cuts and school vouchers and were against national health insurance. Dole's broad and diverse coalition hewed close to the center of the GOP donor pool, exhibiting few distinctive policy positions. For example, Dole donors opposed national health insurance and supported tax cuts, but were divided on abortion and trade. His rivals' donors revealed the deep divisions in the GOP. The moderate candidates' contributors were pro-choice on abortion and against stricter regulation of pornography, opposed to tariffs, and less supportive of increased defense spending. The moderates' supporters also provided slightly more support for environmental spending and national health insurance. The conservative candidates' supporters, by contrast, were pro-life on abortion and less opposed to

Table 6.8

**The Issue Positions of Presidential Donors in 1996** (in percentages)

|  | Clinton | Dole | Moder-ates | Conserv-atives | Buchanan | Moralists |
|---|---|---|---|---|---|---|
| Pro national health insurance |  |  |  |  |  |  |
| Agree | 70 | 14 | 20 | 7 | 6 | 0 |
| Disagree | 19 | 69 | 70 | 87 | 90 | 100 |
| Pro cutting taxes |  |  |  |  |  |  |
| Agree | 17 | 80 | 72 | 88 | 92 | 83 |
| Disagree | 69 | 12 | 17 | 8 | 6 | 9 |
| Environmental protection |  |  |  |  |  |  |
| Spend more | 67 | 15 | 27 | 11 | 6 | 6 |
| Spend less | 6 | 49 | 39 | 39 | 78 | 77 |
| Tariffs to save jobs |  |  |  |  |  |  |
| Agree | 25 | 37 | 21 | 24 | 63 | 20 |
| Disagree | 58 | 44 | 63 | 56 | 21 | 49 |
| Restrict abortions |  |  |  |  |  |  |
| Agree | 6 | 48 | 41 | 63 | 84 | 97 |
| Disagree | 90 | 42 | 54 | 29 | 12 | 0 |
| Anti stricter regulation of pornography |  |  |  |  |  |  |
| Agree | 77 | 61 | 72 | 56 | 49 | 26 |
| Disagree | 19 | 26 | 21 | 36 | 38 | 69 |
| Pro school vouchers |  |  |  |  |  |  |
| Agree | 35 | 77 | 74 | 84 | 84 | 92 |
| Disagree | 53 | 9 | 17 | 10 | 11 | 3 |
| Defense spending |  |  |  |  |  |  |
| Spend more | 7 | 50 | 40 | 55 | 65 | 72 |
| Spend less | 64 | 12 | 20 | 13 | 17 | 6 |

*Source:* Survey by authors.

*Note:* Five-point Likert scale items collapsed; "neutral" category excluded for ease of presentation.

further regulation of pornography, more modest in their opposition to tariffs, and more supportive of increased defense spending. They also backed tax cuts more strongly and were more in favor of reduced federal expenditures, with the exception of defense.

As might be expected, the strongest differences appeared among the Buchanan and moralist donors. Both groups were strongly pro-life on abortion. They were also the most opposed to national health insurance and increased spending on environmental protection, and the most in favor of expanded defense budgets. But there were divisions between these groups as well, especially on trade: Buchanan's supporters strongly opposed free trade, and the moralists' supported it. Indeed, the Buchanan donors displayed considerable economic populism, being the strongest backers of tax cuts, but also favoring a return to the gold standard and immigration restrictions.[5] In contrast, the moralists donors were the only group strongly in favor of stricter regulation of pornography. Overall, the moralist donors were the most consistently conservative on all issues.

The presidential donors were also divided in their proximity to prominent interest groups (see Table 6.9). The Clinton contributors were the most supportive of NOW and the NAACP, reflecting the prominent role of feminists and African Americans in the Democratic Party. The Clinton donors were evenly divided on the AFL-CIO, attitudes that may reflect the high social status of campaign contributors. However, they were even less likely to identify with the Chamber of Commerce, an emblem of the business community. And they were uniformly distant from the Christian Coalition and the NRA.

The Republican donors showed divisions with regard to interest groups that parallel differences on issues. For instance, the Dole donors were found near the center of the GOP, on balance favoring both the Chamber of Commerce and the Christian Coalition, and felt far from liberal groups, such as NOW and the AFL-CIO. The moderate candidates' contributors, however, felt closest to the Chamber of Commerce and most distant from the Christian Coalition and the NRA. Meanwhile, the conservative candidates were less favorable toward the Chamber of Commerce and were much more favorable toward the Christian Coalition.

Nearly all of Buchanan's and the moralist candidates' donors felt close to the Christian Coalition. In fact, about one-fifth of Buchanan's supporters and more than one-third of the moralists' supporters reported being members of the Christian Coalition, compared to less than 10 percent of the other Republican candidates' contributors. Most Buchanan backers also felt close to the NRA, a pattern reminiscent of other right-wing candidates, such as Oliver North (Rozell and Wilcox 1995, 109–32). This positive affect toward the NRA was not shared by the other donors to GOP candidates, even the moralists' supporters who were more divided over the gun lobby. The Buchanan supporters,

Table 6.9

**Interest-Group Proximity of Presidential Donors in 1996** (in percentages)

|  | Clinton | Dole | Moder-ates | Conserv-atives | Buchanan | Moralists |
|---|---|---|---|---|---|---|
| **NOW** | | | | | | |
| Close | 48 | 7 | 6 | 2 | 94 | 94 |
| Far | 32 | 74 | 78 | 92 | 0 | 0 |
| **NAACP** | | | | | | |
| Close | 38 | 4 | 9 | 4 | 1 | 0 |
| Far | 28 | 79 | 73 | 81 | 90 | 85 |
| **AFL-CIO** | | | | | | |
| Close | 34 | 3 | 3 | 0 | 3 | 0 |
| Far | 34 | 88 | 88 | 93 | 92 | 100 |
| **Chamber of Commerce** | | | | | | |
| Close | 25 | 42 | 54 | 40 | 24 | 19 |
| Far | 40 | 23 | 19 | 15 | 33 | 25 |
| **Christian Coalition** | | | | | | |
| Favorable | 3 | 47 | 36 | 72 | 79 | 94 |
| Unfavorable | 90 | 26 | 41 | 11 | 8 | 3 |
| **NRA** | | | | | | |
| Close | 1 | 27 | 15 | 30 | 71 | 38 |
| Far | 97 | 53 | 69 | 44 | 12 | 31 |

*Source:* Survey by authors.

*Note:* Five-point Likert scale items collapsed; "neutral" category excluded for ease of presentation.

however, failed to identify with the Chamber of Commerce, and felt they had little in common with the AFL-CIO, NOW, and NAACP.

In sum, the Clinton donors showed telltale signs of the "New Democratic" image projected by their candidate. They supported liberal social policies and government activism, but with some sympathy for the free market. Absent in 1996 was the intraparty factionalism that has long plagued the Democratic Party. Indeed, Democratic donors showed these kinds of divisions in 1988, when Richard Gephardt and to a lesser extent Albert Gore mobilized more moderate donors, while Jesse Jackson and Paul Simon activated more liberal contributors (Brown, Powell, and Wilcox 1995). The unified Democratic contributor pool in 1996 was the product of a skillful politician who faced no primary opposition, thus eliminating the incentive to mobilize the whole range of potential Democratic donors. It will be interesting to see if more divisions appear in the 2000 nominating contest, when there will be no Democratic incumbent.

In contrast, the GOP was riven by dissension in 1996. Although Dole had wide appeal and was able to assemble a diverse constituency, his rivals were well enough financed to contest the nomination vigorously. Moderate candidates activated a "kinder, gentler" element of the donor pool, who were more socially inclusive and more sympathetic to the public sector, but still exhibited strong support for the free market. Conservative candidates found donors with a stronger emphasis on the market and much less sympathy toward activist government. The Buchanan backers combined "traditional values" with populist economics, whereas the moralists candidate's tapped a more consistently right-wing constituency whose traditional moral values fit more comfortably with free market economics. Although these financiers of Republican politics also agree on many things, their differences demonstrate a persistent factionalism that will surely appear in the 2000 campaign.

## Congressional Contributors: Partisan and Ideological Divisions

Because individual donors frequently give to both presidential and congressional candidates (recall Table 6.3), we would expect both kinds of donors to be similar. The differences between the presidency and Congress lead us to expect some dissimilarities as well, however, based on available fund-raising resources. Ideology is likely to be less important in congressional campaigns because the legislative process is more about the details of policy rather than the grand vision for government. And partisanship and especially incumbency are potent resources: Party leaders and committee and subcommittee members are in good positions to offer both purposive and material benefits to donors. In addition, several hundred congressional candidates routinely seek financial support in an election, as opposed to a few dozen presidential aspirants. Thus, contributors can give to many candidates with diverse ideologies, partisanship, and positions in Congress.

To capture this reality, we sorted the 1996 congressional donors into groups according to the characteristics of the recipient candidates (see Table 6.10). We first divided the candidates by party (Republicans and Democrats) and then by status (incumbents and nonincumbents). Fi-

Table 6.10

**The Demography of Congressional Donors in 1996** (in percentages)

| | Republicans | | | Democrats | | |
|---|---|---|---|---|---|---|
| | Incumbent conservative | Non-incumbent | Incumbent moderates | Incumbent moderates | Non-incumbent | Incumbent liberal |
| Income | | | | | | |
| Less than $100,000 | 8 | 13 | 8 | 17 | 15 | 16 |
| More than $250,000 | 62 | 59 | 62 | 54 | 52 | 57 |
| Education | | | | | | |
| Less than college | 18 | 14 | 14 | 12 | 11 | 9 |
| Postgraduate | 29 | 37 | 44 | 48 | 55 | 56 |
| Age | | | | | | |
| Less than 50 years | 25 | 30 | 22 | 23 | 29 | 19 |
| Greater than 65 years | 42 | 29 | 37 | 39 | 36 | 36 |
| Male | 92 | 86 | 90 | 76 | 75 | 72 |
| White | 97 | 94 | 97 | 96 | 97 | 96 |
| Religion | | | | | | |
| Evangelical | 12 | 14 | 9 | 5 | 5 | 2 |
| Mainline | 47 | 39 | 44 | 25 | 31 | 23 |
| Catholic | 28 | 21 | 32 | 18 | 18 | 24 |
| Jews | 6 | 8 | 13 | 22 | 17 | 27 |
| Secular | 3 | 5 | 3 | 22 | 19 | 16 |

nally, we differentiated the incumbents by ideology, defining "moderates" in both parties and "conservatives" for the Republicans and "liberals" for the Democrats. This sorting produced six categories of candidates, which approximates the partisan and ideological divisions we noted for the presidential donors.[6]

Table 6.10 uses these categories to look at the demographic characteristics of donors to the 1996 congressional candidates, and we see some parallels and divergences from the presidential data (recall Table 6.6). As before, the GOP donors were nearly all male, whereas one-quarter of Democratic donors were female. Most Republican donors were Protestants, with approximately one-quarter Catholics. Democratic donors constitute a more diverse coalition of mainline Protestants, Catholics, Jews, and seculars. Both parties' supporters were overwhelmingly white.

Evangelical Protestants were rare among Democratic donors, but not especially common among Republicans either. The Christian Coalition and allied groups have yet to make the same inroads into the financing of congressional elections as they have made into the financing of presidential nominations. Another difference between presidential and congressional Republicans was region. GOP conservatives raised one-half of their funds in the South, while their moderate counterparts raised nearly the same proportion in the Northeast. A more muted regional divide appears for Democratic supporters' as well.

There were only minor differences in income between donors to the two parties: a majority of donors in all categories had incomes in excess of $250,000, considerably more than for the presidential donors. There were educational differences, however, with Republicans being more likely to have just a college degree, whereas Democrats were more likely to have undertaken postgraduate study. This suggests that the GOP donor base was rooted in the business community, and Democratic large donors were more likely to be professionals. Donors to conservative Republican incumbents were also far less likely to have postgraduate education than were those who gave to moderates. Age was also a significant force in GOP fund-raising, with younger donors more likely to support nonincumbents.

As with presidential donors, congressional contributors overwhelmingly support congressional candidates who shared their party affiliation (see Table 6.11). Conservative contributors also tended to support Republican candidates, especially conservative ones. Liberal donors typically backed liberal Democrats.

Table 6.11

**The Political Identifications of Congressional Donors in 1996** (in percentages)

| | Republicans | | | Democrats | | |
|---|---|---|---|---|---|---|
| | Incumbent conservative | Non-incumbent | Incumbent moderates | Incumbent moderates | Non-incumbent | Incumbent liberal |
| Partisanship | | | | | | |
| Strong Republican | 38[a] | 34 | 29 | 7 | 4 | 4 |
| Republican | 35 | 35 | 32 | 9 | 7 | 9 |
| Independent | 18 | 21 | 17 | 16 | 16 | 18 |
| Democrat | 6 | 5 | 13 | 29 | 39 | 34 |
| Strong Democrat | 3 | 3 | 2 | 40 | 34 | 35 |
| Ideology | | | | | | |
| Extremely conservative | 18 | 14 | 7 | 3 | 2 | 2 |
| Conservative | 58 | 58 | 57 | 17 | 12 | 9 |
| Moderate | 16 | 20 | 22 | 13 | 18 | 21 |
| Liberal | 9 | 17 | 13 | 46 | 55 | 54 |
| Extremely liberal | 1 | 1 | 2 | 22 | 14 | 16 |

*Source:* Survey by authors.
[a]Columns may not add up to 100 percent due to rounding.

These patterns were less consistent than for the presidential contributors, however, with a larger amount of cross-party and cross-ideology contributing. For example, almost 10 percent of donors to conservative Republican incumbents were Democrats, as were 15 percent of those who give to moderate GOP incumbents. Fully 16 percent of those who gave to moderate incumbent Democrats were themselves Republicans, as were 13 percent of those who gave to liberal incumbents. Similar patterns occurred for giving across ideological lines. Almost one-tenth of all donations to conservative incumbent Republicans came from liberal donors, and more than one-tenth of contributions to liberal Democratic incumbents came from conservatives.

There are many reasons for donors to cross party and ideological lines when contributing to congressional candidates. Many 1996 donors contributed because they knew a candidate or were asked to give by a personal friend or a business associate. Moreover, political access knows no partisan or ideological boundaries, and many donors were willing to give to influential legislators' regardless of partisan or ideological differences (see chapter 5).

As was the case with presidential donors, congressional donors held a variety of views on salient issues (see Table 6.12). Republican donors strongly favored tax cuts, free trade, and increased defense spending in 1996. Democrats, on the other hand, strongly favored national health insurance, environmental protection, and maintaining affirmative action programs. Some issues divided each party's financial backers. Republicans were divided over abortion and gay rights, while Democrats had disagreements over free trade and defense spending. Nevertheless, issue-based factionalism was muted among Republican congressional donors compared to the GOP presidential donors. Moreover, donors to congressional Democrats seemed nearly as united as the Democrats' presidential donors in 1996.

Congressional donors also report varying degrees of proximity to interest groups (see Table 6.13). GOP donors felt closer to the Chamber of Commerce, NRA, and Christian Coalition than did the Democrats' donors, and the Democrats felt closer to the Sierra Club, NOW, and the AFL-CIO. There were also some factional divisions within each party. For example, donors to GOP moderates identified less with the Christian Coalition than did their conservative counterparts, and somewhat smaller divisions emerged between backers of Democratic moderates and Democratic liberals on the Sierra Club and

Table 6.12

**The Issue Positions of Congressional Donors in 1996** (in percentages)

| | Republicans | | | Democrats | | |
|---|---|---|---|---|---|---|
| | Incumbent conservative | Non-incumbent | Incumbent moderates | Incumbent moderates | Non-incumbent | Incumbent liberal |
| Pro cutting taxes | | | | | | |
| Agree | 76 | 63 | 60 | 21 | 17 | 13 |
| Disagree | 14 | 11 | 20 | 69 | 75 | 77 |
| Pro national health insurance | | | | | | |
| Agree | 14 | 14 | 22 | 61 | 66 | 68 |
| Disagree | 75 | 74 | 61 | 23 | 21 | 19 |
| Pro environmental protection | | | | | | |
| Agree | 18 | 23 | 31 | 62 | 68 | 66 |
| Disagree | 64 | 65 | 50 | 21 | 15 | 15 |
| Support free trade | | | | | | |
| Agree | 66 | 69 | 76 | 51 | 46 | 55 |
| Disagree | 19 | 15 | 12 | 31 | 34 | 27 |
| Restrict abortion | | | | | | |
| Agree | 35 | 36 | 31 | 10 | 10 | 6 |
| Disagree | 47 | 50 | 55 | 86 | 84 | 89 |
| Gays teach in public school | | | | | | |
| Agree | 27 | 33 | 37 | 80 | 79 | 82 |
| Disagree | 51 | 46 | 43 | 13 | 10 | 11 |

| | | | | | | |
|---|---|---|---|---|---|---|
| **Too far in helping minorities** | | | | | | |
| Agree | 48 | 45 | 35 | 14 | 16 | 13 |
| Disagree | 27 | 28 | 41 | 74 | 73 | 78 |
| **Cut defense spending** | | | | | | |
| Agree | 11 | 16 | 17 | 50 | 53 | 50 |
| Disagree | 81 | 73 | 70 | 37 | 31 | 31 |

*Source:* Survey by authors.
*Note:* Five-point Likert scale items collapsed; neutral category excluded.

Table 6.13

**Interest-Group Proximity of Congressional Donors in 1996** (in percentages)

| | Republicans | | | Democrats | | |
|---|---|---|---|---|---|---|
| | Incumbent conservative | Non-incumbent | Incumbent moderates | Incumbent moderates | Non-incumbent | Incumbent liberal |
| Sierra Club | | | | | | |
| Close | 13 | 13 | 13 | 50 | 52 | 50 |
| Far | 70 | 69 | 61 | 29 | 19 | 22 |
| NOW | | | | | | |
| Close | 13 | 11 | 13 | 44 | 43 | 44 |
| Far | 79 | 76 | 77 | 40 | 40 | 31 |
| AFL-CIO | | | | | | |
| Close | 7 | 6 | 8 | 43 | 39 | 37 |
| Far | 84 | 89 | 82 | 31 | 28 | 26 |
| Chamber of Commerce | | | | | | |
| Close | 16 | 43 | 36 | 12 | 14 | 14 |
| Far | 38 | 25 | 38 | 70 | 65 | 64 |
| Christian Coalition | | | | | | |
| Close | 26 | 28 | 18 | 5 | 4 | 3 |
| Far | 49 | 50 | 63 | 90 | 91 | 92 |
| NRA | | | | | | |
| Close | 32 | 28 | 20 | 6 | 5 | 3 |
| Far | 46 | 49 | 63 | 89 | 90 | 93 |

NOW. Nevertheless, the strongest patterns for congressional donors were their distance from the rival party's core constituencies rather than proximity to their own party's allies.

What accounts for the absence of the sharp ideological divisions among congressional donors? Why don't they resemble the 1996 Republican presidential contributors or contributors who participated in contested Democratic nominations in 1988? It could be that a more nuanced analysis of congressional candidates would reveal more differences among the congressional donors, especially if primary candidates were identified. After all, primary battles between pro-life and pro-choice Republicans, or "new" and "old" Democrats, are more like presidential primaries. Given the power of incumbency, such battles are rare compared to general election contests, which pit one party's candidates against another. The great bulk of the congressional donors were involved in such general election contests in 1996—an election where the partisan control of Congress hung in the balance.

Differences between congressional and presidential campaign politics are also an important source of these differences, however. Congressional fund-raising is more focused on access to policymakers and the narrower details of public programs, whether it be for explicitly material motives or somewhat broader policy preferences. In contrast, presidential politics is more about the great issues of the day, the long-term purposes of government, and contending political philosophies; it is less about access to details of the policymaking process, although such concerns are not entirely absent. From this perspective, the divisions among 1996 Republican presidential donors revealed a fundamental debate about the direction of government, and the more muted division among GOP congressional contributors reflected important but less strident divisions over the details of legislation. In contrast, the financiers of Democratic politics achieved much greater agreement on both kinds of concerns in the 1996 campaign, reflecting their minority status in Congress and coalescing around their one presidential nomination candidate.

## Conclusion

Individual campaign contributors do not look like the general public. They are much wealthier than other Americans and tend to be well-educated, older, white men. They more strongly identify with the Republican Party than nondonors and tend to be more conservative. They also enjoy far more access to policymakers, in large part because of their campaign contributions. Thus, the concern about the impact of individual donors in politics continues to have merit.

Nevertheless, campaign contributors are hardly monolithic. They display considerable variation in motives, issue positions, and affect toward prominent interest groups. In any given election, the interaction of donor characteristics and motives, and the resources and techniques of candidates, produce particular sets of contributors to finance politics. It is mobilized donors who matter most during and after the election.

The individuals who helped finance the 1996 presidential nomination contests tended to reflect the policy views of candidates they backed, suggesting that issues matter in fund-raising. Sometimes these cleavages were subtle, suggesting that donors closely follow the policy pronouncements of candidates, patterns that appear to be most common in presidential politics. However, there was less evidence of intraparty cleavages among congressional donors. This pattern is probably due to the realities of congressional campaigns. The same institutional factors that both structure and differentiate presidential and congressional elections strongly influence the contributing behavior of the individuals who play a major role in financing those contests, and thus how and when their money matters.

## Notes

1. The survey of presidential donors was conducted by mail at the Ray C. Bliss Institute of Applied Politics at the University of Akron in the fall of 1996. It was based on a stratified random sample of 2,400 donors to the 1996 major presidential nomination campaign, drawn from the records of the FEC. The survey produced 1,094 usable questionnaires for a return rate of 50 percent (excluding undeliverable mail). The results were then weighted by the relative size of the funds raised by the sampled presidential campaigns. The survey of congressional donors was also conducted by mail at the Bliss Institute in the fall of 1997. It was based on a random sample of 2,400 donors to 1996 House and Senate campaigns, also drawn from the FEC. The survey produced 1,104 usable returns for a return rate of 50 percent (excluding undeliverable mail). There was no evidence of response bias by region or gender in either survey. The 1996 National Election Study was made available by the Inter-university Consortium for Political and Social Research and was originally conducted at the University of Michigan. All interpretations of these data presented here are the responsibility of the authors.

2. The material, solidary, and purposive scales in Table 6.5 are factor scores derived from an analysis of the motivations battery in the 1996 presidential donor

survey. These results conform with similar analysis in the literature (Brown, Powell, and Wilcox 1995, 86–88). This approach reduces the social desirability effects associated with purposive responses.

3. The unit of analysis for the presidential donors in Tables 6.6 to 6.9 is the *individual contributor*. In 1996, relatively few of these donors contributed to more than one presidential candidate. The Dole campaign was tops with 10 percent having made a donation of $200 or more to one of the other Republican contestants, and the other candidates all showing 2 or 3 percent. This pattern is quite different from 1988, when contributing to more than one candidate was common in both political parties. For example, 44 percent of the 1988 Dole donors gave to another candidate.

4. Only 19 percent of the Clinton donors wanted to cut government aid to business substantially, compared to 21 percent of the Dole donors, 44 percent of contributors to other conservative candidates, and 60 percent of the Buchanan backers.

5. Some 71 percent of the Buchanan donors agreed with a return to the gold standard and limits on immigration. The comparable figures for the Dole contributors were 30 and 57 percent, respectively.

6. ACU scores were used to distinguish the Republican conservatives (greater than or equal 85) from moderates (less than 85), and the Democratic moderates (greater than 15) from liberals (less than or equal 15). The unit of analysis for the congressional donors in Tables 6.10 to 6.13 is the *individual contribution*. So, an individual who gave three contributions would appear as three cases in the analysis. This choice was prompted by the fact that 62 percent of the sample gave to more than one candidate in 1996. Of course, the demographic and political characteristics associated with these contributions are for individual donors.

## 7

ROBERT BIERSACK AND MELANIE HASKELL

# Spitting on the Umpire: Political Parties, the Federal Election Campaign Act, and the 1996 Campaigns

For much of the last half of the twentieth century, political scientists and other observers of American politics have mourned the perceived decline of political parties. In the 1950s, the American Political Science Association commissioned a report called "Toward a More Responsible Two Party System" expressing concern about declining party allegiance in the electorate and diminished party activity in campaigns (American Political Science Association 1950). The most significant factors that caused the decline of the two-party system were rising economic and educational levels, which produced greater voter independence at the polls; primary elections, which replaced party conventions in candidate selection; and candidate-centered campaigns, which operated independently of party officials. By the 1970s, there was a general consensus that the parties were largely irrelevant in modern American campaigns (Crotty 1984).

The one facet of party politics that did not decline was the ability of the parties to raise and spend significant amounts of money. During the late 1970s and early 1980s, the Republican Party found the new technique of direct-mail fund-raising to be a powerful tool for financial growth. They raised large sums by massing the small contributions of thousands of supporters of the Reagan administration. At the same time, Democratic Party organizations followed the lead of their elected officials in forming strong financial relationships with organized interest groups including labor unions as well as corporate and business interests. While the Democrats never matched the fund-raising prowess of the Republicans, there was considerable growth in the financial status of both parties even as their other roles declined. Parties had essentially become financial intermediaries in the political process, using their fund-raising ability to provide campaign related services to candidates who needed both funds and new campaign technology to run for public office (Herrnson 1988).

The 1996 election cycle amply demonstrates the impact of this trend. The combination of new and innovative methods of fund-raising, along with new flexibility in expenditures, placed the parties at the center of the action—and the controversy—in the 1996 campaign. Worry over the decline of party was replaced by concern over the undermining of the party system and the federal campaign finance regime. This concern was exacerbated by the apparent contempt with which the major parties held the Federal Election Commission (FEC), the agency charged with enforcing the campaign finance laws. Indeed, the behavior of many such actors amounted to "spitting on the umpire." This chapter describes and evaluates the financial activities of the two major parties during 1995–96. In so doing, it also tracks the dramatic changes taking place in the campaign finance arena during this period.

The story of party finance in 1996 has two sides, reflecting the federal structure of American government. First, there was the federal funds, or hard money, side of party politics. For about a generation, the involvement of political parties in federal elections has been guided by the limitations and prohibitions contained in the federal campaign finance regulations, culminating in the 1971 Federal Election Campaign Act (FECA) and its 1974, 1976, and 1979 amendments. This law and its precursors prohibit contributions in federal elections (i.e., president, U.S. senators and representatives) from corporations, labor unions, federal contractors, and foreign nationals. The FECA also limits the amounts that may be given to campaigns and political committees by individuals and voluntary organizations commonly referred to as PACs (see Table 7.1). Moreover, the law limits the amount parties and other committees may contribute or spend directly on behalf of candidates for federal office. In 1996, the major parties raised a total of $638 million and expended $623 million in hard money. Second, there were the nonfederal funds, or "soft money," side of party finance. Political parties were also required to operate under the campaign fi-

Table 7.1

**Federal Contribution Limits**

| Donors | Candidate committee | PACs | Recipients Local party committees[a] | State party committees[a] | National party committees[b] | Special limits |
|---|---|---|---|---|---|---|
| Individuals | $1,000 per election | $5,000 per year | $5,000 per year combined limit | | $20,000 per year | $25,000 per year overall limit |
| Local party committees[a] | $5,000 per election combined limit | $5,000 per year combined limit | Unlimited transfers to other party committees | | | |
| State party committees (multicandidate)[a] | $5,000 per election combined limit | $5,000 per year combined limit | Unlimited transfers to other party committees | | | |
| National party committees (multicandidate)[b] | $5,000 per election | $5,000 per year | Unlimited transfers to other party committees | | | $17,500 to Senate candidate per campaign[c] |
| PAC (multicandidate) | $5,000 per election | $5,000 per year | $5,000 per year combined limit | | $15,000 per year | |
| PAC (not multicandidate) | $1,000 per election | $5,000 per year | $5,000 per year combined limit | | $20,000 per year | |

*Source:* August 1996. Campaign guide for political party committees. Federal Election Commission.
[a] State and local party committees share limits unless the local party committee can prove its independence.
[b] A party's national committee, Senate campaign committee, and House campaign committee are commonly called the national party committees and each has a separate limit. See the "Special limits" column for the exception.
[c] The Senate campaign committee and the national committee share this limit.

Table 7.2

**Party Committees' Hard Money Receipts** (federal dollars only, in millions)

|  | 1992 | 1996 | Increase from 1992 |
|---|---|---|---|
| Democrats | $163.3 | $221.6 | 36% |
| Republicans | $264.9 | $416.5 | 57% |
| Totals | $428.2 | $638.1 | 49% |

*Source:* Compiled from Federal Election Commission's "FEC Reports Major Increase in Party Activity for 1995–1996," March 19, 1997.

nance regulations of the fifty states for purposes of state elections. The variations in state campaign finance law combined with the needs of federal campaigns, especially presidential hopefuls, to create a new source of party funds outside of FECA. In 1996, the national party committees raised $252 million and spent some $272 million in soft money.

## One Side of Party Finance: Hard Money

Hard money, which has been regulated and reported at the federal level since 1978, reveals an important part of major party financial activity. Hard money is more difficult to raise and spend because it must meet FECA regulations (Table 7.1). The relevant regulations will be discussed as we review the various aspects of hard money.

### *Receipts of Major Party Organizations*

From January 1, 1995, through December 31, 1996, the national, state and local party committees raised $638 million in federal funds (see Table 7.2). In 1992, the last presidential election year, these same committees raised $428 million. This represents a 49 percent increase in federal receipts for the party committees. The Democrats were responsible for raising $221.6 million of that total, an increase of 36 percent over 1992. Consistent with past years, the Republicans outraised the Democrats with a total of $416.5 million in federal receipts. The Republicans raised 57 percent more than they had in 1992, and their total represented 65 percent of the total federal money raised by

Table 7.3

**Sources of Hard Money Receipts** (federal dollars only, in million $)

| Party committee | 1992 | | 1996 | |
|---|---|---|---|---|
| | Individuals | PACs | Individuals | PACs |
| DNC | 54.8 | 3.0 | 93.2 | 2.0 |
| DSCC | 15.8 | 4.4 | 18.0 | 5.3 |
| DCCC | 5.1 | 3.8 | 16.2 | 5.3 |
| Dem. state/local | 45.7 | 4.0 | 44.0 | 6.7 |
| Total Democrats | 121.0 | 15.1 | 171.0 | 19.2 |
| RNC | 79.0 | 0.86 | 153.0 | 0.68 |
| NRSC | 64.1 | 1.2 | 51.5 | 3.3 |
| NRCC | 26.8 | 1.6 | 62.9 | 8.2 |
| Rep. state/local | 53.1 | 0.87 | 94.8 | 1.6 |
| Total Republicans | 223.0 | 4.5 | 362.2 | 13.8 |

*Source:* Compiled from Federal Election Commission's "FEC Reports Major Increase in Party Activity for 1995–1996," March 19, 1997.

the two parties in 1996. In 1992, Republican committees raised about 62 percent of all party hard money, increasing their financial advantage over their Democratic counterparts in 1996.

*Source of Hard Money*

The parties raised their money primarily from two major sources: individual contributions and political action committees (PACs), as reported in Table 7.3. In 1996 the Democratic Party committees raised $171 million (77 percent) from individual donors and $19.2 million (9 percent) from PACs. In 1992 the Democrats raised $121 million (74 percent) from individual donors and $15.1 million (9 percent) from PACs. The Republican Party committees raised $362.2 million (87 percent) from individual donors and $13.8 million (3 percent) from PACs in 1996. In 1992 Republicans raised $223 million (84 percent) from individuals and $4.5 million (2 percent) from PACs. As usual, the Democrats took more PAC money than the Republicans, but both parties' PAC receipts increased in this last election cycle. The Democratic Party's PAC receipts were up by $4.1 million, while the Republican Party's PAC receipts were up by $9.3 million. Conventional wisdom in Washington in early 1995 contended that Democrats would receive less PAC money than Republicans due to the Republicans'

Table 7.4

**Size of Individual Contributions in the 1996 Election to the National Party Committees** (federal dollars only, in millions)

| Ranges | Democrats | % of Dem. total | Republicans | % of Rep. total |
|---|---|---|---|---|
| $20,000 | 10.4 | 21 | 2.4 | 3 |
| $19,999–$10,000 | 12.9 | 25 | 9.4 | 12 |
| $9,999–$5,000 | 10.1 | 20 | 9.3 | 12 |
| $4,999–$1,000 | 9.9 | 20 | 19.9 | 25 |
| $999–$500 | 2.8 | 5 | 10.7 | 14 |
| $499–$200[a] | 4.4 | 9 | 26.8 | 34 |

*Source:* The numbers in the above table were extracted from the Federal Election Commission's 1996 database on 11/10/98.

[a]Committees only itemize contributions over $200.

gaining majority status in Congress in the 1994 election. It was expected that business interests that had provided at least some support to Democratic committees through the years would switch parties completely when Republicans gained control of the Congress. While there was a measurable shift in PAC support, the well did not run dry for Democratic committees, due in large part to the ongoing and substantial support from labor union PACs, which continued in 1996.

According to the FECA, individuals can give up to $20,000 a year to the national parties; however, individuals are limited to an aggregate contribution total of $25,000 a year. PACs can give up to $15,000 a year to party committees, and there is no total limit. It is often thought that Democratic donors make smaller individual contributions, but that was not true in the 1996 election. When looking at the itemized (over $200) individual contributions in Table 7.4, it will quickly become apparent that Republicans took 34 percent of their individual contributions between $200 and $499, while the Democrats received 9 percent of their contributions in this dollar range. The Democrats reported receiving a majority (66 percent) of individual contributions greater than or equal to $5,000. The Republicans reported receiving only 27 percent of individual contributions greater than $5,000.

Total individual receipts to the three Republican national party committees were $267.3 million, but the itemized total in Table 7.4 sum to only $78.5 million, 29 percent of the Republicans' total individual receipts. The remaining 71 percent ($188.8 million) must have been

Table 7.5

**Party Committees' Hard Money Disbursements**
(federal dollars only, in millions)

|  | 1992 | 1996 | Increase from 1992 |
|---|---|---|---|
| Democrats | 157.5 | 214.3 | 36% |
| Republicans | 251.7 | 408.5 | 62% |
| Totals | 409.2 | 622.8 | 52% |

*Source:* Compiled from Federal Election Commission's, "FEC Reports Major Increase in Party Activity for 1995–1996," March 19, 1997.

reported as nonitemized receipts. This means the Republican Party committees actually received $215.7 million (81 percent of its individual contributions) under $500. As for the three national Democratic Party committees, the ranges in Table 7.4 account for 40 percent ($50.5 million) of the Democratic Party's individual contributions. The remaining 60 percent ($77 million) also must have consisted of contributions under $200. In other words, the Democrats actually received $81.4 million (64 percent of total individual contributions) under $500.

### Disbursements of Major Party Organizations

From January 1, 1995, through December 31, 1996, the national, state and local party committees spent $623 million in federal money (Table 7.5). In 1992, these same committees spent $409 million. This represents a 52 percent increase in federal disbursements for the party committees. The Democrats were responsible for spending $214 million, an increase of over 36 percent compared to 1992. As with receipts, however, the Republicans outspent the Democrats with a total of $409 million in federal disbursements. The Republicans spent 62 percent more than they had in 1992. The Republican committees were responsible for 66 percent of the total federal disbursements made by the two parties in 1996, up from 61 percent in 1992.

### Sources of Hard Money Disbursements

Much of the spending by federal accounts of major party committees was devoted to the maintenance of the organizations themselves. Operating expenses, generic get-out-the-vote activities, fund-raising, and advertising aimed at generating support for Democratic or Republican candidates generally represent the bulk of party spending. The parties also spent their money through three main candidate-related activities: direct candidate contributions, coordinated expenditures, and independent expenditures. In 1996, the Democrats spent $2.2 million (1 percent) in direct candidate contributions, $22.6 million (10 percent) in coordinated expenditures, and $1.5 million (.7 percent) in independent expenditures. The Republicans spent $3.7 million (.9 percent) in direct candidate contributions, $31 million (8 percent) in coordinated expenditures, and $10 million (2 percent) in independent expenditures (Table 7.6).

Independent expenditures were a new phenomenon for party committees in 1996. These are defined as activities that explicitly advocate the election or defeat of a clearly identified candidate, but are made without coordination with the candidates themselves. During previous elections since the passage of the FECA, the law had been interpreted as excluding parties from making independent expenditures. It was presumed that parties and their candidates were inextricably linked, so there could be no such thing as independent behavior by one related to the other. In fact, the law offered parties an opportunity to make limited "coordinated" expenditures instead. Coordinated expenditures are allowed in general election campaigns only, and they permit parties to spend an amount based on population size on behalf of candidates for federal office while coordinating these activities with the candidate. In 1992 the Democrats spent $1.9 million (1 percent) in direct candidate contributions and $28 million (18 percent) in coordinated expenditures. The Republicans spent $3 million (1 percent) in direct candidate contributions and $33.8 million (13 percent) in coordinated expenditures.

*Direct Candidate Contributions*

The FECA restricts direct candidate contributions from party committees to $5,000 per election (i.e., primary, general, and runoff elections) for House candidates. Senate committees can receive up to $17,500 for the entire election cycle from the combination of the national and senatorial campaign committees. In addition, the state parties can give $5,000 per election to Senate candidates. These limits are not adjusted for inflation, as are coordinated expenditure limits.

In the 1996 election, Democrats spent most of their total direct

Table 7.6

**How Federal Money Was Spent** (federal dollars only, in thousands)

| Party committee | 1992 Direct contributions | 1992 Coordinated expenditures | 1992 Independent expenditures | 1996 Direct contributions | 1996 Coordinated expenditures | 1996 Independent expenditures |
|---|---|---|---|---|---|---|
| DNC | 3,101 | 11,269,458 | 0 | 29,287 | 6,695,323 | 0 |
| DSCC | 593,500 | 11,235,712 | 0 | 540,000 | 8,397,129 | 1,386,022 |
| DCCC | 837,828 | 4,135,861 | 0 | 1,035,753 | 5,689,644 | 0 |
| Dem. state/local | 506,464 | 1,409,872 | 0 | 612,805 | 1,793,904 | 109,068 |
| Total, Democrats | 1,940,893 | 28,050,903 | 0 | 2,217,845 | 22,576,000 | 1,495,090 |
| RNC | 785,003 | 11,250,113 | 0 | 486,404 | 22,766,118 | 0 |
| NRSC | 692,195 | 16,477,387 | 0 | 696,500 | 308,319 | 9,734,445 |
| NRCC | 728,444 | 5,189,740 | 0 | 1,259,825 | 7,329,880 | 0 |
| Rep. state/local | 808,834 | 936,195 | 0 | 1,271,041 | 554,834 | 292,096 |
| Total, Republicans | 3,014,476 | 33,853,435 | 0 | 3,713,770 | 30,959,151 | 10,026,541 |

*Source:* Compiled from Federal Election Commission's "FEC Reports Major Increase in Party Activity for 1995–1996," March 19, 1997.

candidate contributions on House challengers, 31 percent (Table 7.7). The Republicans spent most of their direct candidate contributions on House incumbents, 28 percent. The Republican Party held the majority in both branches of Congress going into the 1996 elections, while the Democrats controlled the White House. During the early phases of the campaign the conditions in the economy and the growing support for the reelection of President Clinton made it appear that there would be opportunities for Democratic gains in congressional seats. Thus, Democratic Party committees were aggressive in supporting challengers to the many new Republican members, while Republican committees scrambled to aid their threatened majority.

This is the order in which Democrats spent direct contributions to federal candidates:

1. House challengers, 31 percent
2. House incumbents, 22 percent
3. House open seats, 16 percent
4. Senate open seats, 13 percent
5. Senate challengers, 10 percent
6. Senate incumbents, 8 percent
7. The presidential campaign, 0.1 percent

The analogous Republicans spending pattern was as follows:

1. House incumbents, 28 percent
2. House open seats, 22 percent
3. House challengers, 21 percent
4. Senate open seats, 13 percent
5. Senate incumbents, 8 percent
6. Senate challengers, 6 percent
7. The presidential campaign, 2 percent

*Coordinated Expenditures*

Coordinated expenditures are different from direct candidate contributions because both the party and the candidate decide how these funds are going to be spent. The payment does not come as money to the campaign, as do direct candidate contributions; it comes as services (e.g., polling opposition research). FECA allows coordinated expendi-

Table 7.7

**Party Support of Federal Candidates by Type of Campaign in 1996** (federal dollars only, in thousands)

| Spending type | President — Incumbents | President — Challengers | President — Open seats | Senate — Incumbents | Senate — Challengers | Senate — Open seats | House — Incumbents | House — Challengers | House — Open seats |
|---|---|---|---|---|---|---|---|---|---|
| **Direct contributions** | | | | | | | | | |
| DNC | 1,861 | 0 | | 0 | | 3,115 | 5,352 | 8,754 | 10,205 |
| DSCC | 0 | 0 | | 180,000 | | 245,000 | 5,000 | 0 | 5,000 |
| DCCC | 0 | 0 | | 6,600 | | 6,662 | 366,747 | 410,439 | 243,750 |
| Dem. state/local | 574 | 0 | | 40,306 | | 35,982 | 103,344 | 275,701 | 90,858 |
| RNC | 0 | 0 | | 0 | | 272 | 171,132 | 165,000 | 150,000 |
| NRSC | 0 | 0 | | 140,000 | | 222,500 | 0 | 5,000 | 50,000 |
| NRCC | 0 | 39 | | 14,999 | | 40,400 | 566,282 | 355,546 | 277,559 |
| Rep. state/local | 0 | 69,164 | | 60,055 | | 219,425 | 312,706 | 243,877 | 330,766 |
| **Coordinated expenditures** | | | | | | | | | |
| DNC | 6,665,34 | 0 | | 16,707 | | 0 | 2,458 | 0 | 0 |
| DSCC | 0 | 0 | | 2,351,662 | | 4,784,380 | 353 | 0 | 0 |
| DCCC | 0 | 0 | | 0 | | 0 | 1,130,106 | 3,149,508 | 1,410,030 |
| Dem. state/local | 66,901 | 0 | | 341,937 | | 132,337 | 267,154 | 511,580 | 312,713 |
| RNC | 0 | 11,704,932 | | 2,601,896 | | 3,836,119 | (8,451) | 446,132 | 210,998 |
| NRSC | 0 | 0 | | (119) | | 296,922 | 0 | 0 | 0 |
| NRCC | 0 | 0 | | 0 | | 0 | 2,944,457 | 2,243,418 | 2,142,005 |
| Rep. state/local | 0 | 0 | | 72,649 | | 220,586 | 113,996 | 44,806 | 102,797 |

*Source:* Compiled from Federal Election Commission's "FEC Reports Major Increase in Party Activity for 1995–1996," March 19, 1997.

tures to be made only during the general election campaign. The limits are based on the voting-age population, the office sought, and are adjusted for inflation. In 1996, the national parties were allowed to spend up to $12 million on presidential candidates, $30,910 on most House candidates, or $61,820 on House candidates that represented statewide districts (e.g., Vermont, Montana, Delaware); the amount for Senate candidates varied from $61,820 in small states to $1.4 million in California (Table 7.8). State party committees have additional coordinated expenditure authority with the same limits as the national parties committees for House and Senate races. It should be noted, however, that state parties can engage in what are called "agency agreements." These agreements allow the national party to take over the state party's spending allotment, which doubles the amount the national party can spend (Corrado et al. 1997, 169).

In order to assess fully the impact of the party coordinated expenditures, it is important to look beyond just aggregate spending levels to see how carefully parties target their spending. Table 7.8 shows the relative effort of the parties compared with the closeness of the election and the maximum allowed to be spent. The table shows that this effort generally corresponds with the competitiveness of the election, with those candidates in close races receiving the maximum coordinated spending allowable. The small number of Senate campaigns and special circumstances surrounding these races sometimes reduces the relationship between competitiveness and party spending. For House candidates, however, Table 7.8 shows a strong and consistent relationship between coordinated expenditures and competitiveness for both major parties. In these races, parties can have significant impact on the outcome by marshaling all the resources possible in support of their candidates.

*Independent Expenditures*

In June 1996 the Supreme Court gave party committees the ability to make independent expenditures on behalf of the parties' candidates. The ruling in the case of *Colorado Republican Federal Campaign Committee* v. *Federal Election Commission* (518 U.S. 604 [1996]), commonly referred to as the Colorado case, surprised many political observers who believed the parties could not function independently from their own candidates. The only restrictions on the parties for

Table 7.8

## Party Coordinated Expenditures by Competitiveness
(1996 general election only)

| Office and status/ competitiveness of election | Democrats | | Republicans | |
|---|---|---|---|---|
| | Number of candidates | Percentage maximum allowed | Number of candidates | Percentage maximum allowed |
| Senate incumbents | | | | |
| High[a] | 4 | 73 | 6 | 72 |
| Medium[a] | 1 | 38 | 3 | 98 |
| Low[a] | 2 | 0 | 4 | 26 |
| Senate challengers | | | | |
| High | 3 | 18 | 3 | 93 |
| Medium | 5 | 58 | 3 | 103[b] |
| Low | 6 | 23 | 3 | 61 |
| Senate open seats | | | | |
| High | 6 | 95 | 7 | 99 |
| Medium | 5 | 97 | 3 | 102[b] |
| Low | 2 | 95 | 2 | 63 |
| House incumbents | | | | |
| High | 20 | 57 | 43 | 72 |
| Medium | 28 | 27 | 38 | 34 |
| Low | 116 | 2 | 131 | 1 |
| House challengers | | | | |
| High | 34 | 74 | 11 | 89 |
| Medium | 29 | 48 | 24 | 72 |
| Low | 142 | 12 | 123 | 13 |
| House open seats | | | | |
| High | 20 | 77 | 17 | 92 |
| Medium | 12 | 48 | 17 | 84 |
| Low | 18 | 26 | 16 | 31 |

*Source:* Compiled from Federal Election Commission's "FEC Reports Major Increase in Party Activity for 1995–1996," March 19, 1997, and "FEC Announces 1996 Party Spending Limits," March 15, 1996.

[a]High Competition = 54–46% of general election vote. Medium Competition = 59–55% and 45–41% of the general election vote. Low competition = 60+ and 40 or less % of the general election vote.

[b]Value summed to over 100% due to reporting from national, state, and local party committees. These numbers are subject to a future amendment reattributing the funds to in-kind contributions.

*Note:* Six districts in Texas were excluded from this table. These districts had court-ordered runoffs after the general election due to a redistricting case.

independent expenditures are that disbursements must be paid for with hard money, and the party cannot consult with the candidates.

The ruling came in time to affect some 1996 general election campaigns. Only the senatorial campaign committees and a few state/local committees made independent expenditures in the election. The National Republican Senatorial Committee established a separate office outside the NRSC's headquarters that would be responsible for making independent expenditures. The committee went to this great length to diminish any appearance of coordination. The DSCC did not set up a separate office, but they also tried out the new independent expenditures. The NRSC and the Republican state/local party committees spent $10 million, while the DSCC and the Democratic state/local party committees spent only $1.5 million. The Democrats spent 95 percent of these expenditures ($1.4 million) against Republican federal candidates. The Republicans split the expenditures between supporting (47 percent) their own party's candidates and opposing (53 percent) other federal candidates. The total amount of independent expenditures by all committees reporting to the FEC equaled $22.2 million. This fact is significant because the party committees mentioned above were responsible for a little over one-half of that money $11.5 million (see Table 7.9).

## The Other Side of Party Finance: Soft Money

Apart from the federal funds described to this point, there is another side of party finance. The 1996 campaign is generally seen as the first election conducted largely outside the FECA regime. Twenty years of innovation in campaign techniques and fund-raising have worn holes in the original fabric of contribution limits and restrictions coupled with public financing and expenditure limits that mostly defined presidential campaigns from 1976 through 1992. The snowballing effect of these changes became most pronounced in 1996 when the routes through which people and organizations could circumvent restrictions became common knowledge (Wertheimer 1996).

No single institution came to represent the new financial environment more than the national political parties, and the primary vehicle parties used to break down the facade of campaign finance restrictions was soft money. Throughout much of the 1996 campaign and for more

Table 7.9

**Party Independent Expenditures Supporting and Opposing Federal
Candidates in 1996**
(federal dollars only, in thousands)

| | DSCC | Dem. state/local | NRSC | Rep. state/local |
|---|---|---|---|---|
| Independent expenditure supporting | | | | |
| President | 0 | 569 | 0 | 15,953 |
| Senate | 45,000 | 1,016 | 4,494,597 | 199,065 |
| House | 0 | 31,914 | 0 | 45,475 |
| Total | 45,000 | 33,499 | 4,494,597 | 260,493 |
| Independent expenditure opposing | | | | |
| President | 0 | 569 | 0 | 751 |
| Senate | 1,341,022 | 65,000 | 5,239,848 | 426 |
| House | 0 | 10,000 | 0 | 30,426 |
| Total | 1,341,022 | 75,569 | 5,239,848 | 31,603 |

*Source:* Compiled from Federal Election Commission's "FEC Reports Major Increase in Party Activity for 1995–1996,", March 19, 1997.

than a year after, newspapers were filled with stories of big contributions, sometimes from supposedly sinister sources, pouring into the national parties to be used in the presidential campaign. Hundreds of millions of dollars were raised and spent during 1996 in ways that seemed unthinkably illegal just a few years earlier. Much of the day-to-day reporting from the campaign trail involved speeches made by the two major candidates at fund-raising events where corporations or labor unions or individuals spent sometimes $100,000 or more to have dinner and listen to President Clinton or Senator Dole speak on the issues of the campaign. While this money went into party coffers and not to the campaigns, there was little doubt about the understanding between donor and candidate regarding the value of the money received. The stark contradiction between this frantic and seemingly unlimited fund-raising and the legal framework of financing for presidential campaigns first established in 1971 and implemented in 1976 presented a contradiction that is difficult to explain or understand.

### What Is Party Soft Money?

Party soft money includes funds raised by the parties that fall outside the limits and restrictions of the FECA and its predecessor legislation. Under these laws, the federal accounts of political parties can receive funds only from individuals and political committees (i.e., PACs, other party organizations, and so forth), but not from for profit corporations or directly from dues paid by union members. As discussed earlier in this chapter, the law also restricts money that can be contributed or spent in federal elections (see Table 7.1).

Political parties are involved in many elections at different levels of government, however, and the rules that apply to federal elections cannot be invoked in those campaigns because of the dominant position of states in our federal system of government. Each state is free to develop its own regulations regarding campaign finance, and such regulations run the gamut from strict restrictions on sources of funds and how they can be spent to completely unrestricted systems where unlimited contributions from any source are permissible. Since political parties have legitimate roles in elections at the state and local level, they have traditionally been permitted to use funds that are allowed in state elections for the basic operation of the party organization. In the late 1970s, the use of soft money was expanded to certain generic activities like get-out-the-vote drives that support both federal and state/local candidates (Corrado et al. 1997). National parties, then, have essentially become two organizations, one working under federal law with limited contributions from restricted sources, and another working under the myriad state laws' restrictions and prohibitions. Activities that may affect both federal and state elections (e.g., the basic overhead expenses of running the party, or communications that support the party generally) must use a combination of federal (hard) and nonfederal (soft) money.

Money plays such an important part in politics because it tends to have predictable value and because it can be readily exchanged for nearly anything one can imagine. Neither the predictable value nor the free exchange of money is guaranteed, however, and the development of soft money in American politics is an example of what happens when one type of money has a different value from another. The fact that raising funds from a specific and narrow set of sources in limited amounts is harder than fund-raising where no limits or restrictions apply means that the two kinds of money have, in effect, different values. Funds raised under federal restrictions have a higher value because they are more limited and because they have broader allowable uses. It is not difficult to anticipate at least two reactions to this distinction between hard money and soft: Committees will be willing to exchange soft dollars for hard dollars and pay a premium (because hard dollars are more valuable), and committees will look for ways to make soft money more useful because it is easier to raise. Both reactions are evident in the behavior of the national and state parties during 1995–96.

*Soft Money in 1996*

Table 7.10 shows the total amount of soft money raised and spent by national party organizations during the 1996 election cycle, and the growth in those totals since the 1992 cycle when systematic reporting of soft money began. It should be noted that soft money raised directly by state and local party organizations is not disclosed in any central location, and the rules for its disclosure vary widely from state to state. With this said, several conclusions are apparent from the table. First, soft money is increasingly attractive to parties and is apparently useful in a number of contexts. When it first developed in the 1980s, soft money was described as closely associated with presidential campaigns. It represented an opportunity for presidential candidates to raise funds in large denominations that parties could use to mobilize voters on behalf of the presidential campaign and the rest of the party ticket. If this were the only use for soft money, we would expect to see significant declines in soft money activity during election cycles with no presidential race. The data in Table 7.10 for the 1994 election cycle show that this expectation was not the case. The two national committees (DNC and RNC) both raised and spent more soft money in the 1994 congressional election cycle than they had in 1992. Moreover, the senatorial and congressional campaign committees have apparently discovered that soft money can be useful to them as well, as their totals from these sources have soared from the 1992 election cycle to the 1996 cycle.

The table also clearly suggests that 1996 was a "breakout" campaign for soft money, with totals raised and spent since 1994 more than doubling for the Democrats and the Republicans. Another way of look-

Table 7.10

**Total Soft Money Raised and Spent by the National Party Committees**
(nonfederal dollars only, in millions)

|  | Receipts | | | Expenditures | | |
|---|---|---|---|---|---|---|
|  | 1992 | 1994 | 1996 | 1992 | 1994 | 1996 |
| DNC | 31.4 | 43.9 | 101.9 | 28.4 | 45.1 | 100.5 |
| DSCC | 0.56 | 0.37 | 14.2 | 0.51 | 0.42 | 14.1 |
| DCCC | 4.4 | 5.1 | 12.3 | 4.0 | 5.1 | 11.8 |
| Total | 36.3 | 49.1 | 128.4 | 32.9 | 50.4 | 121.8 |
| RNC | 35.9 | 44.9 | 113.1 | 33.6 | 42.4 | 114.4 |
| NRSC | 9.1 | 5.6 | 29.4 | 7.7 | 6.5 | 29.4 |
| NRCC | 6.1 | 7.4 | 18.5 | 6.2 | 4.7 | 28.7 |
| Total | 36.3 | 52.5 | 123.9 | 46.2 | 48.4 | 149.7 |

*Source:* Compiled from Federal Election Commission's "FEC Reports Major Increase in Party Activity for 1995–1996," March 19, 1997.

*Note:* Totals do not include transfers among committees, so totals may be less than a column's total.

ing at the increasing impact of soft money is to consider the proportion of overall national party fund-raising represented by these unregulated funds. Overall fund-raising of the DNC and RNC for 1996 was $516 million ($301 million hard and $215 million soft money). The increase in funds become more apparent compared with 1992 which was $218 million ($151 million hard and $67 million soft money). While both hard and soft money receipts increased substantially over this period, the relative place of soft money for the parties grew even more, with nearly one-half of all DNC funds coming from unrestricted sources. Soft money is generally more efficient to raise, with no restrictions on size or source, so it is not surprising to find soft money becoming a larger proportion of overall national party financing.

*Sources of Soft Money*

It is not particularly surprising to find that the sources of soft money are the institutions with the greatest financial resources that also have the greatest direct interest in the actions of government. The Center for Responsive Politics has tracked the sources of soft money to national parties by economic interest, and their findings are pretty much what one would expect. Table 7.11 lists the top ten soft money contributors to the Democratic and Republican national committees during 1995–96. As with hard money, the major sources of soft money across the major parties were more similar than one might think. Corporate sources dominate for both Democrats and Republicans (in fact, corporate contributions for the DNC nonfederal accounts—approximately $52 million—were roughly equal to the corporate totals for the RNC's nonfederal accounts), and large-denomination contributions ($100,000 or more) were at least as common at the DNC as their Republican counterpart (Federal Election Commission 1997).

Fund-raising methods are also very similar across the two parties. Much was made during 1995–96 of the efforts of the Clinton administration to "market" access to the White House. Whether one was invited to coffee in the Map Room or to stay overnight in the Lincoln Bedroom, the appearance of trading restricted access to senior officials (including the president) for large contributions to the DNC characterized the "scandal" that was party fund-raising in this period.

Shameless as the Clinton administration may have been in leveraging the time and attention of important officials for political funds, the difference between this program and the efforts of the RNC to provide selective access to congressional leaders was only one of degree. Dinners, weekend outings, and other events were regularly used by both major parties to give major donors a sense that they were close to power. Political scientists have consistently found three different motives for people who participate in the political process, including contributing to political organizations. Individuals either see some tangible benefit for themselves (material motives); or they gain personal satisfaction from close proximity to decision makers (solitary motives); or they believe strongly in issue positions and the political leaders who support those positions (purposive motives) (Wilson 1995). Two of these have one thing in common—the proximity to elected officials is important. Whether contributors seek material benefits (specific legislative or administrative action) or solitary benefits (a psychological satisfaction from associating with important people), the key to raising funds is often establishing proximity between political leaders and contributors while reinforcing the exclusivity of that connection. This connection is not lost on those political professionals who raise funds for parties, and they regularly go to great lengths to reinforce this sense of contact and selectivity for large party donors.

174

Table 7.11

**Top-10 Soft Money Donors to the National Party Committees in 1995–1996 Election Cycle** (in dollars)

| Democrats | | Republicans | |
|---|---|---|---|
| Joseph E. Seagram & Sons | 1,261,700 | Philip Morris Co. | 2,520,518 |
| Communication Workers of America | 1,150,300 | RJR Nabisco | 1,188,175 |
| AFSCME | 1,134,962 | News Corp. | 794,700 |
| Walt Disney Co. | 1,038,050 | Atlantic Richfield Co. | 764,471 |
| Food & Commercial Workers Union | 727,550 | Joseph E. Seagram & Sons | 677,145 |
| Laborers Union | 627,088 | Brown & Williamson Tobacco | 635,000 |
| Lazard Freres & Co. | 624,500 | American Defense Institute | 600,000 |
| MacAndrews & Forbes | 623,250 | U.S. Tobacco Co. | 556,603 |
| MCI Telecommunications | 607,296 | AT&T | 552,340 |
| Association of Trial Lawyers of America | 606,300 | Enron Corp. | 544,500 |

*Source:* Center for Responsive Politics, based on Federal Election Commission data as of May 7, 1997 http://www.crp.org/PUBS/BTL/top10soft.htm.

*Notes:* All totals include parent organizations, subsidiaries, and employers. These figures differ slightly from those reported in Table 8.2, which were compiled by Common Cause.

AFSCME = American Federation of State, County, and Municipal Employees.

The extraordinary pressure to raise soft money during 1995 and 1996 meant in some cases there was less scrutiny of contributors and sources of funds than in previous years. This pattern lead in turn to revelations of questionable contributions that filled the news media beginning at the end of the 1991 campaign and continuing for more than a year thereafter. As is often the case, some of the most "scandalous" revelations had relatively minor impact on soft money fund-raising itself. Perhaps the most important example was the discovery that foreign funds (particularly from Asia) were entering the coffers of the DNC. A provision in the FECA makes it illegal for a foreign national to contribute to any American election campaign (federal, state, or local) either directly or through another program. This apparently clear prohibition was regularly juxtaposed in the press with videotapes of the president welcoming foreign visitors for coffee at the White House and the vice president speaking at a Buddhist temple in California, an event that was later acknowledged to be a fund-raiser. (Some caution is required here because court decisions in 1998 have called into question whether receipts of party soft money accounts should be included in this prohibition). Questions about the activities of John Huang as an administration official and later a DNC fund-raiser, along with others with possible connections to Chinese government and technology officials, were deemed the most newsworthy. After the election, the actual money raised through these channels was found to be a small part of the overall DNC soft money effort. The DNC ultimately returned about $3 million in contributions that appeared to come from foreign sources, about 3 percent of the total soft money take for the DNC (Gravely 1997).

*Soft Money Disbursements*

Party soft money has always been viewed in the context of presidential campaigns. Effective fund-raising in large denominations (like the $100,000 contributions most often seen as basic to the soft money process) requires major national figures like presidential candidates to bring large donors to the party. During the 1984 and 1988 campaigns, these funds were used to develop voter mobilization efforts and conduct activities emphasizing candidates up and down the ballot. Scholars who study political parties have often defended these "party building" activities and have argued that soft money can be an important element in the maintenance of a significant role for parties in the American political system. The funds would be used for party infrastructure—building the tools that parties would use to speak to and mobilize voters (Corrado et al. 1997). In 1996, however, the requirements of the presidential campaigns were somewhat different, and the prospect of using soft money in new ways proved too enticing to avoid.

The Clinton camp realized in 1995 that there was a need to change the president's public image. Newt Gingrich and the new Republican congressional majority were receiving much of the good press, and prospects for the president's reelection were widely held to be slim. Individuals in the White House staff and campaign operatives had a series of discussions beginning in the spring of 1995 that included the president and the vice president. Ultimately, these discussions concluded that a national media campaign of unprecedented proportions would be required to lay a foundation for the reelection of the president (Woodward 1996).

At these discussions it was determined there were essentially two alternatives available to finance this campaign. One option was for the president to reject the public funding program with its (state-by-state and national) spending limits. The second would be to use the national parties with their greater fund-raising flexibility (e.g., using soft money for generic activity) and an emerging legal consensus about ways the parties and others could spend soft monies without violating federal election laws. It was argued that the DNC could pay for ads that described the administration's policy initiatives and argued for their continuation as long as these ads did not explicitly advocate the reelection of the president. A footnote in the Supreme Court decision in *Buckley* v. *Valeo* (424 U.S. 1 [1976]) listed a series of words that the Court deemed to be examples of "express advocacy" (e.g., "vote for," "vote against," "elect," "defeat"). So long as these words were not used, the ads could be paid for partially with soft money, and they would not count against the spending limit imposed on the reelection campaign.

The decision was made that rejecting public funding was politically too risky. A president who had advocated campaign finance reform throughout his term would have a difficult time explaining rejecting the public financing program that represented the most comprehensive of the Watergate-era reforms (Woodward 1996, 234). Thus began the preparation for large soft money contributions to support DNC-financed issue ads supporting the administration. The president himself played a significant role in raising these funds via special meetings of small groups of large donors. In these meetings, he explained to donors how their contributions (which would not be allowed in federal election campaigns) could be used by the DNC to support the administration's political objectives without directly advocating his re-election (Abramson 1997a).

The Dole campaign had a different problem, having spent an amount approaching the national limit by early April 1996 in order to gain the Republican nomination. Dole was faced with several months of enforced silence prior to receiving his general election public funding grant, while the Clinton campaign was free to spend money in primary elections in which the president faced no Democratic opponents. The RNC took up the slack by conducting an advertising campaign broadly supportive of Mr. Dole's efforts, but once again, not (according to the RNC) expressly advocating his election. This meant that, just as for the DNC a year earlier, the funds used to conduct this campaign could be a combination of hard and soft money. The distinction between issue advocacy and express advocacy is legally important because it determines which funds can be used to pay for the advertisement. Many of the commercials aired during the election cycle by the party committees were indistinguishable from campaign ads to the average viewer. In fact, a few ads were run both as "express" ads paid for by the presidential campaigns and "issue" ads run by the party committees. With the exception of a "tag" line, these ads were exactly the same—the only difference was the sponsor. Table 7.12 presents transcripts of issue advertisements paid for by the DNC and the RNC.

The use of soft money by national party committees is not without regulatory requirements. During presidential election years, generic activities (like issue ad campaigns) must be paid for with 65 percent hard money and 35 percent soft money. During nonpresidential years, however, the required ratio for the national committee is 60 percent federal and 40 percent nonfederal. This ratio is fixed by FEC regulations for all administrative expenses and generic activities (including get-out-the-vote drives and other general party promotions). Other party activities including fund-raising and support of specific candidates have different ratios that depend on the amount of federal versus nonfederal involvement for the activity itself.

Table 7.12

## Issue Ads Run by the DNC and the RNC

| Democratic National Committee "Them" Aired August 15, 1996 through August 28, 1996 | Republican National Committee "Surprise" Aired May 1996 |
|---|---|
| "The Oval Office if Dole sits here and Gingrich runs Congress: what could happen? Medicare slashed, women's right to choose gone, education/school drug programs cut, and a risky 550,000,000,000 dollar plan balloons the deficit, raises interest rates, hurts the economy. President Clinton says balance the budget, cut taxes for families/college tuition, stands up to Dole and Gingrich; but if Dole wins and Gingrich runs Congress, there will be nobody there to stop them." | *Announcer:* "Three years ago, Bill Clinton gave us the largest tax increase in history, including a 4-cents-a-gallon increase on gasoline. Bill Clinton said he felt bad about it."<br><br>*Clinton:* "People in this room still get mad at me over the budget because you think I raised your taxes too much. It might surprise you to know I think I raised them too much, too."<br><br>*Announcer:* "OK, Mr. President, we are surprised. So now, surprise us again. Support senator Dole's plan to repeal your gas tax. And learn that actions do speak louder than words." |

*Source:* "Report of the Audit Division on the Dole/Kemp '96 and Dole/Kemp Compliance Committee, Inc (General)." Federal Election Commission. Attachment 1—Text of Advertisements. November 19, 1998. "Report of the Audit Division on Clinton/Gore '96 Primary Committee, Inc." Federal Election Commission. Exhibit 1.

*Note:* These ads do not specifically advocate that the listener vote for or against the presidential candidates. This technicality defines these as issue ads, which means they can be paid for with a mix of hard and soft money.

Once again, however, the relative ease with which soft money can be raised creates strong incentives to find ways to utilize these resources beyond just 35 percent of an expenditure. The path used first by the DNC and later by the RNC to maximize the role of soft money was to make state parties intermediaries in these ad campaigns. Rules for allocating expenditures for state parties are based on the proportion of federal races on the general election ballot, and this often allows for more soft money in state spending than the national party percentage. As a result, national parties transferred to states specific amounts of both hard and soft money, which states then used to pay national advertising consultants for ads to be run in their states. For example, the DNC transferred $2,944,798 soft and $559,940 hard money to the state party committee in North Carolina. This ratio is 81 percent soft and 19 percent hard, significantly less than the 65 percent national hard-dollar requirement. Table 7.13 shows all DNC and RNC transfers of hard and soft money in 1995 and 1996 to the state party committees. Not all of these funds were used on issue ad campaigns for the national elections. Audits conducted by the FEC found a total of $46.6 million spent by the DNC in this manner, while the RNC spent $12.9 million.

Even with the greater soft money percentages allowed for state party organizations, some federally allowable funds were needed to conduct the activities of the parties during the 1996 campaign. We have seen that national committees provided sufficient hard and soft money to conduct the national advertising campaigns they orchestrated through the states, but other spending by state parties was also required. Once again, the ease with which soft money could be raised played a role in how parties generated the funding they needed. In several instances, states with an abundance of soft money made explicit exchanges with other state parties, where hard money was more plentiful. For example, the Florida state Democratic Committee transferred $10,000 in hard money to the Nebraska state Democratic Committee on May 2, 1996. On the same date, the Nebraska state Democratic Committee transferred $12,000 in soft money back to the committee in Florida. In essence, Nebraska was paying extra for hard money that could be used either directly to support federal candidates or as the federal share of some activity that permitted both hard and soft funding sources (Chinoy 1997a).

One argument often made in support of soft money is that these funds are used to develop the basic workings of parties at the state and

Table 7.13

**National Party Transfers to State and Local Party Committees** (in dollars)

| | Federal | | Nonfederal | | Total | |
|---|---|---|---|---|---|---|
| | DNC | RNC | DNC | RNC | DNC | RNC |
| Alabama | 35,823 | 346,194 | 123,904 | 1,196,194 | 159,727 | 1,542,388 |
| Alaska | 22,028 | 29,141 | 5,380 | 54,071 | 27,408 | 83,212 |
| Arizona | 165,124 | 232,848 | 330,636 | 613,453 | 495,760 | 846,301 |
| Arkansas | 336,767 | 190,746 | 399,278 | 1,014,677 | 736,045 | 1,205,423 |
| California | 642,552 | 2,256,289 | 6,808,636 | 7,464,672 | 7,451,188 | 9,720,961 |
| Colorado | 682,224 | 553,335 | 1,275,713 | 1,075,331 | 1,957,937 | 1,628,666 |
| Connecticut | 316,193 | 284,101 | 986,035 | 0 | 1,302,228 | 284,101 |
| Delaware | 19,876 | 31,181 | 80,137 | 243,990 | 100,013 | 275,171 |
| Florida | 1,932,419 | 853,521 | 3,795,371 | 1,334,742 | 5,727,790 | 2,188,263 |
| Georgia | 476,459 | 679,222 | 1,105,686 | 1,980,855 | 1,582,145 | 2,660,077 |
| Hawaii | 10,106 | 27,512 | 56,665 | 35,892 | 66,771 | 63,404 |
| Idaho | 47,957 | 188,391 | 144,700 | 405,150 | 192,657 | 593,541 |
| Illinois | 1,206,181 | 1,056,542 | 1,651,713 | 1,773,683 | 2,857,894 | 2,830,225 |
| Indiana | 40,751 | 133,699 | 530,550 | 1,810,158 | 571,301 | 1,943,857 |
| Iowa | 592,884 | 608,870 | 1,656,528 | 996,227 | 2,249,412 | 1,605,097 |
| Kansas | 48,470 | 218,315 | 40,100 | 23,550 | 88,570 | 241,865 |
| Kentucky | 480,539 | 515,756 | 1,698,119 | 964,506 | 2,178,658 | 1,480,262 |
| Louisiana | 683,769 | 405,233 | 1,395,042 | 345,135 | 2,078,811 | 750,368 |
| Maine | 371,805 | 269,116 | 537,758 | 480,906 | 909,563 | 750,022 |
| Maryland | 97,609 | 27,500 | 339,324 | 44,300 | 436,933 | 71,800 |
| Massachusetts | 74,291 | 152,471 | 1,393,458 | 363,337 | 1,467,749 | 515,808 |
| Michigan | 1,470,516 | 881,726 | 2,708,320 | 2,131,492 | 4,178,836 | 3,013,218 |
| Minnesota | 856,644 | 150,765 | 1,286,037 | 489,412 | 2,142,681 | 640,177 |
| Mississippi | 2,482 | 35,422 | 248,561 | 382,065 | 251,043 | 417,487 |

| | | | | | |
|---|---|---|---|---|---|
| Missouri | 546,125 | 318,915 | 2,200,762 | 1,882,422 | 2,746,887 | 2,201,337 |
| Montana | 47,015 | 174,252 | 221,901 | 288,427 | 268,916 | 462,679 |
| Nebraska | 9,839 | 241,000 | 75,000 | 571,288 | 84,839 | 812,288 |
| Nevada | 245,099 | 400,847 | 553,645 | 774,065 | 798,744 | 1,174,912 |
| New Hampshire | 151,520 | 369,199 | 691,132 | 908,453 | 842,652 | 1,277,652 |
| New Jersey | 335,080 | 309,393 | 61,960 | 117,748 | 397,040 | 427,141 |
| New Mexico | 336,307 | 147,795 | 767,898 | 325,834 | 1,104,205 | 473,629 |
| New York | 190,381 | 53,732 | 0 | 325,332 | 190,381 | 379,064 |
| North Carolina | 559,940 | 445,542 | 2,944,798 | 2,813,230 | 3,504,738 | 3,258,772 |
| North Dakota | 3,000 | 42,200 | 57,000 | 94,255 | 60,000 | 136,455 |
| Ohio | 1,508,542 | 1,441,338 | 4,008,275 | 3,250,534 | 5,516,817 | 4,691,872 |
| Oklahoma | 41,524 | 176,331 | 5,000 | 367,743 | 46,524 | 544,074 |
| Oregon | 667,990 | 395,648 | 1,708,999 | 249,761 | 2,376,989 | 645,409 |
| Pennsylvania | 1,486,757 | 789,278 | 4,627,012 | 2,631,333 | 6,113,769 | 3,420,611 |
| Rhode Island | 4,111 | 15,107 | 0 | 23,398 | 4,111 | 38,505 |
| South Carolina | 39,437 | 65,680 | 80,691 | 266,250 | 120,128 | 331,930 |
| South Dakota | 32,837 | 41,899 | 124,129 | 305,100 | 156,966 | 346,999 |
| Tennessee | 977,682 | 743,543 | 1,430,881 | 1,377,675 | 2,408,563 | 2,121,218 |
| Texas | 418,790 | 499,051 | 896,530 | 1,851,825 | 1,315,320 | 2,350,876 |
| Utah | 51,979 | 46,280 | 159,200 | 217,956 | 211,179 | 264,236 |
| Vermont | 27,118 | 37,224 | 170,133 | 188,120 | 197,251 | 225,344 |
| Virginia | 73,315 | 37,770 | 326,148 | 392,479 | 399,463 | 430,249 |
| Washington | 636,683 | 740,016 | 2,815,097 | 2,686,142 | 3,451,780 | 3,426,158 |
| West Virginia | 50,313 | 5,000 | 0 | 1,000 | 50,313 | 6,000 |
| Wisconsin | 1,081,470 | 369,323 | 1,636,447 | 1,025,766 | 2,717,917 | 1,395,089 |
| Wyoming | 18,792 | 44,022 | 33,208 | 58,774 | 52,000 | 102,796 |
| Total | 20,155,115 | 18,078,281 | 54,193,497 | 48,218,708 | 74,348,612 | 66,296,989 |

*Source:* Compiled from Federal Election Commission's, "FEC Reports Major Increase in Party Activity for 1995–1996," March 19, 1997.

local levels. Since parties are more accountable to voters and more broad based than many other political organizations, some argue that they should enjoy advantages in fund-raising and spending that reflect their special place in the political process. The impact of this argument is reduced, however, if these organizations are really only shells used by the national parties to conduct their business without regard to state and local priorities (Sorauf 1992, 147).

Another way of examining the impact of national party soft money on state and local party behavior is to consider how state and local parties spend their funds. The FEC has descriptive data available on the purpose of all disbursements by state or local parties that include at least some hard money. Even a casual look at these data shows the dramatic impact of the national media campaign on the spending patterns of state parties. Table 7.14 shows the total amount of reported spending by Democratic and Republican state and local parties on administrative and generic expenses during 1991–92 and 1995–96. During the 1992 presidential campaign, only about $1 million of the $55 million spent by Democratic state and local parties used "media" or "advertising" as part of the description. For Republicans, only about $30,000 out of $44 million spent used this description. By 1996, however, approximately $58 million of the $158 million spent by state and local Democratic committees (37 percent of the total) included "media" or "advertising" in the description. For Republicans, about $20 million of the $103 million spent (19 percent) used the term. A sudden and significant share of state and local party spending in 1996 was clearly beyond the control of state and local officials nominally responsible for these organizations. Other spending may have been similarly directed from the national level, but the relationships are more difficult to isolate in these cases. While this plainly suggests that the national parties are able to leverage their fund-raising prowess into control of large parts of the party apparatus at other levels, it calls into serious question the notion that soft money raised nationally has a meaningful strengthening impact on the kinds of party activity at other levels anticipated by supporters of the soft money system.

## The Impact of Soft Money Beyond the 1996 Campaign

The conventional wisdom of political professionals is that the creative use of DNC soft money during 1995 was a major step in the successful

Table 7.14

**Portion of Soft Money Administrative Spending Devoted to Media**
(in million $)

|  | State/local Democrats | | State/local Republicans | |
| --- | --- | --- | --- | --- |
|  | 1992 | 1996 | 1992 | 1996 |
| Total administrative spending | 55 | 158 | 44 | 103 |
| Portion devoted to media/advertising | 1 | 58 | 0.03 | 20 |

*Source:* Compiled by the authors from Federal Election Commission's 1996 Disclosure Database on 12/28/98.

reelection of President Clinton. The advertising campaign conducted by the party set the agenda for the actual campaign that followed and allowed the president to emphasize issues and policies that were most favorable for him. As a result, it serves as a textbook for future campaigns and is likely to help define the relationship between elected officials and national parties and between national and state party organizations for years to come.

One premise of the FECA and its precursors dating to the Tillman Act of 1907 is that funds raised in federal elections must be limited, come from allowable sources, and be disclosed in order to prevent both the reality and the perception of corruption. Inherent in this formulation is also a belief that the process of raising, spending, and disclosing campaign funds is honest (i.e., activities that are campaign related are recognized as such and treated accordingly). Over the course of the past twenty years, the demands of capital-intensive campaigns and the professional staff who manage them have come in conflict with both of these principles. Campaigns today begin with series of surveys, focus groups, and tracking polls that assess the mood of targeted groups of voters, leading to the development and implementation of multimedia presentations running from direct mail to broadcast advertising, intended to persuade and mobilize voters. The one thing all these activities share is the need for funds to pay for them. This need for financial resources creates pressure to circumvent the existing limits and restrictions on sources and amounts of funds.

Moreover, a body of case law has developed that seeks to distinguish between specific electioneering messages (i.e., expressly advocating the election or defeat of a clearly identified candidate) and more general political discourse. The First Amendment to the Constitution protects the right to speak freely on political issues, even (and perhaps most important) to challenge the government directly in the context of debate about public policy. Only in narrow instances can political expression be inhibited, and one of them is to prevent corruption or the appearance of corruption via campaign contributions. How society defines the difference between campaigning and public policy advocacy is critical if campaign finance restrictions are to be meaningful. The literal definition that has evolved in the United States (where specific words must be used for courts to consider expression to be electioneering) has combined with the availability of soft money to create a new campaign finance system based on essentially dishonest manipulations of the process. It is exceedingly difficult (and extremely important) to make justifiable distinctions between general political discourse, whose protection under the First Amendment is critical to democratic government, and active campaigning, where the relationship between candidates and donors is potentially troublesome. The combination of party soft money and its use in advertising structured by lawyers to fall outside the definition of electioneering because it failed to use specific terms has eliminated whatever meaningful distinction may have existed before 1996. The result is a system that is fundamentally dishonest, where limitations and restrictions remain on the books but are ignored with disdain by those who practice the art of politics. Couching what are plainly electioneering messages (so transparent that even the creators of the message acknowledge their electioneering purpose) legally defined as nonelectioneering messages, the applicability of the limits and restrictions call into question the honesty of campaigns.

On October 24, 1996, a group of news reporters waited expectantly in the offices of the FEC for the arrival of the pre–general-election disclosure report of the DNC. The report was the focus of much attention because allegations of illegal foreign contributions and other excesses at the DNC were being widely reported. Late in the day, when no report appeared, a call was made to Democratic Party headquarters asking about the report's status. The caller was informed that no report would be forthcoming because the DNC had conducted no candidate-related activities during the first two weeks in October and therefore the DNC judged that no report was required. Irrespective of the legal nuances that may or may not have justified this decision, this act as much as any other demonstrated the contempt for the spirit of the FECA exhibited by major participants in the 1996 campaign. The simple disclosure of campaign finance activity is generally held to be the least controversial element in the Watergate-era reforms. Indeed, an alternative to comprehensive campaign reform favored by some conservatives is simple disclosure without limits and restrictions. In this case, however, for reasons that were never clearly presented, a national party organization decided that even disclosure was more regulation than it could or should endure.

Ironically, just a month before, the nation was outraged when Baltimore Orioles' second baseman Roberto Alomar spat in the face of umpire John Hirshbeck during an argument at home plate. The failure of a national party organization to submit to the routine public disclosure requirements of the FECA is functionally the same as spitting on the umpire. The ensuing media protest fostered by suspicion of what the DNC might be hiding led to several sleepless nights at DNC headquarters and the eventual submission of the report. While not a momentous or scandalous event in and of itself, it was a striking manifestation of the pervasive attitude among political professionals that campaign finance has become a game without rules—even though the provisions of the FECA remain, technically at least, the law of the land. The cynicism required for this kind of behavior is apparent to the electorate and helps to reinforce the skepticism of all things political that is found throughout the public during this era. While technically the outcome of the legal battles begun during the financing of the 1996 election are yet to be determined, the impact of the conduct of the campaign on the political system will not be decided in federal court. The raising and spending of unregulated funds by party organizations in 1996 is the most compelling argument yet for reform of the existing process. Whether additional restrictions are deemed necessary and can be constructed in a constitutionally defensible manner or whether the remains of the FECA are simply removed from the books, some legislative change is required if honesty is to be restored to federal campaign finance.

## Acknowledgment

The material presented here represents the view of the authors and does not reflect the position of the FEC. The financial data in this chapter, unless noted otherwise, come from FEC press releases, the FEC 1996 Annual Report, and the FEC's 1996 Disclosure Database.

## 8

DIANA DWYRE

# Interest Groups and Issue Advocacy in 1996

*The campaign finance system put in place following the Watergate scandals has been washed away. Though still on the books, campaign finance laws have been replaced by the law of the jungle.*

—Fred Wertheimer,
former president of Common Cause,
November 3, 1996

The activities of candidates, parties, interest groups, and wealthy individuals led many to draw the same conclusion as Fred Wertheimer that the 1996 election season was the "dirtiest ever" (Wertheimer 1996, C1). This chapter is an examination of the campaign finance activities of interest groups[1] during the 1996 elections, and how a variety of groups managed to bend the campaign finance laws without actually breaking them. Indeed, much of this activity fell outside the campaign finance regulatory system and therefore was unlimited and shielded from public scrutiny. These activities may impact American representative democracy negatively by removing responsibility for campaign conduct from candidates, the only political actors who can be held accountable on election day.

Interest-group campaign finance activities in 1996 helped usher in a new era in the financing of federal campaigns, a "postreform" era that rendered the campaign finance reforms of the 1970s virtually meaningless. The high stakes of the 1995–96 election cycle, when control of the Congress hung in the balance for the first time in decades and both parties appeared to have a shot at the presidency, help explain the willingness of political actors to push the envelope on campaign finance. Moreover, the existing campaign finance regulations themselves had become so restrictive that they gave political actors strong incentives to create new channels to collect and distribute millions of dollars.

Interest groups and political action committees (PACs) spent record amounts on federal campaigns during the 1995–96 election cycle. Much of this stepped-up campaign activity was consistent with past practices. For example, PACs continued to give primarily to incumbents and candidates in open-seat races. Yet some of the campaign finance practices of the 1995–96 election cycle were more unusual. For example, interest groups gave political parties record amounts of soft money for the 1996 elections. Soft money, or nonfederal money, is not subject to the source, fund-raising, and contribution limits of the Federal Election Campaign Act (FECA). Thus, soft money can be raised and spent in very large sums and from sources not permitted to make direct campaign contributions, such as corporations and labor unions. Interest groups also spent millions of dollars on issue advocacy communications. Issue advocacy spending is exempt from FECA regulations and is not reported to the Federal Election Commission (FEC) because it is not technically campaign communication. As long as issue advocacy communications do not expressly call for the election or defeat of a particular candidate, interest groups and parties can use unregulated and unlimited funds to pay for them and are not required to report such expenditures to the FEC.

For these reasons, total interest-group spending during the 1995–96 election cycle is difficult to gauge. We do know that regulated interest-group spending—that is, PAC contributions to candidates and parties, PAC independent spending, and PAC organizational spending—totaled $429.9 million, an 11 percent increase over 1994 PAC spending (FEC 1997d). Organized interests, especially corporations and labor unions, also made soft money contributions to political parties. Soft money contributions for 1995–96 totaled $252 million, but it is not clear how much of this money came from organized interests and how much of it came from wealthy individuals (FEC 1997a), many of whom, such as corporate CEOs, were connected to institutions that give soft money. Finally, interest-group spending for issue advocacy communications and other unreported and unregulated activities reached at least $70 million (Marcus and Babcock 1997, A1). Taken together, the various types of spending by interest groups during the 1996 election cycle totaled at least $752 million.

Many of the campaign finance techniques used in 1995 and 1996 have drawn a great deal of criticism for violating the spirit, if not the letter, of the FECA. These criticisms have fueled more intense calls for campaign finance reform. While many of these activities have been documented by the media and were investigated by the House, the Senate, and the Justice Department, there has been little analysis of how and why interest groups raised and spent money in these ways or of the money's impact and consequences. In this chapter, I analyze the campaign finance practices of organized interests and PACs during the 1995–96 election cycle (see chapter 7 for the role of political parties).

## A New Era in Campaign Finance Activity

Many of the 1996 campaign finance practices were fundamentally new techniques that mark a new era in campaign finance. According to Frank Sorauf, "two clear sub-periods can be marked in the flow of money" under the FECA (1992, 13). The first sub-period, from 1974 to 1984, was characterized by rapid growth in the number of PACs and the level of campaign spending. The second period occurred after 1984 when the growth in federal funds leveled off, and was characterized by the redistribution of campaign money to incumbents. Sorauf notes that "behind the emerging stability in American campaign finance is an impressive amount of political learning and adaptation" (1992, 19). In the 1995–96 election cycle, political actors took this learning and adaptation to a new level, beginning a third sub-period in the flow of campaign money in federal elections, one characterized by interest-group and party innovation in directing resources to influence elections. Many of these innovations mark the near collapse of the FECA, with extensive campaign finance activity occurring outside these regulations. It is this departure that defines the "postreform" era (see Herrnson and Dwyre 1999; Herrnson 1998b).

In the postreform era, interest groups and political parties engage in many "indirect campaigning" activities (Faucheux 1998, 21), that is, campaign finance activities that are not directly controlled by the candidates themselves. Such activities have caused major changes in the *sources* of campaign funds for American elections, shifting the nexus of control over individual campaigns away from candidates and toward interest groups and political parties. Moreover, much of this fund-raising and spending was not covered by the campaign finance regulatory system and was thus unlimited and not reported to the public.

While some of the campaign finance practices may be similar to past activities, such as the use of independent expenditures by PACs, increases or changes in these activities affect the larger campaign finance picture. For example, if PACs and interest groups spend substantially more in House districts, and political party spending stays flat or increases only slightly, then the *balance* of PAC and party funds changes, and the amount spent by these other political actors relative to candidate spending also shifts. Such changes in the balance of funds will affect which type of candidates receives more funds, so that if PAC spending increases, incumbents are likely to benefit, and the gap between incumbent and challenger funding will likely increase, further decreasing the competitiveness of these elections.

After a brief overview of the means by which interest groups participate in federal elections, the various interest-group campaign finance developments of 1995–96 are examined in turn and then discussed more generally. Yet it is not enough to document these new developments. It is important to consider their impact on federal elections and their consequences for American representative democracy. Therefore, this chapter concludes with an examination of these issues.

## How Organized Interests Participate in
## Federal Elections

The 1974 FECA, its amendments, and various court and FEC rulings govern the activities of organized interests in federal elections, although there had been restrictions on corporate campaign finance activity since 1907 and labor union campaign finance activity since 1943. The FECA now prohibits labor unions, corporations, and many other groups from making campaign contributions directly to federal candidates. Moreover, interest groups are required to conduct all federal campaign activity through political action committees (an organization qualifies as a PAC by raising money from at least fifty donors and spending it on five or more federal candidates). Therefore, the rise of the modern PAC is a direct result of the FECA.

Political action committees may accept no more than $5,000 per year from an individual, another PAC, or a party committee. The FECA allows a PAC to contribute $5,000 to a congressional candidate for each phase of the election cycle (i.e., $5,000 for the primary, $5,000 for the general election, and another $5,000 if there is a runoff election). A PAC may contribute a maximum of $5,000 to a candidate for a presidential nomination and another $5,000 to a presidential candidate in the general election who opts not to take any federal matching funds. Since presidential candidates are provided public matching funds for individual but not PAC contributions for their nomination contests, the regulations encourage presidential candidates to seek individual rather than PAC contributions.

For the general election, presidential candidates who receive public funding are prohibited from accepting contributions from any source, including PACs. Every major-party presidential candidate since 1976 has accepted public funding, and PACs have thus focused most of their efforts on congressional elections rather than presidential contests. An exception is the rise of leadership PACs, whereby presidential hopefuls have sponsored their own PACs to cover expenses incurred before officially declaring their candidacies (see Corrado 1992, ch. 4). Generally, however, PACs concentrate their campaign finance activities on House and Senate contests; thus this chapter deals primarily with interest-group and PAC activity in congressional races.

Political action committees also may make independent expenditures for or against candidates for federal office. These expenditures must be made without the knowledge or consent of the candidates or their campaigns. Independent expenditures are not limited, but they must be paid for with funds regulated by the FECA and must be reported to the FEC (see below).

Additionally, PACs may contribute a maximum of $15,000 per year to the federal accounts of each of the national party committees.[2] The parties can then use these funds for direct contributions to candidates and coordinated expenditures made on behalf of federal candidates. A new use for party federal dollars was approved in 1996, when the Supreme Court ruled that parties, not just PACs and individuals, can make independent expenditures (*Colorado Republican Federal Campaign Committee* v. *FEC*, 518 U.S. 604 [1996]).

These are the regulated ways by which interest groups may participate in financial activities designed to influence federal elections. Yet, as we later see, organized interests spent enormous amounts of money on activities that are not directly regulated by federal election law, and some of which are not reported to the FEC, for public scrutiny and checking for compliance with the law. These activities, including soft money and issue advocacy, best characterize the postreform era of campaign finance activity.

### Organized Interests in the 1996 Elections

The intensified competition that characterized the 1996 elections led interest groups, parties, and candidates to raise record amounts for campaign activities. Political action committees raised $437.4 million during the 1995–96 election season, a 12 percent increase over 1994 (FEC 1997d). Yet this amount does not reflect all of the money organized interests raised and spent because only PACs are required to report their financial activities to the FEC.

Corporations, labor unions, nonprofit groups, and interest groups with or without PACs all spent money during the 1996 election season, and they all claimed that their spending did not expressly advocate the election or defeat of clearly identified candidates and therefore was not campaigning activity. Nevertheless, much of this money was spent in ways that in effect *did* influence federal elections. Thus much of the campaign finance activity in 1996 occurred outside the regulations that govern federal campaign finance and was hidden from public view.

The *Washington Post* estimates that at least $70 million in unreported and unregulated spending was conducted by interest groups during the 1995–96 cycle (Marcus and Babcock 1997, A1). But because this spending is not reported to the FEC, it is impossible to determine exactly how much money flowed outside the regulated channels. Interest-group campaign activity that is regulated by the FECA and reported to the FEC will be considered first (i.e., PAC contributions and independent expenditures), followed by an examination of campaign finance activities outside the federal campaign finance system (i.e., soft money, issue advocacy, and voter guides).

### PAC Contributions to Candidates and Parties

The most conventional method for interest groups to participate in the campaign finance system is to form a PAC and make contributions directly to candidates and parties. This spending is limited by the FECA and reported to the FEC (see Table 8.1). Political action com-

Table 8.1

**PAC Contributions to Candidates and Parties, 1995–1996** (in million $)

|                         | Democratic | Republican | Total |
|-------------------------|-----------|-----------|-------|
| Senate candidates       | 19.4      | 36.1      | 55.5  |
| Incumbents              | 7.5       | 21.2      | 28.7  |
| Challengers             | 2.8       | 4.6       | 7.4   |
| Open seat               | 9.1       | 10.3      | 19.4  |
| House candidates        | 79.4      | 79.7      | 159.1 |
| Incumbents              | 51.7      | 65.7      | 117.4 |
| Challengers             | 16.7      | 4.9       | 21.6  |
| Open seat               | 10.9      | 9.1       | 20.0  |
| Presidential candidates | 0.03      | 2.4       | 2.43  |
| Political parties       | 19.2      | 13.8      | 33.0  |

*Source:* Federal Election Commission 1997a; Federal Election Commission 1997b.

mittees increased their direct contributions in 1996. Presidential candidates collect very little in PAC money relative to the amounts they receive from individuals because there are no matching funds available for PAC contributions. Indeed, direct PAC contributions constituted only 1 percent of the total money raised by presidential candidates in the 1996 primary season, about $2.5 million (Federal Election Commission 1996a).

Political action committee contributions to House and Senate candidates were much more substantial. Contributions from PACs to House and Senate candidates totaled $201.4 million for the 1995–96 cycle, up $21.8 million over the 1993–94 cycle. The increase was especially large in PAC spending on House races, which jumped over 19 percent from $134.5 million in 1994 to $160.6 million in 1996 (Federal Election Commission 1997d, 2).

Moreover, for the first time in many years, PACs contributed more to Republican than to Democratic congressional candidates. Republican Senate candidates received more in PAC contributions than Democratic Senate candidates for the first time since 1986, when the GOP last controlled the Senate. Republican House candidates received more PAC contributions than their Democratic counterparts for the first time since the FEC began tracking such contributions in 1978. Yet the disparity between the two parties was not as great as it had been when the Democrats controlled both the House and Senate after 1986. In 1996, Democratic and Republican candidates each took about 50 percent of all PAC contributions to House candidates, while the split was

67 percent for the Democrats and 33 percent for the Republicans in the 1994 elections. This shift in PAC contributions to the GOP reflects not only a shift in power on Capitol Hill after the 1994 elections but also a synchronization of some PACs' ideologies with their giving strategies. After years of giving to Democrats because they controlled Congress, business and corporate PACs now give more to the party that offers a policy agenda more consistent with their own. This trend is expected to continue as long as the GOP maintains majority control of Congress.

As one might expect, PACs also continued to give the vast majority of their contributions to incumbent House and Senate candidates, yet to a slightly lesser extent than in previous elections. Incumbents received 67 percent of PAC contributions for the 1996 elections, while they received 72 percent for 1994, 72 percent for 1992, 79 percent for 1990, and 74 percent for 1988. Challengers collected only 15 percent of PAC contributions, and open-seat candidates got 18 percent in 1996, a slight increase for challengers over past years (Federal Election Commission 1997d). The slight decrease in PAC contributions to incumbents probably reflects the high stakes of the 1996 elections, where PACs saw opportunities to elect new senators and House members who agreed more with their policy interests.

Finally, PACs contribute to political parties. Democratic Party committees received $19.2 million, or 9 percent of their receipts from PACs in 1996, up over $4 million from the last presidential election year. Republican Party committees raised $13.8 million from PACs, only 3 percent of their total receipts, but a $9.2 million increase over 1992 PAC receipts (Federal Election Commission 1997a, 1). The lower PAC total for the Republican Party reflects the party's wealthier constituency, which allows it to draw on many more wealthy contributors than the Democrats.

Yet, these PAC contribution figures do not tell the whole story. They only reveal the money given by PACs directly to candidates and parties. Organized interests spent millions more in other, less direct ways, and much of this spending was neither limited in amount or source nor disclosed to the FEC.

## Indirect Campaigning by Organized Interests in 1996

During the 1995–96 cycle, many interest groups spent millions more than the direct contributions they made to House, Senate, and presidential candidates and to political parties. Many of the activities were unreported and unregulated. The indirect campaigning that has come to define contemporary elections includes the increased use of independent expenditures for or against candidates by interest groups and parties, the big jump in interest-group soft money contributions to political parties (especially from corporations and labor unions), and the exponential growth of issue advocacy campaigns by both interest groups and parties.

## Independent Expenditures

An independent expenditure is an expenditure made by an interest group's PAC, an individual, or, since the 1996 Colorado case by a party committee, to influence the outcome of an election without coordination, consultation, or at the suggestion of a candidate or his or her campaign. Since an independent expenditure is a clear attempt to influence an election, it is subject to regulation and reporting requirements. It is a campaign communication made via television, radio, or the mail that *expressly advocates* the election or defeat of a clearly identified candidate. Express advocacy has been defined narrowly by the Supreme Court to include only those communications that use clear indications of advocacy with phrases such as "vote for" or "vote against." Such phrases of express advocacy may be used in an independent expenditure but not in an issue advocacy communication (see below).

While PACs, parties, and individuals must raise the money for independent expenditures in limited increments, independent expenditure spending is not limited, for the Supreme Court ruled in 1976 (*Buckley* v. *Valeo*, 424 U.S. 1 [1976]) that legal limits could be placed only on campaign contributions but not on campaign expenditures. Independent expenditures are reported to the FEC and are regulated by the FECA, for independent expenditures are clearly communications that contain express advocacy.

In 1996 PACs spent more on independent expenditures for and against congressional candidates than they had since 1978, when the FEC began collecting these data (see Figure 8.1). Moreover, this increased independent expenditure spending was characterized by an increase in expenditures *against* candidates, signaling a shift in tone in these campaign communications from positive to negative.

Yet, relative to the amount PACs spend on direct contributions to

Figure 8.1. **Independent Expenditures for and against House and Senate Candidates, 1980–1996**

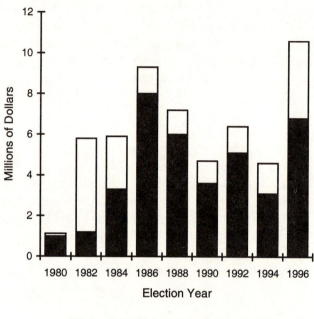

Election Year

☐ Independent Expenditures Against Candidates
■ Independent Expenditures For Candidates

congressional candidates, independent expenditures still constitute a small portion of the PAC spending that is regulated by the FECA and reported to the FEC (see Figure 8.2). In the presidential campaigns, PACs spent only $1.4 million on independent expenditures in 1996, a drop from $4 million in 1992 (Federal Election Commission 1997d, 2).

Despite this relatively low level of independent expenditure spending, it is trending upward in congressional races. Thus, many observers are concerned that independent expenditures are taking some of the control over the dialogue of campaigns away from candidates, the only participants in the electoral process who are held accountable on election day. But the real growth in interest-group campaign finance activity is in the spending that occurs outside the regulations altogether, the millions of soft money dollars that interest groups give to political party committees and the millions of unregulated dollars spent on issue advocacy campaigns. These campaign finance activities add signifi-

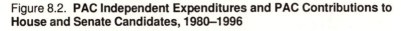

Figure 8.2. **PAC Independent Expenditures and PAC Contributions to House and Senate Candidates, 1980–1996**

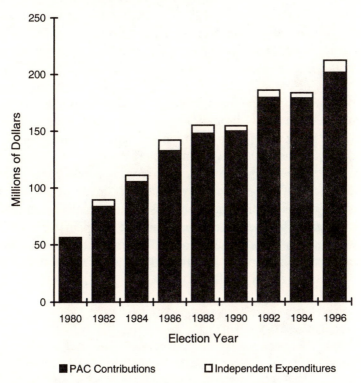

cantly to the amounts spent indirectly by noncandidate groups and further heighten concerns over who controls the dialogue of democracy.

## Organized Interests and Soft Money

*Soft money* (or nonfederal money) is money raised and spent outside the regulations that govern the federal campaign finance system. It can be given by interest groups, corporations, labor unions, or individuals to political party committees in unlimited amounts. Soft money givers do not have to set up separate PACs to make soft money donations. Indeed, corporations and labor unions may give soft money to parties, but they must make direct campaign contributions or independent expenditures through their PACs.

Under the FECA, political parties may not use soft money to promote federal candidates. Soft money may be used to pay for a portion of a party's overhead expenses and for *party-building activities*. Party-building activities include supporting state and local candidates and parties and promoting the party or its candidates as a class without mentioning specific names (e.g., voter registration or get-out-the-vote drives and generic media such as "Vote Republican, For a Change"). Soft money also may be used to pay for a portion of shared expenses that benefit both federal and nonfederal candidates, although the portion of the expense that promotes federal candidates must be paid for with hard money (i.e., federal money subject to contribution and spending limits as well as disclosure requirements).

In 1996, however, much of the soft money spending was virtually indistinguishable from hard money spending. For instance, it was difficult to tell if an advertisement was an issue advocacy ad paid for with soft money or an independent expenditure ad paid for with hard money, for both types of ads appeared to urge a vote for or against particular candidates. The Republican National Committee (RNC) used soft money to pay for this ad (Beck et al. 1997, 54):

> Clinton: I will not raise taxes on the middle class.
> Announcer: We heard this a lot.
> Clinton: We gotta give middle class tax relief no matter what else we do.
> Announcer: Six months later, he gave us the largest tax increase in history. Higher income taxes, income taxes on social security benefits, more payroll taxes. Under Clinton, the typical American family now pays over $1,500 more in federal taxes. A big price to pay for his broken promises. Tell President Clinton: You can't afford higher taxes for more wasteful spending.

While this ad does not expressly tell voters to "vote against" President Clinton, it does send a powerful message that encourages such action.

Soft money is easier to raise than hard money because it can be raised in large, unlimited amounts, while parties must raise hard money in small increments. Moreover, soft money allows parties to reserve their relatively scarce hard money for direct contributions to candidates and independent expenditures (Dwyre 1996). The parties have been using soft money since at least the mid-1980s, yet it was not until the 1996 elections that the parties' soft money fund-raising reached high levels, its sources came under suspicion, and it was regarded as corrupt.

The primary sources of party soft money were corporations, labor unions, and wealthy individuals. In 1996 the parties raised substantially more in soft money than they had since 1991, when the FEC began collecting soft money data (Figure 8.3). The Democratic national party committees raised $123.9 million in soft money, a 242 percent increase over the last presidential election in 1992. Republican national party committees raised $138.2 million in soft money, up 178 percent over 1992 (Federal Election Commission 1997a, 2).

Some of America's leading corporations and labor organizations and their leaders contributed the lion's share of this money (see Table 8.2). For instance, the top soft money contributor to Democratic Party committees was Joseph E. Seagram and Sons (a beer, wine, and liquor company) and its executives, giving a total of $1,180,700 during the 1995–96 cycle. The tobacco firm of Philip Morris Company and its executives were the top Republican Party soft money contributors, with a total of $2,517,518 in soft money contributions (Common Cause 1997). Table 8.2 shows the top-ten soft money contributors to each party for the 1996 elections.

Soft money is given in very large increments, which is one reason it is so controversial. Soft money contributions are not limited, raising the potential for corruption. The argument is that big contributors may receive favorable treatment in exchange for their large soft money donations to political parties. Halting the unregulated flow of large amounts of corporate, labor union, and other money was one of the goals of the reforms instituted in the FECA. Soft money has all but undone these reforms. Indeed, the Democratic Party's soft money fund-raising practices became a significant issue in the last weeks of the 1996 elections, and the increasing size of soft money contributions and the sources of these donations made soft money the number-one campaign finance reform item after the 1996 elections (see chapter 9). Moreover, soft money donations to political parties have not only skyrocketed but also have come to constitute an increasingly larger portion of interest-group donations to political parties. Figure 8.3 shows both of these trends.

Some of the soft money that the parties raised from interest groups, corporations, and labor unions was redistributed to other groups. For instance, the parties funded a number of tax-exempt organizations that

Table 8.2

**Top Soft Money Contributors to Political Party Committees, 1995–1996** (in dollars)

| Democratic Party | | Republican Party | |
|---|---|---|---|
| Contributor | Amount | Contributor | Amount |
| Joseph E. Seagram & Sons Inc./MCA Inc. (beer, wine, liquor) | 1,180,700 | Philip Morris Co. Inc. (tobacco) | 2,517,518 |
| Communications Workers of America (labor union) | 1,128,425 | RJR Nabisco Inc. (tobacco) | 1,188,175 |
| AFSCME (labor union) | 1,091,050 | American Financial Group (insurance) | 794,000 |
| Walt Disney Co. (entertainment) | 997,050 | Atlantic Richfield Co. (oil and gas) | 766,506 |
| United Food & Commercial Workers (labor union) | 714,050 | News Corp. (communications) | 744,700 |
| Revlon/MacAndrews & Forbes Holding Inc. (securities and investments) | 673,250 | Union Pacific Corp./Southern Pacific Corp. (transportation) | 707,393 |
| Lazard Freres & Co. (securities and investments) | 617,000 | Joseph E. Seagram & Sons Inc./MCA Inc. (beer, wine, liquor) | 682,145 |
| Laborers International Union of No. America (labor union) | 610,400 | Brown & Williamson Tobacco Corp. (tobacco) | 635,000 |
| Loral Corp. (aerospace and defense) | 606,500 | U.S. Tobacco Co. (tobacco) | 559,253 |
| MCI Telecommunications Corp. (communications) | 593,603 | AT&T (communications) | 546,440 |

*Source:* Common Cause 1997.
*Note:* Amounts include contributions from executives and/or subsidiaries. These figures differ slightly from those reported in Table 7.11, which were compiled by the Center of Responsive Politics.

Figure 8.3. **Party PAC and Soft Money Receipts, 1992–1996**

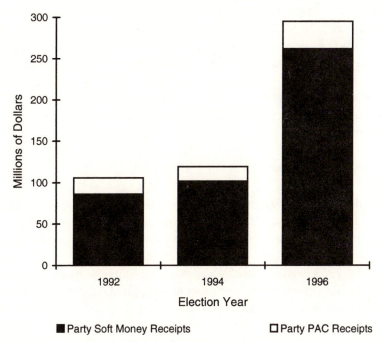

are, by law, not permitted to engage in partisan campaign activities. The RNC redistributed about $6 million to other groups in this way. Most of that soft money, $4.6 million, was given to Americans for Tax Reform, an antitax organization with ties to RNC chairman Haley Barbour, to conduct a direct mail and telephone bank operation in 150 congressional districts (Committee on Governmental Affairs, United States Senate 1998, 5928). The RNC gave the National Right to Life Committee $650,000, which used the money to run advertisements that benefited Republican candidates (Committee on Governmental Affairs, United States Senate 1998, 6033). The Democratic National Committee (DNC) redistributed only $185,000 to nonprofit groups such as the Rainbow Coalition to mobilize minority voters, who generally vote Democratic (Committee on Governmental Affairs, United States Senate 1998, 5927; Herrnson 1998b, 155).

What is disturbing about these soft-money transfers to nonprofit organizations, and what caused the Senate Committee on Governmental Affairs to investigate them, is the fact that these nonprofit organizations are tax exempt and therefore are not permitted to engage in partisan campaign activities. It now appears that many of their election-related activities indeed *were* partisan and/or expressly advocated the election or defeat of clearly identified candidates, even if they did not use words such as "vote for" or "vote against." Thus, since these organizations are tax exempt, their political activities were, in effect, subsidized by the federal treasury, while other interest groups that legally engaged in partisan campaign activities were required to pay federal taxes.

### Interest-Group Issue Advocacy Campaigns

Issue advocacy campaigns were perhaps the most controversial campaign finance activity of 1996. Yet these are also the most difficult activities to track and measure because the groups that run them are not subject to any financial limits or disclosure requirements.

In the 1976 case of *Buckley* v. *Valeo*, the Supreme Court ruled that contribution and spending limits would be applied only to expenditures that "in express terms advocate the election or defeat of a clearly identified candidate for federal office" (424 U.S. 1 [1976], 44). The Court explained in a footnote that limitations would apply only to communications that contain express words of advocacy, such as "vote for or against," "elect," "Smith for Congress," or "defeat" (424 U.S. 1 [1976], footnote 52). If a communication does not contain any of these *magic words*, that is, if it does not expressly advocate the election or defeat of a clearly identified candidate, it is not considered a campaign communication and therefore is not subject to contribution and spending limits or to disclosure requirements. Such communications have come to be known as "issue advocacy" ads, because they are designed to educate the public about certain policy issues or about a candidate's position on a particular issue.

As one might expect, this test of express advocacy has caused a good deal of controversy because the Supreme Court's interpretation of express advocacy is so narrow that virtually any communication by a noncandidate group that does not include such phrases as "vote for" or "vote against" falls outside the definition of express advocacy. Anything outside that definition is considered issue advocacy, and it may be paid for with unregulated, unlimited, and undisclosed interest-group funds or party soft money dollars.[3]

Therefore, the Court's interpretation of express advocacy leaves quite a lot of room for groups to run television and radio ads that look and sound like campaign ads but technically are not considered campaign ads. So if a group can achieve virtually the same effect with an issue advocacy ad, why run an express advocacy ad that is constrained by contribution limits and disclosure requirements? In 1996 a number of corporations, labor unions, interest groups, tax-exempt organizations, and political party committees came to this conclusion and spent millions of dollars on issue advocacy campaigns that were unregulated and therefore shielded from public scrutiny.

The Annenberg Public Policy Center of the University of Pennsylvania found that over two dozen interest groups and parties ran issue advocacy advertisements during the 1995–96 election cycle and that they spent an estimated $135 million to $150 million on them (Beck et al. 1997, 3). Candidates themselves spent about $400 million on campaign advertising, money subject to contribution limits and disclosed to the public. Thus issue advocacy advertising constituted almost one-third as much as candidates spent on communications with the public during the election. The Annenberg Center also found that 41.1 percent of the issue ads run during the 1996 elections were pure attacks, while only 24.3 percent of presidential candidate ads were attack ads (Beck et al. 1997, 9).

Perhaps the most controversial of these issue advocacy campaigns was the AFL-CIO's *Labor '96* effort. The labor federation announced that it would spend $35 million nationally aimed almost exclusively at unseating GOP House members. About $25 million of this went into paid media communications aired in forty-four congressional districts, including the districts of thirty-two of the House Republican freshmen elected in 1994. The remainder was spent on direct mail and other organizing activities (Beck et al. 1997, 10). None of this spending was reported to the FEC because the AFL-CIO's efforts were considered issue advocacy, not express advocacy campaigning. Federal law forbids unions to spend membership dues on political advertising that contains express advocacy, but the AFL-CIO issue advocacy ads and voter guides did not call for the election or defeat of any candidates. So, the union was able to use membership dues to pay for these activities.

Here is an AFL-CIO ad that ran in a number of congressional districts in 1996 (Beck et al. 1997, 10):

Carolyn: My husband and I both work. And next year, we'll have two
children in college. And it will be very hard to put them through, even
with the two incomes.
Announcer: Working families are struggling. But Congressman X voted
with Newt Gingrich to cut college loans, while giving tax breaks to the
wealthy. He even wants to eliminate the Department of Education. Congress will vote again on the budget. Tell Congressman X, don't write
off our children's future.
Carolyn: Tell him, his priorities are all wrong.

While this ad clearly falls outside the narrow definition of express
advocacy, for it does not use magic words such as "vote for" or "vote
against," it does seem likely that it was designed to influence the
outcome of the election.

After some rather public prodding from RNC chairman Haley Barbour, the business community responded to the AFL-CIO's efforts
with a counterattack sponsored by the national Chamber of Commerce
and a group called The Coalition: Americans Working for Real
Change, a coalition of thirty-two business groups formed by the Chamber. Together these groups spent an estimated $7.1 million on issue
advocacy and direct mail to group members (Clymer 1996, B14). The
National Federation of Independent Businesses added about $5 million
in spending on candidates and to train members in political action
(Dine 1996, 20A).

It is impossible to know exactly how much labor and business spent
in unregulated funds on federal races in 1996, for these examples
represent only the most highly publicized cases. We do know, however, that corporate PACs contributed $50.4 million directly to Repub-
lican House and Senate candidates and only $19.1 million to their
Democratic opponents, while labor PACs gave $43.3 million in contri-
butions to House and Senate Democratic candidates and only $3 mil-
lion to GOP candidates (Federal Election Commission 1997d). Yet, the
full extent of labor and business 1996 election activities will never be
known, for we cannot determine how much was spent on issue advocacy activities.

Much of the issue advocacy activity in 1996 occurred in House
districts that featured the nation's closest elections, particularly the
districts of the seventy-three GOP House freshmen up for reelection.
For instance, in Arizona-6, the AFL-CIO spent an estimated

$2,130,638 in television ads from April to November 1996 and The Coalition and the National Republican Congressional Committee responded with over $630,000 in television ads to help GOP freshman J.D. Hayworth, who won by only 1 percent over Democratic challenger Steve Owens (National Republican Congressional Committee 1996a). Clearly, interest groups found a way to direct far more resources to targeted House races than they had in past elections through the use of issue advocacy campaigns.

Other organized interests also spent unregulated and undisclosed money on issue advocacy during the election. Most of the groups that ran issue advocacy campaigns produced communications with clear partisan messages. The Annenberg Center found that 97.2 percent of all issue advocacy ads run in 1996 were partisan in nature, with an even split between the two major parties (Beck et al. 1997, 7). For example, Citizen Action, a tax-exempt grassroots consumer and environmental group, spent $7 million on issue ads, mailings, and telephone calls that were critical of GOP freshmen on environmental issues, education, and Medicare. The Sierra Club spent $6.5 million on issue ads and voter guides, while its PAC gave only $750,000 in contributions to congressional candidates[4] (Marcus 1996b, A1). The Sierra Club issue advocacy communications targeted primarily freshman Republican members of Congress. The Ralph Nader–sponsored group, Public Citizen, also ran issue advocacy ads and sponsored video voter guides in seven House districts in 1996 (Noel 1996, A21).

The Coalition for Our Children's Future, a group established by RNC chairman Haley Barbour to promote the Republicans' legislative agenda, spent over $700,000 on issue advocacy media campaigns, mailings, and telephone banks in the final weeks of the election. The television ads were paid for by an anonymous contributor (Beck et al. 1997, 30). Citizens for Reform, a tax-exempt group run by a conservative Republican activist who also runs the Conservative Campaign Fund, spent an estimated $2 million on issue advocacy ads against Democratic candidates in fifteen congressional districts during October and November of 1996. One of the Citizens for Reform issue advocacy ads was an attack ad that accused Democratic candidate Bill Yellowtail of Montana of being a convicted criminal and a wife beater. While all these groups ran issue advocacy campaigns that did not contain express advocacy as narrowly defined by the Supreme Court, their communications were targeted in a partisan manner, and their messages featured the name and/or likeness of candidates running for federal office.

Producers of issue advocacy ads are careful *not* to advocate the election or defeat of a federal candidate expressly, and, in fact, the ads generally do not refer to the election at all. All issue advocacy ads mention some issue or issues; the most popular ones in 1996 were Medicare, "big-labor bosses," and welfare. Many urge citizens to call an officeholder or a party to tell them to do something, such as vote a certain way or support a certain policy.

The "call your elected representative" appeal in issue advocacy ads actually may have mobilized some citizens to lobby their senators or House members, but the more likely reaction of viewers was to gain the negative or positive impression of the candidate highlighted in the ad. Indeed, 31.3 percent of the issue advocacy ads that suggested some action did not provide a phone number or an address of the appropriate person, group, or party to contact (Beck et al. 1997, 7). Moreover, negative issue ads often featured the familiar ominous background music, code words such as "liberal" and "radical," and grainy, un-flattering black-and-white pictures so common in campaign attack ads. Positive issue ads used cheery music, code words such as "trust," and family-values pictures, while praising some policy stand of an official or party (Herrnson and Dwyre 1999). These are exactly the same tech-niques used in conventional campaign television ads (West 1997, 4–9; Jamieson 1992), making issue advocacy ads virtually indistinguishable from campaign ads. Therefore, issue advocacy advertisements aired during the campaign season clearly have the potential of influencing voters' opinions of candidates running for office. Indeed, why else would interest groups and parties run them?

Another way organized interests can spend unlimited, unregulated, and undisclosed money without dipping into the scarce funds raised in small increments by their PACs is by distributing *voter guides*. Voter guides can be paid for directly out of union membership or corporate funds, and the amounts spent do not have to be reported to the FEC as long as the voter guide does not expressly advocate the election or defeat of a clearly identified candidate. Interest groups claim that voter guides are not campaigning but issue advocacy, that the guides are nonpartisan attempts to educate voters about candidates' stands on issues. Groups have distributed printed voter guides for years. In 1996, more groups distributed voter guides, and some groups improved on the voter-guide idea by airing "electronic" or "video" voter guides on television.

Voter guides have been controversial because the interest groups that use them claim the guides are not campaign activity. Yet, voter guides make it quite clear which candidate agrees with the interest group and therefore which candidate should be supported in the election. Indeed, voter guides are most often partisan, such as those used by the Christian Coalition that favor GOP candidates almost exclusively and those used by labor unions that virtually always benefit Democratic candidates.

The Christian Coalition voter guides distributed in churches across the country have long been controversial, particularly because of the group's application for tax-exempt status. In 1996 the Christian Coalition distributed more than 54 million voter guides that favorably portrayed conservative Republican candidates (Herrnson 1998b, 161). Other groups that distributed voter guides in 1996 include the National Federation of Independent Business, which mailed almost 240,000 voter guides that favored probusiness candidates; the National Rifle Association, which sent voter guides to its large membership; and the AFL-CIO, which distributed 11.5 million voter guides in 114 House, 15 Senate, and 2 gubernatorial elections (Herrnson 1998b, 160–61). One 30-second long AFL-CIO video voter guide that ran in Arizona was part of the labor union's "working family" voter-guide campaign:

> Announcer: Where do the candidates stand? Congressman J.D. Hayworth voted to cut Medicare funding by $270 billion. Steve Owens opposes those Medicare cuts. When it comes to Medicare, there is a difference.

Viewers were then asked to call a union information number to get printed voter guides that address a number of issues (Marcus 1996b, A16). It should be clear which candidate merits one's vote.

Video voter guides were a new development in 1996. With televised voter guides, interest groups enjoy a far wider reach for their messages than printed voter guides can provide and therefore potentially a far greater influence over the outcome of an election. Printed voter guides distributed only to a group's membership or in churches by the Christian Coalition reach an audience that most likely already agrees with the issue positions presented by the group. Video voter guides do not merely preach to the choir, but attempt to swell its ranks.

Voter guides feature information about both candidates in a race and one or more issues selected by an interest group, not by one of the candidates. An interest group therefore can take some control of the campaign dialogue by partially defining the issue or issues around which the campaign will revolve. When third-party campaigners such as interest groups exercise a great degree of influence over the campaign dialogue, the electoral contest becomes less of a competition between two candidates and more of a battle between interest groups, or worse, a campaign waged by a single special-interest group against one of the candidates.

Indeed, interest groups and parties nearly outspent some candidates in 1996. For example, in the twenty-first congressional district in Pennsylvania (Erie and surrounding areas), where GOP freshman Phil English was defending his seat against Democratic challenger Ron DiNicola, interest groups and parties spent at least $1.4 million on both regulated and unregulated activities in the district, and the two candidates spent $1.7 million combined (Gugliotta and Chinoy 1997, A1). Most of the interest-group and party money was spent on media, no doubt exceeding the $833,000 spent collectively on media by the two candidates. A local television station manager in Erie captured the sentiment that these other campaigners were like modern-day "carpetbaggers" in this race: "I have a real problem as a citizen to have outside influences from Philadelphia, Washington, wherever. . . . They have no interest after the election in how the economy and business of our community will be affected" (Gugliotta and Chinoy 1997, A1).

Indeed, issue advocacy ads are not always welcomed by the candidates they are intended to help. For example, in the Pennsylvania race mentioned above, the National Republican Congressional Committee sponsored an antiunion ad that featured a heavy-set "union boss" in a smoke-filled room reaching into a briefcase and handing stacks of cash across a table. The narrator announced, "The big labor bosses in Washington, D.C., have a big scheme to buy the Congress. . . . They've spent $150,000 here on ads favoring Ron DiNicola" [the Democratic challenger for the House seat] (Gugliotta and Chinoy 1997, A1; National Republican Congressional Committee 1996b). The incumbent, Republican Representative Phil English, did not appreciate the party's help: "If they had asked me, I would have told those guys that attacking big labor is not a particularly effective strategy in Erie" (Gugliotta and Chinoy 1997, A1).

Mike Enzi, the Republican candidate for the seat of retiring U.S. Senator Alan Simpson (R-Wyo.), was stung by an issue advocacy ad as well. The National Republican Senatorial Committee ran an ad criticizing his opponent for supporting a state sales tax increase, but Enzi had also supported the tax increase as a member of the state Senate Revenue Committee (Obey 1996, 11). As candidates lose control of more and more of the campaign dialogue to outside campaigners, such as interest groups and parties, they may be hit more often by friendly fire.

## Some Explanations

Why were there so many interest-group campaign finance developments in the 1995–96 election cycle, particularly the huge amount of spending that fell outside the regulatory reach of the FECA? One reason is the FECA itself. Most of the limitations on raising and spending campaign funds were set in 1974 and have not been changed since then. For example, the amounts that individuals can contribute to PACs have not increased, nor has the maximum that PACs can contribute directly to candidates. The 1974 FECA Amendments limit PAC contributions to $5,000 per candidate per election, but that $5,000 had a real value of less than $2,000 by 1996. Indeed, many campaign professionals argue that the cost of campaigns has risen at a faster rate than the general cost of living. Thus, contribution limits have not kept pace with the true cost of running campaigns for office. It is no wonder interest groups and PACs looked for new ways to direct funds to their favored candidates in 1996.

Another reason that organized interests raised so much more money (both regulated and unregulated) and found new, innovative ways to spend it is that the stakes were higher in 1996 than they had been in a very long time. Moreover, all involved realized the elections' importance, unlike 1994, when virtually every political observer was surprised when the GOP took control of Congress. For the first time in decades, partisan control of the House and Senate was realistically and obviously up for grabs. The race for the White House appeared to be competitive as well. Furthermore, the 1996 elections were to determine who would control the outcome of policy battles over major issues such as Medicare, health care reform, environmental policy, welfare reform, and education. With such important and far-reaching policy areas under consideration, many different interest groups and both parties felt compelled to pull out all the stops in order to influence the outcome of the 1996 elections. When the stakes are this high, the players will look for new ways to increase gains and cut losses. Out of such a competitive environment grows innovation (Kolodny and Dwyre 1998).

These conditions motivated interest groups and parties to behave differently under the campaign finance regime in place since 1974. This chapter has shown that their behavior during the 1995–96 election cycle differed in significant ways from their past campaign behavior. Their campaign innovations are different enough from past practices to constitute the beginning of a new era in the federal campaign finance regulation. The 1996 elections ushered in the postreform era whereby the reforms of the 1970s all but collapsed.

This new stage in the evolution of the campaign finance system is characterized by changes in the *sources* of campaign funds. The shift has occurred on two fronts. First, noncandidate campaigners (i.e., interest groups, corporations, labor unions, tax-exempt organizations, and parties) are playing a larger campaign finance role in federal elections, making them more significant sources of campaign resources. Second, much of their campaign finance activity has moved from inside the campaign finance system of regulations to outside it.

The United States has a long tradition of campaign finance reforms that attempt to ensure that campaign money is raised and spent in a manner that can be publicly observed (Sorauf 1992, ch. 1). In 1996, however, the amount of money that was publicly observable may have paled in comparison to the amount that was not reported to the FEC and therefore was shielded from public scrutiny. These changes gave interest groups and parties more control over individual campaigns and candidates less control over their own contests. This trend makes it more difficult to place responsibility for the conduct of campaigns, for it is only the candidates that can be held responsible for the campaign on election day. In the final section, I examine some of the consequences of this move to the postreform era of the federal campaign finance system.

## Consequences and Conclusions

A number of consequences may result from this shift to the postreform era. For instance, the perceived need for campaign finance reform increased after the election and led to passage of a campaign finance reform bill in the House of Representatives in 1998. The reforms proposed directly addressed the campaign finance practices of the postreform era, rather than the standard reforms proposed for many years.

Additionally, all those involved with federal campaigns are likely to respond and react to the new campaign finance environment. Candidates, interest groups, parties, and others will adjust their strategies and look for ways to take advantage of the opportunities offered by indirect campaigning and unregulated activities. And unless the Supreme Court loosens the connection it has made between campaign spending and free speech, the trends toward indirect campaigning and unregulated activities will continue and grow. An increasing amount of money spent on campaigns will be shielded from public scrutiny by this constitutional protection. Thus, the campaign dialogue is likely to degrade, for these noncandidate campaigners cannot effectively be held accountable for their campaign messages.

One consequence of the 1996 elections was increased attention to reforming the laws that govern the financing of federal elections. The 1996 elections reinvigorated and changed the push for campaign finance reform (see chapter 9). The campaign finance activities discussed in this chapter are some of the developments that mobilized many reform groups, editorial boards, and elected officials to call more vigorously for campaign finance reform legislation. The push for reform is due in part to the fact that many of these campaign finance activities have removed much of the control over the raising and spending of campaign dollars from the candidates and put it in the hands of outside campaigners, namely, interest groups and parties. One Democratic media consultant recently noted, "As candidates lose control and as advocacy groups take over, candidates become props in the campaign process" (Faucheux 1998, 20). A Republican consultant predicted, "We'll reach a point in the future where you may see the bulk of the campaign being run from outside [candidate] campaigns" (Faucheux 1998, 21).

These emerging trends motivated some elected officials to design campaign finance reform proposals to curb these indirect campaigning techniques by, for example, banning soft money and restricting unlimited and undisclosed spending on issue advocacy. Meanwhile, traditional reforms such as public funding and spending limits, which aim to address the incumbency advantage and special-interest influence, have been put on the back burner. Indeed, the main features of the Shays-Meehan Bipartisan Campaign Reform Act that passed the House (but not the Senate) in 1998 were a soft money ban and an expansion of the definition of express advocacy. The expanded definition would have deemed communications run in the last sixty days before an election that feature the name or likeness of a federal candidate to be campaign communications and therefore subject to FECA regulations and reporting requirements. This would have, in effect, turned issue advocacy ads into independent expenditures, which at least are regulated and disclosed. As more candidates are faced with a barrage of issue advocacy ads during their own campaigns, more members of Congress may be inclined to support such reforms. Indeed, these reforms do not attempt to curb their advantages as incumbents, as traditional reforms do. Instead, they aim to return more control over the campaign dialogue to candidates.

A major impediment to such reforms, however, is the Supreme Court's interpretation of the First Amendment in its evaluation of campaign finance laws. The Court's narrow definition of express advocacy is designed to protect the free speech rights of interest groups, parties, and individuals. Yet this interpretation of the First Amendment allows for unlimited spending on communications that in fact do advocate the election or defeat of candidates. Anyone could make a campaign ad that does not include the magic words of express advocacy such as "vote for" or "vote against," and it would still be a campaign ad.

Unless the Supreme Court reexamines its express advocacy definition, many House and Senate members are unlikely to join the effort to reform the campaign finance laws. Indeed, one of the most potent arguments against the leading campaign finance reform bills of 1998 (the McCain-Feingold bill in the Senate and the Shays-Meehan bill in the House) was that the bills were quite likely unconstitutional because they attempted to expand the Supreme Court's definition of express advocacy.

Thus interest groups, corporations, labor unions, parties, and wealthy individuals will continue to be free to spend more and more unlimited and undisclosed money on House and Senate contests. And candidates no doubt will respond to these noncandidate campaign messages. A barrage of issue advocacy advertising may free some candidates from attacking their opponents, allowing them to concentrate on positive messages in their own advertising. Thus, while the campaign may be full of negative advertising, the mudslinging will not come from the candidates but from these other campaigners. Candidates can disavow any knowledge of or responsibility for the negative campaigning while reaping the electoral benefits of it. In the end, no one is held accountable for the tone of the campaign dialogue because the dialogue is no longer controlled primarily by the candidate, the only campaigner who will be judged on election day.

Noncandidate organizations that fund an increasingly larger part of the campaign dialogue are further removed from responsibility for their messages because often it is impossible to know who exactly is running an issue advocacy ad, since the sponsors are not required to report the activity to the FEC. Indeed, interest groups may come to prefer unregulated spending over spending that they must conduct through PACs and report to the FEC. Unregulated spending on issue advocacy allows interest groups to control the message completely without the approval of the candidate, and it can be paid for with funds that are much easier to raise than regulated money.

If this unregulated spending is not curbed by reform, organized interests may eventually shift so much of their campaigning from reported to unreported activity that their role in federal elections will escape scrutiny and therefore any potential prosecution for wrongdoing. As long as the courts distinguish issue advocacy from campaigning as a constitutionally protected form of free speech, these trends are likely to continue. Such constitutional questions point to the difficulty of reforming the system.

Another consequence of the new developments in campaign finance in 1996 is that the massive effort by labor has awakened the business community, much like the rise of citizen groups during and after the 1960s was met with the rapid growth of business lobbying and campaign activity (Berry 1989, ch. 2). David Magleby has predicted that while labor may have outdone business in 1996, in the future labor's 1996 effort "will prompt a much greater effort by business and trade associations that labor will not be able to match" (Clymer 1996, B14). Future elections may effectively challenge any hope of achieving some sort of pluralism in the sources of campaign money.

What 1996 will be remembered for is the extent to which campaign finance players pushed the system to its limits and discovered clever new ways to raise and spend money that did not violate the law. That much of this campaign finance activity took place outside the confines of the FECA has motivated reformers to call for changes to the law that will bring the financing of elections back into the light of day and under regulatory control. Yet it appears that most of these extraregulatory activities were legal political activities under current interpretations of the law and the Constitution. Thus, while the impact and consequences of these activities may be undesirable, addressing them will be a very difficult task.

## Acknowledgments

I would like to thank Frank Sorauf for his insightful comments on an earlier draft of this work, Robert Stanley for his many helpful suggestions, and Joe Picard for his moral support and editorial assistance.

## Notes

1. The term "interest group" is a broad one that covers organizations that clearly engage in campaign activities (i.e., political action committees) as well as those that purport not to be advocating the election or defeat of specific candidates but instead to educating the public about issues (e.g., nonprofit organizations, labor unions, and corporations). As the discussion of issue advocacy will show, it is often difficult to distinguish between the two types of activities.

2. A party's national committee, Senate campaign committee, and House campaign committee are each considered national party committees, and each may accept the maximum contribution from a PAC.

3. Note that parties may use soft money to pay for only a *portion* of an issue advocacy communication, while interest groups and individuals may use all unlimited and undisclosed money to pay for issue advocacy expenditures.

4. The Sierra Club's 1996 PAC contributions to candidates (regulated and disclosed spending) were nearly double what the PAC gave in 1994, but, like other groups, the club's unregulated issue advocacy spending far outstripped its PAC giving.

## 9

ROBERT E. MUTCH

# The Reinvigorated Reform Debate

The congressional debate over campaign reform underwent two significant changes in the mid-1990s: Republican victories in the 1994 midterm elections changed its politics, and freewheeling fund-raising in
the Democrats' 1996 presidential campaign altered its content. Republicans in the House of Representatives, the center of their party's 1994
"revolution," turned out to be deeply split on campaign reform. Yet it
was determined Republican rebels who made it possible to pass the
only reform bill to get through either house since the GOP takeover. In
the Senate, on the other hand, the politics and the outcome of the
reform debate remained essentially unchanged despite the change in
party control. That Republican conservatives kept the reform debate
alive after 1994 was unexpected. What raised the profile of that debate
to new highs was something more familiar: a presidential fund-raising
scandal.

The first press reports of questionable fund-raising practices in Bill
Clinton's reelection campaign appeared in the weeks before the 1996
elections. These reports probably hurt Democrats at the polls, but they
heartened reformers as well as their opponents: For opposing reasons,
both wanted a Watergate-size scandal. Reformers hoped a scandal
would spark the kind of public anger that could compel Congress to
pass a reform bill; their opponents hoped it would discredit President
Clinton by disclosing violations of existing law. Neither side got its
wish. What press coverage and the ensuing congressional investigations did was broaden the debate and shift its focus.

The familiar reform groups, Common Cause and Public Citizen,
continued to be active, but a profusion of task forces, forums, and
working groups sprang up to bring academics, journalists, and activists

together to seek agreement on new combinations of reform ideas. What all had in common was a shift away from the issues that had dominated the debate before 1996—PACs, public funding, and spending limits—and toward the issues the 1996 campaigns had pushed to the front—soft money, issue advocacy, and foreign contributions.

These debates also had something in common with those of the previous two decades: They still divided those who want to limit the role of money in elections from those who do not. Tightening the restrictions on the raising and spending of campaign money is the traditional meaning of reform, and is most likely to attract support from Democrats; their mostly Republican opponents usually aim to loosen those same restrictions. The enormous sums of money raised in 1996 and the inventive, and often unaccountable, ways devised to spend that money did cause opinion to shift slightly toward more regulation, but not enough to pass new legislation.

## Reform Legislation in Congress After 1994

In the absence of a Watergate-size scandal that raises public pressure to the point where the two sides see the virtues of compromise, the result of the reform debate has been deadlock. The Republican victory in the 1994 congressional elections promised to continue that deadlock.

### Bills and Tactics in the 104th Congress (1995–1996)

The Republicans had telegraphed their lack of concern with campaign reform in the manifesto of their revolution, the Contract with America. The Contract made no mention of campaign reform, so it was no surprise that its chief author, newly elected Speaker Newt Gingrich, took no initiative on the issue. In preceding Congresses, Democratic majorities in both houses had introduced reform bills early, giving them the low bill numbers that carried the prestige, or at least the appearance, of leadership commitment. This did not happen in the 104th Congress. Senate Minority Leader Tom Daschle (D-S. Dak.) did introduce S.10, a comprehensive bill that combined lobbying and campaign reform, but it was stillborn.

The reform bills that mattered were not introduced until late in the first session, when it had become clear that neither President Clinton nor congressional party leaders were going to take action. The Senate bill was a revised version of the last of the measures sponsored by Senator David Boren (D-Okla.), who had led the reform effort in the upper chamber since the mid-1980s. Boren's retirement left it unclear who would take his place. That question was answered in September 1995, when Senators John McCain (R-Ariz.) and Russell Feingold (D-Wis.) introduced S.1219.[1] Although the McCain-Feingold bill did attract three more Republican cosponsors, it was, like the Boren bills before it, a Democratic measure. Action in the House, though, did not follow earlier patterns.

Speaker Gingrich's indifference to campaign reform sparked another Republican "revolution"—against the new House leadership. This revolt was surprising on at least two counts: It took place less than a year after the GOP's stunning rise to power, and it happened in the face of a consolidation of power in the Speaker's office so unusual that observers compared it both to a prime minister's power in a parliamentary system and to the turn-of-the-century "czar rule" Speakers (Fenno 1997, 31; Evans and Oleszek 1997, 90–91). Another surprise was that the leader of the revolt, Representative Linda Smith (R-Wash.), was a freshman and a conservative. Representative Smith attracted a bipartisan group of supporters in the House as well as the public backing of Ross Perot (Yang 1995). She and her chief cosponsors, Representatives Christopher Shays (R-Conn.) and Martin T. Meehan (D-Mass.), introduced H.R.2566, the House version of McCain-Feingold.[2]

### *Senate and House Versions of McCain-Feingold I*

Like their predecessors, the Senate and House versions of the McCain-Feingold bill (here labeled McCain-Feingold I to distinguish it from the 105th Congress measure) provided broadcast discounts, free air time, and postal deductions to candidates who complied with voluntary spending limits. Unlike their predecessors, they did not include other forms of public funding for complying candidates.

Both bills also prohibited PACs from contributing to candidates for federal office, with a backup provision should the ban be found unconstitutional. The fallback was to reduce the limit on PAC contributions to the same $1,000 per candidate per election that applies to individuals. They also prohibited leadership PACs and placed severe limits on bundling individual contributions.

The two bills restricted independent expenditures by amending its legal definition and specifying the conditions that would indicate collaboration between spenders and candidates. On the increasingly contentious issue of soft money, they provided that all "generic" party activities (e.g., voter registration and get-out-the-vote drives) must be financed by hard money.

Both bills also included a provision that had never been popular with House Democrats: a limit on out-of-state contributions. They differed from the Boren bill of the previous Congress, which had required Senate candidates to raise all their money in-state except for the two-year cycle in which their own election fell. The Senate and House bills reduced this provision to 60 percent but applied it to every cycle.

S.1219 was similar in most respects to Senator Boren's bill and met the same fate. On June 25, a Republican filibuster prevented it from coming to a vote. A cloture attempt failed by a vote of 54–46, falling six votes short of the sixty needed to end the Republican filibuster. All but one Democrat voted to end debate, but only eight Republicans joined them.

Despite the change in party control, this pattern was very similar to that of 1994. As in 1994, the filibuster was led by Senator Mitch McConnell (R-Ky.). Business and labor groups again opposed the PAC ban, and conservative groups objected to the restrictions on independent spending. President Clinton announced his support for the bill, but was no more active on its behalf than he had been two years earlier. Senator Trent Lott (R-Mass.), who had just replaced the retiring Senator Bob Dole (R-Kans.) as majority leader, pulled the bill after only one cloture vote (Dewar 1996). The Senate vote also killed any hope that the Smith-Shays-Meehan bill would come to a vote in the House. But House GOP leaders had their own agenda, which included a vote on a Republican campaign finance bill.

### Republican and Democratic Leadership Bills in the House

It was something of a surprise that the House GOP would bring any campaign reform bill to the floor, especially after the Senate killed McCain-Feingold I. But back in November, party leaders had decided they must respond to the Smith-Shays-Meehan effort. Shortly after the GOP rebels and their Democratic allies introduced their bill, Speaker Gingrich assigned Representative Peter Hoekstra (R-Mich.) to head a seventeen-member task force to come up with an alternative. That alternative was to be the centerpiece of what the speaker called Reform Week, during which the House would vote on several reform measures.

The task force did draft its own reform proposals, but accompanied them with a report that all but predicted their failure. After polling Republican House members, the task force bluntly described the new politics of campaign reform in a GOP-controlled House:

> In plain English, none of the . . . topics has a greater amount of disagreement within the Conference than Congressional reform. . . . [T]he greater the length of service in the House, the less likely the Member is to prioritize Congressional reform. (Quoted in Burger and Sheffner 1996)

Republicans had won control of the House by electing seventy-three new members. But many of those freshmen had campaigned on reform platforms that now pitted them against senior members of their own party. The senior members, long accustomed to voting against campaign reform bills in Democratic-controlled Congresses, saw no reason to vote differently now that they were finally in the majority (Rae 1998, 173–74). Although many freshmen criticized the task force proposals for being weak, and senior members attacked them as too restrictive, party leaders remained committed to bringing up a version of those proposals as their own bill.

On July 9, that bill came out of the Committee on Government Reform and Oversight, sponsored by committee chair Bill Thomas (R-Calif.) and cosponsored by the top GOP leaders. Two months earlier, Democrats had drawn up their own bill, cosponsored by Minority Leader Dick Gephardt (D-Mo.) and other party leaders. The Reform Week vote was to be a contest between these two bills.

Neither bill banned PACs, but the GOP bill imposed the more severe restrictions on contributions: $2,500 per election cycle, as opposed to the Democratic bill's limit of $8,000. Both bills would have eliminated leadership PACs, the Democratic bill immediately, the Republican after two years. Thomas's bill prohibited all PACs from bundling contributions, but the Democratic bill, in a gesture of support for committees such as EMILY'S List, prohibited bundling only by connected PACs.

Both measures raised the overall amount individuals could contribute per year to candidates and parties, the Democratic bill to $50,000, the Republican to $117,000. The Democrats kept the $1,000 limit on individual contributions and limited the amount candidates could receive in large donations (above $200). Thomas's bill imposed no limit on large contributions and raised the individual limit to the same $2,500 applied to PACs. Thomas would, however, have required candidates to raise at least one-half of their funds from individual residents of their congressional districts. Both bills imposed further restrictions on independent spending, but only the Republican bill, like Smith-Shays-Meehan, prohibited the use of soft money for generic campaign activities.

On July 17, the day these measures were supposed to come up for a vote, GOP leaders abruptly pulled their bill from the schedule and postponed debate. The reason for this unusual action became clear under the even more unusual circumstances under which the bill finally came to the floor on July 25.

The Rules Committee reported a rule on the Thomas bill, but in a rare, perhaps unprecedented, move, did so without a recommendation. Rules Committee Chair Gerald B. H. Solomon (R-N.Y.) said the action reflected "a sincere difference of opinion among our members over the proper course of action to take on this issue" (*Congressional Record* July 25, 1996, H8458). Thomas admitted that the leadership had been unable to secure the backing of Republicans on the Rules Committee: "Even our majority Members in the committee were torn about what is the best way to go" (*Congressional Record* July 25, 1996, H4861). The leaders themselves were so torn that they revised their bill to meet objections they themselves did not agree with.

The amended version kept the PAC contribution limit at $2,500 per election, but reduced the individual contribution limit back to the $1,000 limit provided for in existing law. It also reduced the overall yearly limit on individual contributions to $50,000, the same as in the Democratic bill. Speaking on behalf of his measure, Thomas said the amendments improved the bill, "most notably by sending a stronger signal that we want to control the flow of money into campaigns" (*Congressional Record* July 25, 1996, H4861).

Thomas's remarks were surprising, as they seemed to indicate a Republican shift away from their own leader's highly publicized opinions about the role of money in politics. The previous November, Speaker Gingrich had said that "one of the greatest myths of modern politics is that campaigns are too expensive. The political process, in fact, is underfunded." He explained the source of that myth this way:

"Most modern campaign critique . . . is simply a nonsensical socialist analysis based on hatred of the private enterprise system" (Gingrich 1995, 12, 13).

The revisions did not save the GOP bill, which failed 162–259. Every Democrat voted against it, but so did almost one-third of Republicans. Among the GOP defectors were Representative Solomon, two other majority members of the Rules Committee, and 40 percent of the freshman class. The Republican split also reflected an ideological difference: The majority who voted for the Thomas bill were slightly, but noticeably, more conservative on economic issues than the defectors.[3]

There was no debate on the Smith-Shays-Meehan bill, as the rule permitted a vote only on the Democratic alternative. That alternative also failed—by a vote of 177–243—but further embarrassed the GOP leadership by attracting more votes than the Thomas bill.

## The Issue Divide: Reformers' Concerns
## Before and After the 1996 Elections

The issues that occupied reformers in the 104th Congress were for the most part the same that had occupied them since the late 1970s: PACs, public funding, spending limits, and independent expenditures. All but independent expenditures receded in importance after the 1996 campaigns, to be replaced by soft money, issue advocacy, and foreign contributions. None of these were new issues, of course, but all assumed new significance during the 1996 campaigns

### *Political Action Committees*

Political action committees were the primary target of mostly Democratic congressional reformers from the late 1970s through the early 1990s. This focus was in accord with public opinion: PACs are the very embodiment of special-interest giving, so throughout the 1980s and 1990s, large popular majorities supported measures that would restrict the committees (Magleby and Patterson 1994, 421,426).

It was alarm at the explosive growth of corporation and trade association committees that prompted House Democrats to propose restrictions on PAC contributions in 1979. Republicans, cheered by the same PAC phenomenon that so disconcerted Democrats, defended the new business committees as a reform in themselves.

As it became clear that the Democrats were able to use their as yet unbroken control of the House to attract business money to their own campaigns, Republicans began to sour on PACs and called for a prohibition against them. Newt Gingrich succinctly expressed the GOP's sense of betrayal less than a year after becoming speaker of the House: "The political action system has become an arm of the Washington lobbyists, and in fact simply follows power without ideology" (Gingrich 1995, 3).

Yet by the time the Speaker made these remarks, he and his party had already abandoned their drive to ban PAC contributions. Just as House Democrats' early fear of business PACs lessened as they learned how to attract business money, so too did the Republicans' 1994 victory dilute their desire to eliminate PACs. By 1995, only Democrats supported a PAC ban, an idea they had adopted five years earlier only to prevent Republicans from outflanking them on this popular issue (Dewar 1990). The idea had never been popular with House Democrats, though, as they were far more dependent on PAC donations than were senators.

Before 1994, Republicans called for banning PAC money because too much of it was going to Democrats; Democrats backed the idea to retain their leadership on the reform issue. After 1994, the GOP dropped the idea because PAC money was now flowing to them; Democrats still backed it, again to retain their status as reform leaders. The 1996 campaigns ended this charade by taking people's minds off PACs altogether.

### Public Funding and Spending Limits

Public financing had almost entirely disappeared as a reform goal by the time McCain-Feingold I was introduced. Spending limits had not yet disappeared, even though they were tied to public financing.

Public funding has been a Democratic idea since the first bill to institute U.S. Treasury financing for presidential elections was introduced in 1904. Watergate weakened GOP opposition, but could not overcome it. Campaign spending limits, on the other hand, had been part of federal law from 1911 to 1971. After Watergate, majorities of both parties in both houses of Congress restored and strengthened spending ceilings. In response to a conservative-libertarian challenge to the post-Watergate law, however, the Supreme Court interpreted the First Amendment to prohibit such limits.

In *Buckley* v. *Valeo* (424 U.S. 1 [1976]), the Court upheld limits only for presidential candidates who voluntarily accepted them as a condition for receiving public funding. While Republicans began portraying limits as an infringement of free speech, Democrats began trying to reinstate them in congressional elections by trying to enact public funding for those elections. Year after year, Republican opposition doomed these attempts. By 1995, in McCain-Feingold I, the only public financing congressional candidates would have received for agreeing to limit their spending was reduced postage rates. McCain-Feingold II dropped even those provisions.

### Independent Expenditures

McCain-Feingold I addressed this issue, but like the Boren bills before it, addressed practices of the 1980s. In the 1980s, independent spending was as much a weapon in a struggle for control of the Republican Party as a campaign tactic. But as the conservative groups who pioneered the attack ads of the early 1980s gained power in the GOP, independent spending decreased as a percentage of spending in both presidential and congressional campaigns.

The new wrinkle that McCain-Feingold II had to address was less the result of a new campaign practice than the Supreme Court's attempt to clarify an old one. The question before the Court in *Colorado Republican Federal Campaign Committee* v. *Federal Election Commission* (518 U.S. 604 [1996]) was whether party spending on behalf of its candidates could be independent of those candidates and thus unlimited. The Court found that it could, but did so in a fragmented ruling consisting of a plurality opinion and three concurring and dissenting opinions.

The justices rejected FEC arguments that all party spending on behalf of its candidates should be presumed to be coordinated, noting that the Commission's judgment did not "represent the outcome of an empirical investigation" (518 U.S. 604 [1996], 2318). They also rejected the argument that parties and their candidates are in a sense identical. "We cannot assume ... that this is so," they wrote (518 U.S. 604 [1996], 2319). The justices buttressed their conclusion by citing a college text that describes parties as " 'coalitions' of differing interests," and dismissed the claimed identity of parties and candidates as "metaphysical" (518 U.S. 604 [1996], 2319). After this decision, both parties created independent spending committees for use in the 1996 congressional campaigns.

In 1995, McCain-Feingold I dealt with this issue in one line, providing that the term "independent expenditures" did not include those made by a party committee. The 1997 bill retracted that definition. In a two-page section devoted to the matter, McCain-Feingold II did not dispute the Court's ruling that it was possible for parties to make independent expenditures—it just provided that they would not be permitted to do so.[4] Once a party has nominated a candidate, the bill would have allowed party committees to make only coordinated expenditures, which, unlike independent expenditures, are subject to FECA limits.

It was these limits that were the real issue behind the Colorado case: The Colorado Republican Party had claimed that ceilings on party spending violated its free speech rights. The plurality opinion in Colorado did not address that issue, although two of the concurring opinions did and agreed with the Colorado GOP.

It is unlikely that many members of Congress actually believe that parties can act independently of their candidates. But many of them do believe, as did the Colorado Republican Party, that party spending on behalf of those candidates should not be limited. Limits on party spending have always sparked disagreements, even among reformers, and lifting them has been a Republican goal since at least the early 1980s (Alexander and Haggerty 1987, 21). During and after the 1996 elections, party spending became more important as it became entwined with two other high-profile issues: soft money and issue advocacy.

### Party Spending and Soft Money

Soft money has a dual origin: In a 1978 advisory opinion, the FEC permitted parties to mix state and FECA-regulated funds for activities that involved candidates for both state and federal office. In the 1979 FECA amendments, Congress permitted state parties to spend unlimited sums on such generic party activities. State and local party activity was noticeably subdued in the 1976 presidential campaign, and there was broad bipartisan agreement that this was because of its doubtful legality under the 1974 FECA amendments (Mutch 1988, 111–13). Congress designed the 1979 amendments to revive grassroots political participation. What they did, in fact, in combination with the 1978

advisory opinion, was to create an ever-growing pool of money not subject to the FECA regulations enacted only five years earlier (Corrado 1993, 63).

As a reform issue, soft money has been through several changes. It was Republicans who first understood the fund-raising potential of the new law and used it as back-door private funding for Ronald Reagan's 1980 presidential campaign. Democrats complained loudly, and Common Cause soon came out against the practice. By 1988, though, the Democrats had become as adept as the Republicans at raising soft money, and Democrats began defending the unregulated funds as being necessary to strengthen parties. It was at this point that Republicans began to propose that political parties be prohibited from receiving soft money contributions (Alexander and Bauer 1991, 118).

After the 1992 elections, Bill Clinton proposed a ban on the very soft money contributions of which he himself had been such a successful solicitor. Both the House and Senate passed reform bills that included Clinton's proposals, but never managed to agree on a conference bill to send to the president (Alexander and Corrado 1995, 266–80). Similar provisions appeared in McCain-Feingold I. It was the unprecedented explosion of soft money in 1996—the parties raised more than $260 million, three times what they raised four years earlier—that made soft money into the primary reform issue.

One measure of the increased importance of soft money to reformers is the difference between McCain-Feingold I and II. Title I of McCain-Feingold I was still about spending limits; Title II, "Reduction of Special Interest Influence," still began with a PAC ban. These provisions vanished after 1996. Title I of McCain-Feingold II went directly into a ban on the use of soft money in federal election activity. The two bills were not dramatically different in their provisions, but McCain-Feingold II did define "federal election activity" in a way that severely restricted even state and local party use of funds not regulated by the FECA.

Groups outside of Congress issued similar proposals. A nine-member task force created by Herbert Alexander and the Citizens' Research Foundation recommended the abolition of soft money. Although task force members, all political scientists, supported strong parties, they found the parties' use of soft money in 1996 went well beyond "the 'party building' envisioned by the authorizing legislation" (Citizens' Research Foundation 1997, 6). A six-member group associated with the Brookings Institution agreed. Saying that the original, party-building role of soft money "has been mangled beyond recognition," they advised a ban on soft money for national parties (Ornstein et al. 1997, 4).

What most offended these groups in 1996 was the parties' use of issue advocacy advertisements. Like independent spending, issue advocacy is usually associated with nonparty interest groups, and it, too, was a prominent feature of the 1996 campaigns.

## Issue Advocacy

Until the 1996 elections, issue advocacy was a relatively little-used evasion of federal election law. Before and after 1996, reformers dealt with the problem by expanding the definition of independent expenditures, the difference being that the post-1996 efforts were far more detailed and comprehensive.

In the 1974 FECA amendments, Congress defined independent expenditures as those that expressly advocate the election or defeat of identified candidates. Express advocacy was defined as ads using such terms as "vote for" and "vote against." Ads that expressed an opinion on public policy issues but did not use such terms about candidates were not considered campaign expenditures (Mutch 1988, 72–76). The members of Congress who drafted this law were experienced campaigners who knew how easy it is to disguise campaign ads as issue ads. They nonetheless regarded the distinction between the two as one that "controls undue influence by a group or individual" while preserving "inviolate every citizen's ability to communicate his views." (Senate Report 93–689, 19)

In retrospect, it is surprising that 1996-style issue advocacy campaigns did not appear earlier. Because federal law does not regard issue advocacy as campaign spending, contributions to and expenditures by groups engaging in it are not regulated and need not be reported. This freedom from regulation proved to be powerfully attractive, and increased use of the tactic in 1996 drew attention from reformers within and outside Congress.

McCain-Feingold II dealt with this problem by expanding the definition of express advocacy to include ads that "when taken as a whole," express "unmistakable and unambiguous support for or opposition to" identified candidates or ads that appear within sixty days of an election. Groups outside Congress agreed. The six-member Brookings group made the slightly stronger proposal that such an ad appearing within ninety days of an election "be considered a campaign ad . . . and be covered by the same rules governing independent expenditure campaigns" (Ornstein et al. 1997, 5). The Citizens' Research Foundation task force recommended that spending for such ads be reported when it exceeds $50,000 per election and that labor unions, corporations, and trade associations be required to finance issue ads from voluntary contributions that also would have to be reported (Citizens' Research Foundation 1997, 7).

Redefining independent expenditures to cover the kind of issue advocacy that marked the 1996 campaigns would ensure that they are financed by hard money that is subject to FECA limitations and must be publicly disclosed. The chances of enacting an expanded definition seem slight, largely because of the Supreme Court's ruling in *Buckley* v. *Valeo*. The *Buckley* court did realize it would not be difficult to devise "expenditures that skirted the restrictions on express advocacy . . . but nevertheless benefited the candidate's campaign" (424 U.S. 1). But it also endorsed the equation of money and speech that underlies opposition to the proposals outlined above. Senator McConnell attacked the issue advocacy provisions in McCain-Feingold II as "unconscionable assaults on the first amendment" (*Congressional Record* October 6, 1997, S10343).

### Foreign Contributions

Most of the contributions labeled "foreign" were actually soft money, which created problems for those seeking legislative remedies for the problem. Of course, not everyone was looking for legislative remedies. The Republican position was that Democratic fund-raising practices were violations of existing law and should be prosecuted as such.

The illegality of many of the disputed contributions to the DNC, however, remains in doubt. Although the law prohibits foreign nationals from making political contributions, it does permit legal permanent residents to do so. Moreover, the law refers to contributions "in connection with an election to any political office," a definition that can easily be read to exclude soft money. For a contribution to be illegal under this law, it probably should be in hard money and either the money or the donor must be foreign. This proved a hard case to make.

The Republicans' most dramatic charge was that Democrats had endangered national security by accepting contributions from the People's Republic of China (PRC). In the words of the Senate Governmental Affairs Committee's report on its investigation into the Clinton fund-raising scandal:

> In the frenzied drive to raise . . . campaign money, the Democratic Party dismantled its own internal vetting procedures, no longer caring . . . where its money came from and who was supplying it (Senate Report 105–67, 33).

The committee's investigation revealed plenty of frenzied fund-raising and much evidence that donors were poorly screened.

The committee was unable, however, to substantiate the charges of Chinese government influence. The PRC evidently did intend to move beyond its already extensive lobbying efforts by trying to influence U.S. elections (Woodward and Duffy 1997; Senate Report 105–67, 2501–12). That the PRC actually carried out such a plan, or that it was the source of any of the contributions received by the DNC, is in doubt.

The Justice Department also had a difficult time substantiating charges it brought against Democratic donor Yah Lin Trie, who was alleged to have funneled foreign money into the DNC. In September 1998 the federal judge hearing the case ruled that the law banning foreign contributions does not apply to soft money (Suro and Miller 1998).

McCain-Feingold II would have made that law apply to soft money. By expanding the federal prohibition to cover "a contribution or donation to a committee of a political party," it would have banned soft money from foreign donors (S.25, sec. 506).

## Reform Legislation in Congress After 1996

### *Bills and Tactics in the 105th Congress (1997–1998)*

Reformers lost no time in the 105th Congress. Senators McCain and Feingold and Representatives Shays and Meehan (with Linda Smith in a supporting role this time) introduced the Senate and House versions of McCain-Feingold II on January 21, 1997, just two weeks after the 105th Congress opened. Two days later, President Clinton added to the appearance of gathering momentum by inviting the four sponsors to the White House to pledge his support. After the meeting, the optimistic legislators said public pressure for reform was mounting and predicted floor votes that year (Carr 1997a).

If public pressure to pass a reform bill was mounting—and it is not clear it was—it was doing so for the same reason that further emboldened Republican opposition to reform: questionable fund-raising practices in Clinton's just-completed reelection campaign. Many were convinced that both parties' use of unprecedented sums for spending that evaded federal law underscored the need to reform that law (Wilcox and Joe 1998; Citizens' Research Foundation 1997, 1–2; Ornstein et al. 1997, 1). Senator Feingold, for example, pointed to both parties' use of soft money, issue advocacy, and nonprofit groups as proof that "the few remaining pillars holding up our crumbling federal election system finally collapsed" (Feingold 1997). Reform opponents pointed to the Clinton campaign's activities to argue that the problem was not in the FECA but in Democratic violations of that law. As Senate Majority Leader Trent Lott put it: "The problem is that laws have been broken. And I think we should enforce the laws before we start running off to change the laws" (Quoted in Doherty 1997a, 2447).

### Congress Investigates Democratic Fund-Raising

Even as the 105th Congress opened, it was gearing up for highly publicized investigations into the fund-raising practices of Clinton's reelection campaign. The focus on Democrats was not universally welcomed, however, and Senate GOP attempts to limit the scope of that chamber's inquiry resulted in the kind of rank-and-file rebellion hitherto seen only in the House.

The reason for the rancor was Senator Fred Thompson (R-Tenn.). In one sense, he was his party's ideal choice: Besides enjoying bipartisan respect, he was also a former Hollywood actor who had been the Republican counsel to the Senate Watergate Committee. What dampened Republican glee at the prospect of the camera-friendly former Watergate counsel grilling Clinton campaign staff was the grimmer prospect that he would not restrict his inquiry either to Democrats or to presidential campaigns. Thompson, after all, was also a cosponsor of McCain-Feingold II and an outspoken advocate of campaign reform.

In mid-February, Thompson and Senator John Glenn (D-Ohio), the ranking minority member of the Governmental Affairs Committee, reached common ground on the scope of the investigation, which they agreed would cover "illegal and improper" activities. But their agreement had to be approved by the Rules Committee, whose Republican majority opposed the Thompson-Glenn understanding. By a party-line vote, the committee issued a rule restricting Thompson's inquiry to "illegal" activities (Carr 1997b, 572–74). The rule would keep the investigation focused on Clinton and the Democrats and keep it from promoting discussion of campaign reform.

This vote did not bind Senate Republicans outside the committee, however. When the rule came up for a vote five days later, at least ten senators objected to it during a contentious party caucus. Dissenters were so adamant in their opposition to the rule that Majority Leader Lott agreed to amend it on the floor. The amended rule, which reinstated the Thompson-Glenn agreement to investigate "illegal and improper" activities, passed unanimously (Carr 1997c, 617).

House GOP leaders never feared that the House investigation, conducted by Representative Dan Burton (R-Ind.), would be used to promote reform. As it turned out, neither chamber's investigation was of much help to either reformers or their opponents. Republicans did succeed in embarrassing Democrats by publicizing the White House coffees, sleepovers in the Lincoln bedroom, and poorly screened donations, but they did not manage to convince their audience that these events were part of a pattern of rampant illegality. Democrats appear to have been more successful in their less ambitious goal of insisting that they were no worse than the Republicans. The press gave front-page coverage to both sets of hearings, but the public soon tuned out. This reaction was not the kind of wave reformers could ride to a legislative victory.

### Action and Inaction in the Senate

Seven months after Senator Thompson won his battle for a broadened investigation, the reform bill he cosponsored fell before the expected filibuster. By this time, McCain-Feingold II had undergone a transformation. As originally introduced, it and its Shays-Meehan counterpart (S.25 and H.R.493, respectively) were almost identical to the bills that had gone down to defeat the previous summer. But times had changed, and the bills had changed with them.

The original bills emphasized the issues that had been highest on the reformers' agenda for well over a decade: benefits to candidates who voluntarily limited their campaign spending, limits or outright bans on PACs, and restrictions on bundling. The 1996 presidential campaign changed those priorities in just a matter of months. When they finally got to the floor, the two bills had dropped spending limits, PAC bans, and bundling curbs, focusing instead on the new "hot button" issues of soft money and independent spending.

Another new feature was that Senate Democrats mounted their own filibuster. The dueling filibusters came about as the result of Republican anger over the AFL-CIO's issue ads on behalf of Democrats in the 1996 elections. Senator Lott offered a "paycheck protection" amendment to McCain-Feingold II that would have required labor unions to get written permission from members before spending treasury money for political purposes. This move put Republicans in the same position the Democrats had been in for most of the last decade: Their majority was large enough to pass the measure but too small to bring it to a vote. On October 7, Republican leaders failed, 52–48, to impose cloture on debate of their amendment. The reformers then failed, 53–47, to stop debate on McCain-Feingold II. Minority Leader Tom Daschle (D-S. Dak.) forced two more cloture votes on the next two days with similar results (Doherty 1997b).

Three cloture votes were more than most of McCain-Feingold II's predecessors had endured, but Democrats did not relent. Perhaps emboldened by hopes of rising public pressure for reform after months of testimony before Senator Thompson's committee, Democrats stalled other legislative business to force Republican leaders to allow another vote on campaign reform. They went so far as to block a highway bill that was popular with constituents and Congress, sustaining a filibuster through four cloture votes. Republican leaders finally relented, agreeing to a vote on campaign reform legislation early in 1998 (Doherty and Koszczuk 1997, 2664).

That vote, on a Republican motion to table McCain-Feingold II, came on February 24. Seven Republicans joined the Democrats to defeat the motion 51–48. This vote opened the way for Senators Olympia Snowe (R-Maine) and James M. Jeffords (R-Vt.) to offer an amendment they hoped would bridge partisan differences over the Lott-McConnell "paycheck protection" proposal. Their amendment would have prohibited unions and corporations from airing broadcast ads attacking specific candidates within sixty days of a general election and thirty days of a primary. After weeks of effort, Snowe and Jeffords managed to get Democrats to support their compromise. That support was enough—just barely, by a 50–47 vote—to defeat a Republican attempt to table the amendment. It was not enough to change the lineup on McCain-Feingold II, though: Although the modified bill again survived a Republican attempt to table it, the bill attracted no new votes to defeat the continuing GOP filibuster. Republicans also gained no new votes for their "paycheck protection" measure: They failed, 55–45, to impose cloture on that proposal (Dewar 1998a, 1998b, 1998c). "It's over," Senator McConnell was quoted as saying. "We'll move on to things people care about" (Dewar 1998b). As it turned out, campaign reform was something people cared about on the other side of the Capitol.

### Republican Rebels Gain Strength in the House

In the previous Congress, the minority of House Republicans willing to buck their leaders over campaign reform had been larger and more vocal than its Senate counterpart. That pattern continued in the 105th Congress, and against a weaker leadership. Speaker Gingrich was tarnished by an Ethics Committee investigation and eventual reprimand. He won reelection as Speaker, but not unanimously, and in the summer of 1997 he faced an attempted coup (Yang 1997a, b, c). One of the rifts party leaders did not bridge was that over campaign reform.

GOP leaders, who had pledged to bring a reform bill to the floor before April 1998, scheduled a vote for March 26 or 27. On March 26, they announced the vote would be delayed, reportedly because reformers in their own ranks resisted a plan to prevent a vote on Shays-Meehan. Through a spokesman, Majority Leader Armey predicted there would not be a vote until late April (Mitchell 1998).

Late the next day, a Friday, after many members had already left for the weekend, Majority Leader Armey announced that the vote would take place the following Tuesday. Normally, most members would have been back at the Capitol by then, but the funeral of former Representative Steve Schiff (R-N. Mex.) was scheduled for Monday, which meant that many would still be en route to Washington when debate began.

The inconvenient scheduling was not the only slap at reformers. The vote would be only on four leadership-backed bills, one of them another comprehensive bill sponsored by Representative Thomas. Moreover, the vote would be taken under suspension of the rules, a procedure usually used for such noncontroversial measures as resolutions honoring persons or groups. It permits only twenty minutes of debate per bill with no amendments and requires that a bill get a two-thirds majority to pass (Holmes 1998).

Not included among the bills to be voted on were two bills that had already garnered considerable support: the Shays-Meehan measure and one drawn up by a twelve-member bipartisan freshman task force led by Representatives Asa Hutchinson (R-Ark.) and Tom Allen (D-Maine). Purposely avoiding the comprehensiveness of Shays-Meehan, this mercifully brief bill focused on banning soft money and strengthening disclosure.

The "freshman bill," as it came to be known, also met with resistance from GOP leaders in both chambers. Majority Whip Tom DeLay (R-Tex.) and Senator McConnell (R-Ky.) reportedly blocked House Republican freshmen from formally endorsing the bill. According to the *Washington Post*, "GOP leaders objected to any crackdown on soft money that did not also include curbs on election-related spending by labor unions" (Dewar 1997).

Representative Armey's surprise announcement of the vote, and the news that the Shays-Meehan and Hutchinson-Allen bills would not come to the floor, prompted a sharp exchange between Representative Shays and the majority leader. Asked to explain this decision, Armey replied that the "sense of urgency" expressed by "those people who have been so vocal on this matter" suggested "that haste was more important to their concerns than the substance of the matter . . . and certainly for those of my colleagues who are so anxious to have this opportunity, I look forward to watching them as they vote for this" (*Congressional Record* March 27, 1998, H1683).

On the day of the vote, debate consisted largely of attacks on the voting procedure as a "fraud," a "mockery," and a "sham." Even Republicans formally speaking for the bill were critical either of the bill or the voting procedure. Representative Hutchinson said the leadership's tactic "reflects the dark side of this institution, and both sides of the aisle have contributed to this darkness. The last minute move to put a few bills on suspension sent a message to the American people that we are afraid of reform, and that we will undermine it at any price" (*Congressional Record* March 30, 1998, H1734).

When the Thomas bill came up for the long-awaited vote, it failed by a lopsided 74–337. The huge number of Republicans who voted against the bill—140, including Majority Leader Armey, Majority Whip DeLay, and all but two majority members of the Rules Committee—reinforced suspicions that GOP leaders never had intended the measure to pass. Unlike the intraparty split that marked the vote on Thomas's 104th Congress bill, the division on this bill reflected no discernible ideological difference.[5]

Another GOP attempt to require labor unions to get written permission from members before spending treasury money for political purposes also went down in defeat. Two smaller bills did pass by large majorities—one banning campaign contributions from noncitizens and one strengthening disclosure—but these died in the Senate.

The GOP leaders' heavy-handedness gave new life to a petition to discharge Shays-Meehan. A group of mostly southern, conservative Democrats calling themselves the Blue Dogs had begun collecting signatures a few months earlier and were only 30 short of the 218 needed to force Shays-Meehan to the floor when Representative Armey announced the surprise vote. That announcement prompted more members to sign. By April 21, when the House reconvened after the spring recess, 204 had signed, including 12 Republicans. The following day, after a contentious Republican caucus, Speaker Gingrich agreed to bring a campaign finance bill to the floor within weeks (Katz 1998a).

The GOP leadership may have given in, but they had not given up. The bill they brought up on May 21 was the Hutchinson-Allen "freshman" bill, a clever move that pitted its supporters against those of the better-known Shays-Meehan bill. They also brought it up under a rule that permitted eleven amendments in the form of substitutes (including Shays-Meehan), every one of which was itself open to multiple amendments. According to Rules Chairman Solomon, nearly 600 amendments had been filed, more than for any other bill in the history of the House of Representatives (Katz 1998b). Representative John Linder (R-Ga.), the Rules Committee member who introduced the rule, said it would "create the most open debate process in the history of campaign reform, as was promised by the Speaker" (*Congressional Record* May 21, 1998, H3723).

One month of debate later, Representative Linder, "in order to allow for consideration of as many amendments as possible," introduced a second rule that permitted at least 258 more amendments (*Congressional Record* June 18, 1998, H4773; Katz 1998c). Representative

Martin Frost (D-Tex.), ranking minority member on the Rules Committee, denounced both rules: "No longer will the Senate be able to lay sole claim to ownership of the filibuster. . . . The Republican leadership has kept its promise to allow debate on campaign finance reform, but this process is too clever by half. This is a ruse" (*Congressional Record* June 18, 1998, H4773). Majority Whip Tom DeLay (R-Tex.) remarked on Frost's "chutzpah" in complaining that the "open and honest debate" Democrats had been demanding for months was now "too open, too comprehensive, too complete" (*Congressional Record* June 18, 1998, H4774).

In the end, the Republican strategy failed. During the ten weeks of debate, the House voted down nearly all GOP amendments, often by large margins. Finally, when it came to the showdown between Shays-Meehan and Hutchinson-Allen, Shays-Meehan won.

The Hutchinson-Allen bill was defeated 147–222: Republicans narrowly supported it, 121–102. There were leaders and reformers, moderates and conservatives on both sides of the vote, but GOP freshmen supported it almost 3–1.

The Hutchinson-Allen vote was a tough one for Democrats, sixty of whom voted "present" rather than oppose the bill or give it a vote that would imperil Shays-Meehan. Almost three-fourths of the Democratic votes for the "freshmen" bill came from the party's freshmen. Although six Democratic members of the class of 1996 voted against the bill (as did nine GOP freshmen), the remainder divided evenly between votes of "yea" and "present." But Democrats' decisions on how to vote were as much ideological as tactical. Those who voted for the bill were significantly more conservative than other Democrats; there was almost no difference between those who voted "nay" and those who voted "present." The freshmen who cast most of the "yea" votes were themselves a relatively conservative group, but even they showed an ideological split: The one-half who voted "present" were noticeably more liberal than the half who voted "yea."[6]

There were two votes on Shays-Meehan: On August 3, the House agreed 237–186 to accept it as an amendment in the form of a substitute to Hutchinson-Allen; on August 6, Shays-Meehan as the amended bill passed 252–179. Fifty-one Republicans joined all but eleven Democrats to agree on Shays-Meehan on August 3; the same fifty-one, plus another ten Republicans, joined all but fifteen Democrats to pass the final bill on August 6. The GOP ideological split that first appeared in the vote on the GOP leadership's 104th Congress bill was evident again in these votes: Republicans voting against Shays-Meehan were noticeably more conservative than those voting for it.[7]

It was the first time either house had passed a campaign reform bill since the Republicans took power, and Democrats, joined by some Republicans, loudly cheered the final tally. Over the next several days, reformers predicted the House vote would change the vote in the Senate. It did not. On September 10, Senate Republicans led another successful filibuster against McCain-Feingold II (Dewar 1998d).

## Reform in the States

While campaign reform was grinding to its usual standstill in Congress, reform groups were taking action in the states. But while these groups have succeeded in getting their laws enacted, the laws themselves have not always succeeded. Courts have struck down some of the new laws, and others have inspired the same kinds of circumvention seen on the national level.

States have only recently encountered the problems besetting federal law because they have only recently enacted restrictions similar to those in the FECA. Although the states produced their own burst of reform legislation in the wake of Watergate, the resulting laws tended to be less ambitious than the FECA, concentrating on disclosure and limiting only the largest contributions (Malbin and Gais 1998, 13–15). In the 1980s, this trend began to reverse.

Through the 1990s, more states began enacting limits on contributions from individuals and PACs. Most of these states still had laws that were more lenient than the FECA. For example, twenty-seven states permit corporations to make political contributions, and thirty-five allow labor unions to do so (*The Council of State Governments* 1997, 177–83). Twenty-four states either have individual and PAC contribution limits that are more generous than that in the FECA or have no limits at all (Malbin and Gais 1998, 17–18) The relative leniency of these laws did not, however, prevent interest groups and parties from evading them with the same methods pioneered in congressional and presidential elections. Independent spending, soft money, and issue advocacy campaigns now are features of state as well as federal campaigns (Malbin and Gais 1998, 88–89; Alexander 1991, 32–35).

Another factor promoting the rise of these evasive techniques is public funding programs, which can now be found in twenty-six states. Sixteen states enacted public funding laws in the 1970s, when Congress established the presidential campaign fund. Such programs became less popular in the 1980s, when they were established in only seven states (Alexander 1991, 109). But their popularity may be returning. Maine, Nebraska, and Vermont enacted similar laws in the mid-1990s, and Massachusetts and Arizona voters did the same in 1998 (Malbin and Gais 1998, 22–23; Booth 1998).

It is the Maine program that is most noteworthy because it resembles the FECA in prohibiting candidates who accept public funds from receiving any private money. The Maine law was the result of an initiative and appears to be part of a new trend toward enacting stricter regulations. Some of the contribution limits, for example, are substantially more restrictive than those in the FECA, and this has caused them to run afoul of the courts. Just as interest groups, parties, and candidates evade restrictive campaign funding laws, so, too, do reform groups use initiative campaigns to circumvent unfriendly legislatures (Alexander 1991, 74).

That voters approved these initiatives suggests that people do want to change the way we finance our elections. But they want to do so by enacting measures—spending limits, low contribution limits, even public funding—that are unpopular with legislatures. The reluctance of legislatures to act on measures that have public support can be explained only partly by the realization that the courts will not allow them. Another part of the explanation lies in the nature of that public support. Merely knowing that a majority of voters would approve of a measure is not in itself reason to enact it, particularly if it would change the rules under which legislators run for office. Lawmakers probably would rush to enact those measures if public support for them took the form of the outrage produced by past scandals. But it is precisely that outrage that is missing.

## Conclusion: The End of the Scandal-Reform Cycle?

Reformers and their opponents agreed on two things: There was no strong public demand for reform legislation, and Congress was unlikely to pass a reform bill in the absence of such a demand. Historically, the public has demanded reform only in response to scandal, and congressional reformers hoped revelations about the financing of the 1996 Clinton campaign would provoke enough popular outrage to overcome Republican opposition to their bills. That this did not happen raises the question whether the scandal-reform cycle is a thing of the past.

Most of the law the McCain-Feingold bills were intended to revise was enacted in response to just two presidential election funding scandals, one involving Theodore Roosevelt's 1904 campaign, the other Richard Nixon's 1972 campaign (Mutch 1988, 1–53; Mutch 1991, 105–6). Scandal is the sudden revelation that prominent politicians have been engaging in, and concealing, widely disapproved practices. All three elements must be present: The practice (corporate contributions in 1904, large personal gifts in 1972) must be one the public finds improper, whether or not illegal; those engaged in it therefore conceal their involvement; and involvement is nonetheless revealed. Revelation causes public outcry, and Congress hastens to appease the voters. This was the pattern in 1904 and 1972, but the situation in the 1990s is quite different.

Secrecy breeds scandal, but it is disclosure that feeds today's discontent. When Congress strengthened disclosure in 1974, it institutionalized revelation: Disclosure is showing us for the first time how our politics have been financed for the last 100 years, and many people do not like what they see. Still, there is no explosion of public anger. Although disclosure gives us the same kind of dismaying news that was at the heart of past scandals, it does so in a steady stream, year after year. The occasional revelation made people angry; routine disclosure produces chronic, low-level dissatisfaction.

Congress may have put an end to the scandal-reform cycle not only by eliminating the element of secrecy but also by making the 1974 FECA amendments so comprehensive. The more complex the law, the more ingenious the methods of circumventing it, and the more difficult it becomes to make clear distinctions between what is and what is not legal. The result is that even headline-making revelations, like those about soft money and foreign contributions, dissolve quickly into quibbles over legal minutiae. The public response to prolonged bouts of bickering among lawyers is more likely to be cynicism than righteous anger. Reformers continue to hope for a scandal that will compel Congress to pass their bills, but the record of the 105th Congress makes the possibility of such a scandal seem remote.

## Notes

1. Senator Boren retired in 1994 to become president of the University of Oklahoma. His successor as reform leader, Senator McCain, began his Senate career opposing Boren. In his second year in the Senate, McCain called Boren's S.2 "an ill-founded piece of legislation" that would be "disastrous . . . not only to the Republican Party but to the political process as we know it" (*Congressional Record* February 23, 1988, 2032). But later in 1988 McCain became publicly associated with the more unsavory side of that political process as one of the "Keating Five" (Alexander and Bauer 1991, 79–81). In 1990 Senator McCain switched sides on campaign reform by voting for Boren's S.137, a position he has maintained ever since. Senator Feingold, who was elected to the Senate in 1992, voted for S.3, the last of the Boren bills.

2. With ties to the Christian Right and militia groups, Representative Smith was strikingly different from the liberal Democrats who had worn the mantle of reform for the previous two decades. But she also had closer ties to Ross Perot than any other House Republican and had spearheaded an initiative to reform campaign ethics in Washington state (Rae 1998, 172–73; *Congressional Quarterly Weekly* report, January 7, 1995, 102). Conservative columnist Robert D. Novak (1995) wrote that House GOP leaders were "terrified" of this "right-winger" and did not know what to do about her. Representative Shays, one of the party's dwindling number of social moderates, had backed every campaign reform bill that had come up for a vote since his election to the House in 1987. Representative Meehan, elected in 1992, voted for H.R.3, the 103rd Congress reform bill.

3. The difference, as measured by 1995–96 U.S. Chamber of Commerce ratings, was Mean for Yea votes: 94.4 (n: 150; sd: 4.9); Mean for Nay votes: 85.9 (n: 61; sd: 12.9). "Conservative" and "liberal" are relative terms here—the mean Chamber of Commerce rating for House Democrats in the 104th Congress was 32.7.

4. The wording of the bill is important in light of the Colorado ruling. That case involved spending by the Colorado Republican Party in the 1986 campaign for the U.S. Senate seat being vacated by Gary Hart. The party ran campaign ads against then Representative Tim Wirth during his primary election campaign for the Democratic nomination. That the ads appeared before either party had formally chosen a candidate was an important factor in the Supreme Court's ruling. The Court based its opinion in part on the absence of "any factual finding that the Party had consulted with any candidate in the making or planning of the advertising campaign" (518 U.S. 604 [1996], 2317) McCain-Feingold II prohibited parties from making independent expenditures "[on] or after the date on which a political party nominates a candidate" (S.25, sec. 204).

5. The difference, as measured by U.S. Chamber of Commerce 1997 ratings, was Mean for Yea votes: 87.67 (n: 73; sd: 10.40); Mean for Nay votes: 86.58 (n: 137; sd: 13.07).

6. The differences among all Democrats, as measured by U.S. Chamber of Commerce 1997 ratings, were Mean of Yea votes : 56.61 (n: 26; sd: 19.85); Mean of Nay votes: 41.55 (n: 119; sd: 16.85); Mean of Present votes: 42.90 (n: 58; sd: 19.23). The difference between Democratic freshmen was Mean of Yea votes: 50.05 (n: 19; sd: 19.19); Mean of Present votes: 45.62 (n: 16; sd: 15.48).

7. The difference, as measured by U.S. Chamber of Commerce 1997 ratings, was August 3: Mean of Yea votes: 84.8 (n: 48; sd: 13.2); Mean of Nay votes: 94.5 (n: 143; sd: 5.5). August 6: Mean of Yea votes: 86.1 (n: 57; sd: 12.7); Mean of Nay votes: 94.6 (n: 135; sd: 5.5).

# References

Abramson, Jill. 1997a. "Tape Shows Clinton Involvement in Party-Paid Ads." *New York Times,* October 21, A20.

———. 1997b. "Cost of 1996 Campaigns Sets Record of $2.2 Billion." *New York Times,* November 25.

———. 1998. "Election Panel Refuses to Order Repayments by Clinton and Dole." *New York Times,* December 11.

Adams, Jane Meredith. 1996. "Perot, Citing Insider Politics, Blasts Decision." *Boston Globe,* September 19.

*Advertising Age.* 1997. "100 Leading National Advertisers." September 29.

Alexander, Herbert E. 1962. *Financing the 1960 Election.* Princeton, N.J.: Citizens' Research Foundation.

———. 1966. *Financing the 1964 Election.* Princeton, N.J.: Citizens' Research Foundation.

———. 1971. *Financing the 1968 Election.* Lexington, Mass: Heath Lexington Books.

———. 1979. *Financing the 1976 Election.* Washington, D.C.: CQ Press.

———. 1991. *Reform and Reality: The Financing of State and Local Campaigns.* New York: Twentieth Century Fund.

Alexander, Herbert E., and Monica Bauer. 1991. *Financing the 1988 Election.* Boulder, Colo.: Westview Press.

Alexander, Herbert E., and Anthony Corrado. 1995. *Financing the 1992 Election.* Armonk, N.Y.: M.E. Sharpe.

Alexander, Herbert E., with Eugenia Grohman, Caroline D. Jones, and Clifford Brown. 1976. *Financing the 1972 Election.* Lexington, Mass.: Lexington Books.

Alexander, Herbert E., and Brian A. Haggerty. 1983. *Financing the 1980 Election.* Lexington, Mass.: Lexington Books.

———. 1987. *Financing the 1984 Election.* Lexington, Mass.: Lexington Books.

American Political Science Association Committee on Political Parties. 1950. "Toward A More Responsible Two-Party System." *American Political Science Review* 44: Supplement.

Associated Press. 1996. "Vice-Presidential Debate Viewership Half That of '92." Press Release, October 11.

Babcock, Charles R., and Ruth Marcus. 1996. " 'Dole, Inc.': The Rise of a Money Machine." *Washington Post,* August 20, A1.

Balz, Dan, and Howard Kurtz. 1996. "Two Top Media Advisers Quit as Dole Operation Suffers Another Shake-Up." *Washington Post,* September 6.

Beck, Deborah, Paul Taylor, Jeffrey Stanger, and Douglas Rivlin. 1997. *Issue*

*Advocacy Advertising during the 1996 Campaign.* Philadelphia: Annenberg Public Policy Center.

Bennet, James. 1996. "Another Tally in '96 Race: Two Months of TV Ads." *New York Times,* November 13.

Berke, Richard L. 1987. "Heeding Plato, Greek Americans Aid in Effort to Raise Money for Dukakis." *New York Times,* December 20, A20.

———. 1996. "With Studied Calm, Democrats Feverishly Attack the Dole Plan." *New York Times,* August 6.

Berry, Jeffrey M. 1989. *The Interest Group Society,* 2d ed. New York: HarperCollins.

Beyle, Thad. "Reading the Tea Leaves." 1998. *State Government News,* August 1998.

Biersack, Robert. 1996. "The Nationalization of Party Finance." In *The State of the Parties,* ed. John C. Green and Daniel M. Shea. 2d ed. Lanham, Md.: Rowman & Littlefield.

Booth, William. 1998. "The Ballot Battle: Initiatives Bypass Traditional Lawmaking." *Washington Post,* November 5, A33.

Brown, Clifford Jr., Lynda Powell, and Clyde Wilcox. 1995. *Serious Money: Fundraising and Contributing on Presidential Nomination Campaigns.* New York: Cambridge University Press.

Buell, Emmett Jr. 1996. "The Invisible Primary." In *In Pursuit of the White House,* ed. William Mayer. Chatham, N.J.: Chatham House.

Burger, Timothy J., and Benjamin Sheffner. 1996. "House Task Force Warns of GOP 'Division' on Campaign Reform." *Roll Call,* February 26, 1.

Carr, Rebecca. 1997a. "Thompson Widens Scope as Investigation Begins." *Congressional Quarterly Weekly Report,* February 1, 274.

———. 1997b. "Narrowed Scope Paves the Way for Approval of Senate Probe." *Congressional Quarterly Weekly Report,* March 8, 572–74.

———. 1997c. "The Deal That Got Out of the Bag." *Congressional Quarterly Weekly Report,* March 15, 617.

Ceaser, James W., and Andrew E. Busch. 1997. *Losing to Win: The 1996 Elections and American Politics.* Lanham, Md.: Rowman & Littlefield.

Chinoy, Ira. 1997a. "In Trades between Party Committees, Not All Dollars Are Equal." *Washington Post,* February 18, A7.

———. 1997b. "In Presidential Race, TV Ads Were Biggest '96 Cost by Far." *Washington Post,* March 31.

Citizens' Research Foundation. 1997. *New Realities, New Thinking: Report of the Task Force on Campaign Finance Reform.* Los Angeles: Citizens' Research Foundation.

Clymer, Adam. 1996. "Politics: The Contributors; Labor Flexes Financial Muscle to Raise Stakes Against G.O.P. in Congressional Fights." *New York Times,* October 31.

Commission on Presidential Debates. 1995. "Commission on Presidential Debates Recommends Four Debates." Press Release, October 31.

Common Cause. 1996. "Statement of Common Cause President Ann McBride at News Conference Asking for Independent Counsel to Investigate Campaign Finance Activities of Clinton, Dole Campaigns." Press Release, October 9.

————. 1997. "The Soft Money Laundromat" at www/commoncause.org /soft_money/ topdem.htm and topgop.htm.

Corrado, Anthony. 1992. *Creative Campaigning: PACs and the Presidential Selection Process.* Boulder, Colo.: Westview Press.

————. 1993. *Paying for Presidents.* New York: Twentieth Century Fund Press.

————. 1997a. "Financing the 1996 Elections." In *The Election of 1996,* ed. Gerald Pomper. Chatham, N.J.: Chatham House.

————. 1997b. "Party Soft Money." In *Campaign Finance Reform: A Sourcebook,* Anthony Corrado et al., pp. 165–177. Washington, D.C.: Brookings Institution.

Corrado, Anthony, Thomas E. Mann, Daniel R. Ortiz, Trevor Potter, and Frank J. Sorauf. 1997. *Campaign Finance Reform: A Sourcebook.* Washington, D.C.: Brookings Institution.

The Council of State Governments. 1997. *The Book of the States.* Lexington, Ky.: Council of State Governments.

Crotty, William J. 1984. *American Parties in Decline.* Boston: Little Brown.

Dewar, Helen. 1990. "Senate Democrats Accept Republican Proposal to Outlaw PACs." *Washington Post,* July 28, A4.

————. 1996. "Senate Kills Campaign Finance Bill." *Washington Post,* June 26, A4.

————. 1997. "Campaign Finance Bills Pile Up, Votes Don't." *Washington Post,* July 4, A4.

————. 1998a. "Sen. Lott Tries to Block Action on Campaign Finance Reform." *Washington Post,* February 25, A4.

————. 1998b. "Campaign Fund Bill Is Doomed, Foes Say." *Washington Post,* February 26, A12.

————. 1998c. "Campaign Finance Bill Dies in Senate." *Washington Post,* February 27, A1.

————. 1998d. "Campaign Finance Bill Buried for Year." *Washington Post,* September 11, A4.

Dine, Philip. 1996. "Labor, Business Groups Battle, Try to Advance Their Agenda." *St. Louis Post-Dispatch,* November 6.

Doherty, Carroll J. 1997a. "Death Rattle Sparks Search for Signs of Political Life." *Congressional Quarterly Weekly Report,* October 11, 2447–48.

————. 1997b. "Votes a Good Indicator of Depth of Feeling on Both Sides." *Congressional Quarterly Weekly Report,* October 11, 2449.

Doherty, Carroll J., and Jackie Koszczuk. 1997. "Deal Smoothes Path for Senate Exit; House Still Caught in Gridlock." *Congressional Quarterly Weekly Report,* November 11, 2664.

Drew, Elizabeth. 1983. *Politics and Money: The New Road to Corruption.* New York: Macmillan.

————. 1997. *Whatever It Takes.* New York: Viking.

Dwyre, Diana. 1996. "Spinning Straw into Gold: Soft Money and U.S. House Elections." *Legislative Studies Quarterly* 21: 409–24.

Eismeier, Theodore J., and Philip H. Pollock III. 1988. *Business, Money, and the Rise of Corporate PACs in American Elections.* New York: Quorum Books.

Epstein, Leon D. 1986. *Political Parties in the American Mold.* Madison: University of Wisconsin Press.

Evans, C. Lawrence, and Walter J. Oleszek. 1997. *Congress under Fire: Reform Politics and the Republican Majority.* Boston: Houghton Mifflin.

Faucheux, Ron. 1998. "The Indirect Approach: How Advocacy Groups Are Muscling Their Way into the Ring—and What Candidates Are Doing About It." *Campaigns and Elections,* June, 18–24.

Federal Election Commission. 1994. *Annual Report 1993.* Washington D.C.: Federal Election Commission.

———. 1995. Advisory Opinion. August 24.

———. 1996a. "Financing the 1996 Presidential Campaign" at http://www.fec.gov/pres96/ presgen1.htm.

———. 1996b. "Dole, Clinton, Perot Receive Public Funds." *Record* 22:10 (October).

———. 1996c. Advisory Opinion. June 14.

———. 1997a. *Presidential Candidate Summary Report.* Washington, D.C.: Federal Election Commission.

———. 1997b. "FEC Reports Major Increase in Party Activity for 1995–96." Press Release, March 19.

———. 1997c. "Congressional Fundraising and Spending Up Again in 1996." Press Release, April 14.

———. 1997d. "PAC Activity Increased in 1995–96 Election Cycle." Press Release, April 22.

———. 1997e. *Annual Report 1996.* Washington D.C.: Federal Election Commission.

———. 1998a. *Report of the Audit Division on Clinton/Gore '96 General Election Committee, Inc. and Clinton/Gore '96 General Election Legal and Accounting Fund.* Agenda Document 98–86, November 19.

———. 1998b. *Report of the Audit Division on the Dole/Kemp '96 and Dole/Kemp Compliance Committee, Inc.* Agenda Document 98–88, November 19.

*Federal Election Commission Broadcast Media Public Education Program on the Tax Checkoff: Final Report.* 1991. Washington, D.C.: Washington Independent Productions.

Feingold, Russell. 1997. "Money Can't Be the Biggest Question for Candidates." *Roll Call,* January 9. Special section on campaign reform.

Fenno, Richard F. Jr. 1997. *Learning to Govern: An Institutional View of the 104th Congress.* Washington, D.C.: Brookings Institution.

Fineman, Howard, and Mark Hosenball. 1996. "The Asian Connection." *Newsweek,* October 28.

Fritsch, Jane. 1995a. "Money Problems Hobble Gramm Campaign." *New York Times,* October 18.

———. 1995b. "Dole Overtakes No. 1 Rival in Raising Money for '96 Race." *New York Times,* July 1.

Fritz, Sarah, and Dwight Morris. 1992. *Gold-Plated Politics: Running for Congress in the 1990s.* Washington, D.C.: CQ Press.

"Frontline: Washington's Other Scandal." 1998. Produced by the Public Broadcasting System, aired October 6.

Gerth, Jeff, and Stephen Labaton. 1996. "Wealthy Indonesian Businessman Has Strong Ties to Clinton." *New York Times,* October 11.

Gimpel, James G. 1995. *Fulfilling the Contract: The First 100 Days.* Boston: Allyn and Bacon.

Gingrich, Newt. 1995. "Testimony of House Speaker Newt Gingrich before the Committee on House Oversight." November 2.

Goldstein, Josh, and Frank Greve. 1996. "$425,000 Give-and-Run Mystery Has Democrats Puzzled." *Philadelphia Inquirer,* August 25.

Goldstein, Kenneth M. 1997. "Political Commercials in the 1996 Election." Paper prepared for the 1997 annual meeting of the Midwest Political Science Association, Chicago.

Gravely, Bob. 1997. "From Arms to Buddhists to Coffee: The ABCs of the Investigations." *Congressional Quarterly Weekly,* April 5, 800.

Green, John C., and James L. Guth. 1986. "Big Bucks and Petty Cash: Party and Interest Group Activists in American Politics." In *Interest Group Politics,* ed. Allan Cigler and Burdett Loomis, 2d ed., pp. 91–113. Washington, D.C.: CQ Press.

———. 1993. "Controlling the Mischief of Faction: Party Support and Coalition Building Among Party Activists." In *Politics, Professionalism, and Power,* ed. John C. Green, pp. 234–264. Lanham, Md.: Rowman & Littlefield.

Gugliotta, Guy, and Ira Chinoy. 1997. "Money Machine: The Fund-Raising Frenzy of Campaign '96." *Washington Post,* February 10.

Hall, Mimi. 1996. "Perot Accepts Taxpayer Funding." *USA Today,* August 20.

Harris, John F. 1996. "President Sidesteps Funds Flap." *Washington Post,* October 22.

Heard, Alexander. 1960. *The Costs of Democracy.* Chapel Hill: University of North Carolina Press.

Herrnson, Paul S. 1988. *Party Campaigning in the 1980s.* Cambridge: Harvard University Press.

———. 1998a. *Congressional Elections: Campaigning at Home and in Washington.* 2d ed. Washington, D.C.: CQ Press.

———. 1998b. "Parties and Interest Groups in Postreform Congressional Elections." In *Interest Group Politics,* ed. Allan J. Cigler and Burdett A. Loomis, 5th ed. Washington, D.C.: CQ Press.

Herrnson, Paul S., and Diana Dwyre. 1999. "Party Issue Advocacy in Congressional Elections." In *The State of the Parties,* ed. John C. Green and Daniel M. Shea, 3d. ed. Lanham, Md.: University Press of America.

Herrnson, Paul S., and Clyde Wilcox. 1997. "The 1996 Presidential Election: A Tale of a Campaign That Didn't Seem to Matter." In *Toward the Millennium: The Elections of 1996,* ed. Larry J. Sabato, pp. 121–42. Boston: Allyn & Bacon.

Hertzke, Allen D. 1993. *Echoes of Discontent.* Washington, D.C.: CQ Press.

Holmes, Stephen A. 1996. "Lugar Struggles to Revive Campaign." *New York Times,* February 2.

———. 1998. "House GOP Shifts on Campaign Bills." *New York Times,* March 28, A8.

Humphries, Craig. 1991. "Corporations, PACs, and the Strategic Link between Contributions and Lobbying Activities." *Western Political Quarterly* 44: 357–72.

Internal Revenue Service. 1994. "1992 Taxpayer Usage Study." Report 13.

Jackson, Brooks. 1997. "Financing the 1996 Campaign: The Law of the Jungle."

In *Toward the Millennium: The Elections of 1996,* ed. Larry J. Sabato, pp. 225–60. Boston: Allyn & Bacon.

Jacobson, Gary C. 1980. *Money in Congressional Elections.* New Haven: Yale University Press.

Jamieson, Kathleen Hall. 1992. *Dirty Politics: Deception, Distraction, and Democracy.* New York: Oxford University Press.

Jones, Ruth S. 1990. "Contributing as Participation." In *Money, Elections, and Democracy: Reforming Congressional Campaign Finance,* ed. Margaret Latus Nugent and John R. Johannes. Boulder, Colo.: Westview Press, 1990.

Katz, Jeffrey L. 1998a. "Petition Pushes House GOP Leadership to Schedule Campaign Finance Debate." *Congressional Quarterly Weekly Report,* April 25, 1057–58.

―――. 1998b. "Supporters of Campaign Finance Overhaul Grow Wary as House GOP Leaders Signal a Summer of Protracted Debate." *Congressional Quarterly Weekly Report,* May 31, 1379.

―――. 1998c. "Campaign Finance Proposal Survives a Key Vote as House Debate Continues." *Congressional Quarterly Weekly Report,* June 20, 1688.

Kolodny, Robin, and Diana Dwyre. 1998. "Party-Orchestrated Activities for Legislative Party Goals: Campaigns for Majorities in the US House of Representatives in the 1990s." *Party Politics* 4: 275–95.

Koopman, Douglas L. 1996. *Hostile Takeover: The House Republican Party, 1980–1995.* Lanham, Md.: Rowman & Littlefield.

Kranish, Michael. 1996a. "Debate Panel Asks Perot Be Excluded." *Boston Globe,* September 18.

―――. 1996b. "Post-Convention Gains Come to Naught in Polls." *Boston Globe,* September 4.

Kurtz, Howard. 1996. "The Latest Story Ever Told." *Washington Post,* November 11.

Lewis, Neil A. 1996a. "Answer to 'Will Perot Debate?' Depends on 'Can He Win?' " *New York Times,* September 17.

―――. 1996b. "Judge Rejects Suit by Perot to Join Presidential Debates." *New York Times,* October 2.

Lowry, Brian. 1996. "Debate Attracts a Third of Potential TV Audience." *Los Angeles Times,* October 9.

Magleby, David B., and Kelly D. Patterson. 1994. "Poll Trends: Congressional Reform." *Public Opinion Quarterly* 58: 419–27.

Magleby, David B., Kelly D. Patterson, and Stephen H. Wirls. 1994. "Fear and Loathing of the Modern Congress: Public Manifestations of Constitutional Design." Paper presented at the annual meeting of the Midwest Political Science Association, Chicago.

Malbin, Michael J., and Thomas L. Gais. 1998. *The Day After Reform: Sobering Campaign Finance Lessons from the American States.* Albany, N.Y.: Rockefeller Institute Press.

Marcus, Ruth. 1996a. "Who Picks Up the Tab Now?" *Washington Post Weekly Edition,* May 20–26, 12.

―――. 1996b. "Taking 'Voter Guides' to the TV Audience: AFL-CIO Tries New Approach in 28 Districts." *Washington Post,* October 17.

Marcus, Ruth, and Charles R. Babcock. 1995. "Alexander Raised Millions for TV Project." *Washington Post,* December 30, 1995, A1.

———. 1997. "The System Cracks under the Weight of Cash; Candidates, Parties and Outside Interests Dropped a Record $2.7 Billion." *Washington Post,* February 9.

Market Decisions Corporation. 1990. *Presidential Election Campaign Fund Focus Group Research.* 1990. Portland, Ore.: Market Decisions Corporation.

Miller, Alan C. 1996. "Democrats Return Illegal Contribution." *Los Angeles Times,* September 21.

Mitchell, Alison. 1998. "GOP Defections Delay House Vote on Campaign Bill." *New York Times,* March 27, A1.

Morris, Dwight, and Murielle E. Gamache. 1994. *Gold-Plated Politics: The 1992 Congressional Races.* Washington, D.C.: CQ Press.

Moncrief, Gary F. 1998. "Candidate Spending in State Legislative Races." In *Campaign Finance in State Legislative Elections,* ed. Joel A. Thompson and Gary F. Moncrief. Washington, D.C.: CQ Press.

Mundy, Alicia. 1996. "Spot TV: Jamie Sterling." *Brandweek* 37: 47 (December 9).

Mutch, Robert E. 1988. *Campaigns, Congress, and Courts: The Making of Federal Campaign Finance Law.* New York: Praeger.

———. 1991. "The Evolution of Campaign Finance Regulation in the United States and Canada." In *Comparative Issues in Party and Election Finance,* ed. F. Leslie Seidle. pp. 57–111. Toronto: Dundurn Press.

Nagourney, Adam. 1996a. "Dole Urges Action on Campaign Gifts." *New York Times,* October 21.

———. 1996b. "Doles Warms to Task of Attacking Clinton." *New York Times,* October 19.

National Republican Congressional Committee. 1996a. "AFL-CIO/NRCC Total Television Ad $ (Targeted Districts—Estimated)." November 20.

National Republican Congressional Committee. 1996b. "Chapter Two." NRCC-sponsored issue advocacy advertisement, produced by Sipple Strategic Communications.

Noel, Don. 1996. "Costly 'Issue Ads' Tilt the 5th District Playing Field." *Hartford Courant,* sec. A.

Novak, Robert D. 1995. "Linda Smith: Raising a Stink." *Washington Post,* September 28, A29.

Novotny, Patrick. 1997. "Cable Television, Local Media Markets, and the Post-Network Trends in Campaign Advertisements in the 1990s." Paper presented at the 1997 annual meeting of the American Political Science Association, Washington, D.C.

Obey, Doug. 1996. "Independent Spending May Decide Outcome of Wyoming Campaign." *The Hill,* October 9.

Ornstein, Norman, Thomas Mann, and Michael Malbin. 1998. *Vital Statistics on Congress, 1997–1998.* Washington. D.C.: CQ Press.

Ornstein, Norman J., Thomas. E. Mann, Paul Taylor, Michael J. Malbin, and Anthony Corrado. 1997. *Five Ideas for Practical Campaign Reform.* Washington, D.C.: Brookings Institution.

Pomper, Gerald M. 1997. "The Presidential Election." In *The Election of 1996*, ed. Gerald M. Pomper et al., pp. 173–204. Chatham, N.J.: Chatham House.

Rae, Nicol C. 1998. *Conservative Reformers: The Republican Freshmen and the Lessons of the 104th Congress*. Armonk, N.Y.: M.E. Sharpe.

Republican National Committee. 1996. "RNC Announces $20 Million TV Advertising Campaign." Press Release, May 16.

Rozell, Mark J., and Clyde Wilcox, ed. 1995. *God at the Grassroots*. Lanham, Md.: Rowman & Littlefield.

Sabato, Larry J. 1997. "The November Vote—A Status Quo Election." In *Toward the Millennium: The Elections of 1996*, ed. Larry J. Sabato, pp. 143–61. Boston: Allyn & Bacon.

Seelye, Katharine Q. 1996. "Dole Replaces 2 Aides to Sharpen Message." *New York Times*, September 6.

Simpson, Glenn R., and Jill Abramson. 1996. "Legal Loopholes Let Overseas Contributors Fill Democratic Coffers." *Wall Street Journal*, October 8.

Sorauf, Frank J. 1988. *Money in American Elections*. Glenview, Il.: Scott, Foresman.

———. 1992. *Inside Campaign Finance: Myths and Realities*. New Haven: Yale University Press.

Suro, Robert, and Bill Miller. 1998. "Judge: 'Soft Money' Not Covered by Foreign Political Donor Ban." *Washington Post*, October 10, A3.

Thomas, Evan, et al. 1996. "Victory March." *Newsweek Special Election Issue*, November 18.

Twentieth Century Fund Task Force on Presidential Debates. 1995. *Let America Decide*. New York: Twentieth Century Fund Press.

U.S. Department of Commerce. Bureau of Economic Analysis. *Survey of Current Business*, August 1998.

Verba, Sidney, Kay Lehman Schlozman, and Henry E. Brady. 1995. *Voice and Equality*. Cambridge: Harvard University Press.

Verhovek, Sam Howe. 1996. "Strategic Mistakes Brought Down Gramm." *New York Times*, February 15.

Waldman, Peter. 1996. "By Courting Clinton, Lippo Gains Stature at Home in Indonesia." *Wall Street Journal*, October 16.

Wayne, Stephen. 1998. "Interest Groups on the Road to the White House: Traveling the Hard and Soft Routes." In *The Interest Group Connection*, ed. P. Herrnson, R. Shaiko, and C. Wilcox. Chatham, N.J.: Chatham House.

Wertheimer, Fred. 1996. "The Dirtiest Election Ever." *Washington Post*, November 3, C1.

West, Darrell M. 1997. *Air Wars: Television Advertising in Election Campaigns, 1952–1996*. 2d ed. Washington, D.C.: CQ Press.

Wilcox, Clyde. 1991. "Financing the 1998 Prenomination Campaigns." In *Nominating the President*, ed. E. Buell and L. Sigelman. Knoxville: University of Tennessee Press.

———. 1992. *God's Warriors*. Baltimore: Johns Hopkins University Press.

———. 1999. "Follow the Money: Clinton, Campaign Finance, and Reform." In *Understanding the Presidency*, ed. James P. Pfiffner and Roger Davidson. 2d ed. New York: Addison-Wesley Longman.

Wilcox, Clyde, Robert Biersack, Paul Herrnson, and Wesley Joe. 1998. "Contribution Strategies of Large Congressional Donors: 1978–1994." Los Angeles: Citizens' Research Foundation.

Wilcox, Clyde, and Wesley Joe. 1998. "Dead Law: The Federal Election Finance Regulations, 1974–1996." *PS: Political Science & Politics,* March, 14–17.

Wilson, James Q. 1995. *Political Organizations.* Princeton, N.J.: Princeton University Press

Woodward, Bob. 1996. *The Choice.* New York: Touchstone Books.

Woodward, Bob, and Brian Duffy. 1997. "Chinese Embassy Role in Contributions Probed." *Washington Post,* February 13, A1.

Yang, John E. 1995. "House Coalition Presses Campaign Reform Vote." *Washington Post,* September 20, A2.

———. 1997a. "Gingrich Reelected Speaker Despite Defections." *Washington Post,* January 8, A1.

———. 1997b. "Ethics Panel Supports Reprimand of Gingrich." *Washington Post,* January 18, A1.

———. 1997c. "House GOP Leadership Comes Apart at Seams." *Washington Post,* July 19, A1.

# Index